REFRAMING THE EMOTIONAL WORLDS OF THE EARLY CHILDHOOD CLASSROOM

This volume examines the emotional world of the early childhood classroom as it affects young children (whose emotional well-being is crucial to successful learning), educators (for whom teaching is never a solely cognitive act), parents, and administrators. In a culture where issues such as bullying and teacher burnout comprise major challenges to student success, this book brings together diverse voices (researchers, practitioners, children, and parents) and multiple perspectives (theoretical and personal) to refocus attention on the pivotal role of emotion in schools.

To do so, editors Samara Madrid, David E. Fernie, and Rebecca Kantor envision emotion as a dynamic, fluid, and negotiated construct, performed and produced in the daily lives of children and adults alike. A nuanced yet cohesive analysis, *Reframing the Emotional Worlds of the Early Childhood Classroom* thus presents a challenge to the overriding concern with quantifiable classroom achievement that increasingly threatens to push the emotional lives of classroom participants to the margins of educational and public discourse.

Samara Madrid is an associate professor in the Department of Elementary and Early Education at the University of Wyoming.

David E. Fernie is professor of early childhood education and former dean of education at Wheelock College.

Rebecca Kantor is dean of the School of Education and Human Development at University of Colorado, Denver.

REFRAMING THE EMOTIONAL WORLDS OF THE EARLY CHILDHOOD CLASSROOM

Edited by
Samara Madrid, Ph.D.
UNIVERSITY OF WYOMING

David E. Fernie, Ed.D.
WHEELOCK COLLEGE

Rebecca Kantor, Ed.D.
UNIVERSITY OF COLORADO, DENVER

Routledge
Taylor & Francis Group

NEW YORK AND LONDON

First published 2015
by Routledge
711 Third Avenue, New York, NY 10017

and by Routledge
2 Park Square, Milton Park, Abingdon, Oxon, OX14 4RN

Routledge is an imprint of the Taylor & Francis Group, an informa business

Library of Congress Cataloging-in-Publication Data
CIP data has been applied for

ISBN: 978-0-415-83384-4 (hbk)
ISBN: 978-0-415-83385-1 (pbk)
ISBN: 978-0-203-49600-8 (ebk)

Typeset in Bembo
by Apex CoVantage, LLC

MIX
Paper from
responsible sources
FSC
www.fsc.org   FSC® C013056

Printed and bound in Great Britain by
TJ International Ltd, Padstow, Cornwall

Dedicated to those who recognize that the path between the head and the heart should be well traveled.

CONTENTS

FOREWORD

Of all the new scientific discoveries with implications for education, in my opinion, the most critical and underappreciated concern the role of emotions in thinking and the inherently social nature of the human mind. Science is proving with empirical evidence what good teachers and effective parents have known all along—that emotions are not add-ons that interfere with clear-headed thinking, perhaps influencing cognition from time to time, but otherwise separate from cognitive abilities. Instead, both psychological science and neuroscience are demonstrating that the emotions we experience are foundational to *why* thinking and learning happen in the first place, including to why and how we engage with traditional academic skills. And, after all, this makes sense! The human brain is evolved to be efficient—it only attends to, deeply processes, and remembers information that *matters*.

This newly evolving scientific appreciation of the centrality of emotion to thinking, and of the centrality of social relationships to emotion, has profound implications for how we educate children. Successful classrooms are those that establish an inclusive culture of positive expectation, where learners come implicitly to believe that difficult tasks, even when they are initially frustrating, are worthwhile and something that "people like me" do. In this way, access to resources alone is not sufficient to build a successful classroom, even though students may have high levels of intellectual potential. It is the emotions children and their teachers subjectively experience in the classroom, like enthusiasm, interest, and frustration followed by renewed resolve, that harness intellectual potential and yoke this potential to momentary engagement and future success.

Following from this, yet sadly contrary to the assumptions underlying many policies and teacher training approaches, teachers' abilities to orchestrate lessons effectively and children's abilities to learn productively are not simply dependent on access to materials and information. Instead, they are also tied to both teachers' and students' abilities to make strong and appropriate social relationships. Through connecting with others in the school community who also value academics and who expect *everyone* to have trials but eventually to succeed, students learn to dig in rather than give up. Indeed, among the most compelling modern educational findings is that general intelligence does not predict students' academic and personal success as well as do students' capacities for socio-emotional resilience and relationship building—their abilities to get going when success is uncertain, to consider alternative paths when an initial course seems blocked, and to persist when tasks become difficult. These, in turn, are dependent on students effectively seeking out (and finding) social resources that support and promote these capacities.

And hence the need for this thoughtful, courageous, and important book. Recent scientific research has demonstrated unequivocally that emotions are complex and dynamic but scientifically tractable. Put another way, the research has demonstrated that emotions are mental and behavioral patterns that can be studied. They are not random, but instead have systematic and predictable effects on how individuals behave and think. However, to discover and describe how these emotional dynamics play out specifically in the classroom context will take much thoughtful observation, documentation, and interpretation on the parts of educators and practitioner researchers. This book engages just such a discussion for early childhood educators. Each chapter thoughtfully frames and interprets a learning space, context, or domain in terms of its emotional and social dimensions. In so doing, each also provides a generative example of how early childhood educators can understand and leverage emotions and relationships in the classroom and in the school, both among adults and between adults and children.

It is clear that appropriate social bonding is a critical foundation for the emotions that undergird meaningful learning and achievement, and especially so in early childhood. The chapters in this volume explore this instrumental connection between social bonds, emotions, and learning, and in so doing move the conversation forward from *whether* to *how*. I look forward to hearing about the impact of the conversations this volume starts on early childhood educators' thinking and practice.

Mary Helen Immordino-Yang, Ed.D.
Associate Professor of Education,
Psychology, and Neuroscience,
University of Southern California

1

INTRODUCTION TO REFRAMING EMOTION

Samara Madrid, David E. Fernie, and Rebecca Kantor

UNIVERSITY OF WYOMING, WHEELOCK COLLEGE,
AND UNIVERSITY OF COLORADO, DENVER

The main purpose of this volume is to provoke new and productive thinking about the emotional lives of young children, parents, teachers, and administrators as they experience a range of emotions in early childhood settings. Attention to emotion has always been a part of the early childhood commitment to support all aspects of a child's development. However, recent heightened attention to emotion in early childhood education has focused largely on developing curricula for young children in order to develop socio-emotional expression skills and strategies for self-regulation, or to implement intervention strategies intended to change or manage children's behavior and promote socio-emotional learning (Bronson, 2000; Copple & Bredekamp, 2009; Epstein, 2009; Hyson, 2004; Jalongo, 2013; Salovey & Sluyter, 1997; Thompson, 2002; Webster-Stratton, 1999). These approaches seek to improve children's behavior, promote their participation in group life as a student, and enhance their readiness to learn and preparation for kindergarten and later schooling.

Emotion in This Volume

This book, however, shifts the focus from looking at pedagogy's role in the socio-emotional learning of young children toward a broader examination of the role of emotion in the early childhood world, for both adults and children, as emotion is embedded in relationships and daily contexts. Further, the purpose of this book is not to define emotion, to propose where emotion is located, or to debate the merits of various theoretical perspectives on emotion. Rather, the goal is to show how a wide range of emotions informs, affects, and directs children's and adults' *lived* experiences within early childhood. Markus and Kitiyama (1994) help us to confirm and articulate the focus of this book and the role of emotion as we see it:

> We are not assuming that emotions are not felt or that they are not biological or even universal for that matter. The main argument is that emotions are not neutral to the social systems that exist in a culture. The ways emotions are organized within a particular culture are very much dependent upon the moral and social order, as well as ideological and political systems. Emotions, regardless of the location, are part of relationships. In short, emotions are social actions.
>
> *(p. 6)*

This reframing and shift in focus move us away from examining only individual emotion or emotional self-regulation and management toward examining how emotions are lived, experienced, and negotiated in daily life among multiple social participants in early childhood educational settings.

Emotion has recently been shown to be a key factor in social functioning, decision making, and cognition, providing direction and serving as a "rudder" for our further experiences, actions, and transfer of knowledge. For example, Immordino-Yang (2011), in her study of the role of emotion in her young daughter's poetry, highlights the importance of the social mind in learning and creating knowledge:

> By virtue of its evolutionary connection to bodily feeling and survival, our social mind motivates us to create things that represent the meaning we have made by processes of noticing, feeling, and understanding so that others can notice and feel and understand what we have.
>
> *(pp. 134–135)*

This perspective reveals how cognitive processes are profoundly affected by the emotional processes that Immordino-Yang and Damasio (2007) call "emotional thought." These new advances in neuroscience research allow us to reconceptualize and to "look differently" at the complex and nuanced nature of how emotion is taken up, reproduced, enacted, and engaged with as children, teachers, administrators, and parents act and react to one another within social and cultural contexts.

During this time, when the current political context is focused primarily on the learning of disciplinary knowledge and academic skills, there is an increased need to shed light on the role of emotion, both in learning and in the overall well-being of children, teachers, and other educational participants (Boler, 1999; Day & Lee, 2011; Schutz & Pekrun, 2007; Schultz & Zembylas, 2009; Zembylas, 2005, 2007). In the last decade, an overriding concern with achievement and accountability threatens to push the emotional lives of classroom participants to the margins of educational and public discourse. Children, parents, teachers, and administrators feel the increased pressure, monitoring, and time constraints associated with standardization (Shutz & Pekrun, 2007). Has this focus on high-stakes accountability pushed the joy, wonder, and spontaneity out of the school and classroom space? What discourses of emotion are circulating now? What are the related effects on teachers', children's, parents', and administrators' well-being and happiness? How important are emotions to learning and academic achievement?

Along with valid concerns over the effects of this pushdown on young children's educational life, there is a related concern about the quality and reality of adults' emotional lives in classrooms. Teacher and administrator burnout and the low retention rates of new teachers in urban settings (and elsewhere) have been tied to the emotional dimensions of teachers' experiences, to accountability pressures, and to teachers' perceived lack of control—all of which can lead to "emotional exhaustion and depersonalization" (Larrivee, 2012, p. 22).

The co-editors concur with others who recognize that teaching is not solely a cognitive act: The emotional engagement of teachers matters, and is a primary factor in their personal well-being in the teacher role, teacher identity, job satisfaction, and job retention (Bullough, 2009; Day & Qing, 2009; Hargreaves, 1994, 1998; Larrivee, 2012; Meyer, 2009; Nias, 1999; Noddings 2011; Zembylas, 2005). Day and Lee (2011) suggest that teachers often report feeling positive emotions such as joy, love, and compassion, but also frequently experience negative emotions such as guilt, frustration, disappointment, anxiety, and fear when their hard-fought-for "professional identity is threatened by mandated reform, rather than renewal efforts" (p. 2).

This research is consonant with a related body of literature that suggests that early childhood teachers spend a great deal of time navigating the "emotional labor" of the job and dealing with the consequences of this process (Colley, 2006; Jacobson, 2003, 2008; Hargreaves, 1994, 1998; Osgood, 2006, 2010; Taggart, 2011; Troman, 2000; Tucker, 2010). For example, Madrid and Dunn-Kenney (2010) found the most common emotions discussed by a small group of early childhood educators were stress, worry, and frustration. Tucker (2010) also found that mental and physical breakdowns were predominant themes related to the stress and isolation of teaching.

At the same time, there is common discourse that discourages teachers from overtly sharing or overtly demonstrating the discomforting emotions that come with the daily interactions in classroom life and with children, colleagues, and parents. Teacher preparation is supposed to make teachers ready to teach and to arm them with professional knowledge and dispositions intended to dispel uncertainties and discomforts, to provide answers rather than to provoke questions. Stress and anxiety are often pushed underground because teachers worry about being viewed as unprofessional and/or incompetent and, sadly, there simply are few opportunities permitting difficult feelings to be examined, considered, and discussed in the workplace (Elfer & Dearnley, 2007; Jacobson, 2008)

Yet within the early childhood education field, both now and in its history, the traditional view is that love and caring motivate and dominate the emotional lives of early childhood teachers. Moyles (2001) notes that it can be difficult to separate the head from the heart, as well as the mother role from the formal teacher role, and it is necessary to combine them in order to meet the needs of the child and the teacher. Goldstein (1997), Noddings (1984, 1993), and Liston and Garrison (2004) have attempted to move this discussion of love toward a definition that is based on critical and feminist pedagogies, but the discourse has been slow to shift within the mainstream early childhood education field. Shields (2002), in her analysis of gender and emotion, outlines how women have been positioned as the loving "caregiver" because of the link between females and maternal emotions. Relatedly, Page (2011) found this discourse to exist not only among professionals in the field, but also among parents whose children attend early childhood centers. She found that mothers placed "vital importance" on the relationship between the caregiver and the child, noting that "the mothers in this study appeared to want adults who cared for their children to love them, though they don't always call it love" (p. 11). Teachers' valuing and feeling love and nurturance are not necessarily problematic, but this assumption does become problematic when teachers are positioned as natural caregivers because of being female, rather than as professionals who draw upon care as an aspect of their intentional teaching.

The emotional worlds of classrooms are more complex than any *one* particular emotion. Competing and contradictory narratives and paradoxes exist, particularly in early childhood education, because a "good teacher" is linked to the display of love and care, while being a professional is linked to emotional neutrality (Taggart, 2011; Moyles, 2001). Being a *non-emotional* professional, however, runs "counter to the beliefs and practices of the early-years professional, and this poses a very real threat to the professional integrity that practitioners cling to . . ." (Osgood, 2006, p. 191). And herein lies the conundrum: There is a current "call" for early childhood teachers to display love, care, and passion and to display professional emotional detachment, while also coping with the stress and demands inherent in working with colleagues, families, and children. Colley (2006) highlights these contradictions:

> Alongside this prescribed curriculum, and the unwritten curriculum of emotional bonding, a further 'hidden' curriculum emerged as students talked about what they had learned as they participated in their work placements. Their narratives centered on coping with the emotional demands of the job, and revealed a vocational culture of detachment in the workplace, which contrasts somewhat with the nurturing ideal that is officially promoted.
>
> *(p. 21)*

In the chapters and commentaries that follow, we present diverse stories that illustrate the emotional demands, emotional possibilities, and emotional realties of the early childhood world. Our stories illustrate what emotions mean within the everyday lives of people in these educational spaces. As noted at the beginning of this introductory chapter, we center on multiple responses/voices and refocus on emotions broadly, viewing them not solely as internal affective states, but as fluid, dynamic, negotiated, and social and cultural constructs that act as a guide in our daily lived experiences. In terms of reframing emotion, the co-editors identify three ways in which we are trying to shift the focus and lens in early childhood around emotion in this volume:

1) *Location of emotion in social action:* In these stories, the authors examine emotions as they are used, performed, and negotiated within social relationships and social action among children, teachers, administration, and parents. This reframing shifts the focus to emotions as they exist, are learned, and are communicated in the course of "social action."

2) *Multiple participants/voices:* By combining the perspectives of teachers, children, parents, administrators, and researchers across and often within individual chapters, we reframe the reader's vision of the complex nature of the emotional life of the classroom, not just simply looking at it from one social perspective, but from complementary perspectives that collectively create a more holistic sense of emotion in educational venues.

3) *Expanded role of emotion and types of emotion:* We examine what it feels like to be in one of the participant roles noted earlier, moving past "love and care" to illustrate how various emotional responses, including emotional discomfort, are also part of teaching and learning. The reframing of the diverse roles and types of emotion also resists thinking about emotions in binary or dualistic terms.

By looking across locations and roles, and by including multiple voices, we hope to complicate the idea of emotion and see the nuanced meaning of emotion as it is yoked to social action.

Structure and Themes of the Book

While we oriented the book to highlight the elements of location, voice, and roles/types, the invited authors naturally brought their own unique topics, stories, questions, and perspectives on emotion in the early childhood world. Our authors include parents, teachers, researchers, and administrators, along with experts who, through their insightful commentaries, provide yet another perspective on the chapter topics. As we worked with the chapter authors and expert commentaries as they took shape, we organized chapters under three section themes that emerged from the stories and data in the chapters: Just practices and emotional discomfort, places and spaces for emotional intimacy and challenge, and understanding emotion within roles and relationships.

Just Practices and Emotional Discomfort

Are justice and emotion two constructs that belong together? In considering the relationship between justice and emotion, we must first understand how our emotional investments and attachments guide how we conceptualize what is "best," "good," and "fair" for our young children and families in early education. Anyone who has been a social advocate can testify that justice and emotion are not separate: Often, our emotional responses and reactions motivate us to fight for the rights of those who are oppressed or subjected to inequitable regulations, policies, or practices. What role does emotion play when considering just and unjust early childhood practices and policies? How do teachers, children, administrators, and parents experience practices and policies that invoke emotional comfort and discomfort?

The first three chapters examine these questions as they illustrate how just practices and related emotion are lived and recounted by teachers, administrators, children, and parents. Each chapter shows that constructing emotion is a process that exists *in situ* and within systems of power and dominance; some of these systems oppress, and others transform. Justice is not simply an outcome, but is a continual process of reflection, resistance, and change. In contexts where oppressive policies and practices are prevalent, reflection and change engender people's resistance and promote a self-focused concern with what feels "right" and "best" for them (i.e., this feels right to me so it must be just). In contrast, in settings where policies and practices focus on community problem-solving, people arrive at what is "right" for the "greater good" and are able to critically reflect on their emotional responses (Ahmed, 2004; Jacobson, 2003; Mackenzie, 2002; Madrid, Baldwin, & Frye, 2013; Zembylas, 2008). The first three chapters illustrate both scenarios—how communities use emotion and reflection to resolve dilemmas experienced by their members and how schools also can be places of oppression.

Chapter 2, *A family, a fire, and a framework: Emotions in an anti-bias school community,* highlights the ways in which a school's anti-bias stance can be the catalyst for the community's emotional growth. Caryn Park, Debbie LeeKeenan, and Heidi Given make visible how a family's tragedy and their teachers' and students' emotional work, within an anti-bias stance and focused on equity, create the conditions for emotional learning. The chapter powerfully recounts the family's response—reaching out to the school as the initial support system when facing this personal crisis. This chapter demonstrates how trust can be built among families and schools when a school community recognizes and actively resists bias and oppressive practices.

The school culture created in this consciously anti-bias setting made it possible for the school community to explore their individual and group identities, emotions, and functioning in society. Socially just learning and the emotions that come with it require both comfort and discomfort as various members of school communities come together with often competing emotional attachments to a particular issue. Each stakeholder must ask: What are the just practices for this community? It also requires the further understanding that feeling emotional discomfort is just as necessary and valuable as feeling emotional comfort when in the role of advocate.

In contrast to Chapter 2, whose anti-bias curriculum sets the tone for parents and children to be emotionally supported and comforted, Chapter 3, *Guinea pigs,*

Asperger's syndrome, and my son: When teachers struggle to recognize humanity, demonstrates the emotional turmoil and discomfort of a parent exposed to school systems that did not promote fair and just practices toward him and his son. Steve Bialostock's story chronicles a deeply personal account of his son, diagnosed at age three with Asperger's, and his experiences in school through fifth grade. The chapter describes their emotional experiences and the unjust and oppressive interactions with teachers and administrators, which caused schooling to be a painful journey for both of them. Bialostok suggests that the emotions of children on the autism spectrum involve a distinctive style of communication that is not always understood. Perhaps more importantly, he eloquently shows through his own experience that the emotions of parents of children with autism are not understood. His chapter leaves us asking questions about the inequalities in school curricula and polices that ostracize and devalue ways of knowing that challenge the mainstream and leave little room for children and parents who resist the norm. It provides an intimate view of the life of a parent advocating for his child and the emotional loss that occurs when being an advocate causes further tensions and struggles.

Chapter 4, *Food fight: Difficult negotiations between adults in an early childhood center,* chronicles year-long discussions at a community childcare program around food policies and the emotional tensions that existed and were created when discussing and attempting to arrive at "fair" and "just" food polices. Susan Twombly illustrates how a routine examination of the school's current practices and policies concerning "good" nutrition standards for young children evolved into something much more complex and difficult. Discussions elicited strong emotional responses from both parents and teachers. These conversations, recounted by Susan (the center director), exemplify the many complicated issues that teachers and parents must negotiate and the intense emotions that arise in such negotiations. Here, we see that teachers must understand their own deeply held beliefs about food and examine them in light of their roles as a partner with parents and as an advocate and supporter of a healthy foundation for children. Parents, too, must compromise some of their cultural practices and beliefs in the best interests of the community of children in each classroom. Teachers must also negotiate with their colleagues and mesh their various individual beliefs with the culture of the program. Overall, this chapter shows how strong emotional reactions to policy change signal a complexity of competing values that need to be unpacked by all those invested if a fair and equitable outcome is to be achieved.

Places and Spaces for Emotional Intimacy and Challenge

Do the places and interactional spaces we co-construct offer distinctive and innovative possibilities for emotional growth and work? The next three chapters demonstrate how physical and interactional spaces and places can provoke and support desired emotional learning, expressions, and possibilities.

These three chapters share several commonalities. In all three, we see inspirational examples of teachers' intentional decisions to establish innovative educational venues, either physical venues such as the woods, or interactional venues such as conflict and story-sharing, and shape them to make positive differences in the emotional lives of young children. All three chapters build on and depend upon one definition of intimacy as "a close, familiar, and usually affectionate or loving personal relationship with another person or group"—in this case, with their teachers (http://dictionary.com). All three provided classroom participants the opportunity to enhance relationships and the challenge to grow emotionally by attending to and caring for each other in ways made eminently possible by the creation of these spaces and places.

In this section, we see what can happen when teachers' early childhood practices reflect a deep respect for children and their abilities and possibilities, no matter what their age or life situation. More specifically, each chapter in this section echoes the image of the child embraced in the programs of Reggio Emilia, of a child with both impressive abilities and potentials (Malaguzzi, 1994). This is not surprising, as each of the authors has studied and visited the programs of Reggio Emilia and developed Reggio-inspired programs in the United States and, as a result, this guiding image has become deeply and now subtly interwoven into their thinking and current work. Still, it is impressive to hear about these programs and practices in action and the real emotional (and other) benefits the authors describe.

Across these chapters, we see children solve problems, resolve conflicts, grow in their peer relationships, meet physical and social challenges that develop an early natural empathy, and envision new possibilities for sharing and building their current and future lives. In these chapters, the authors extend beyond their past interests and those prevalent in the research and pedagogical literatures to shed light on new contexts for supporting children's social and emotional life. Topics are viewed from a different angle, in a new light, and in relation to specific contexts with the emotional lens as orientation.

In Chapter 5, *Recognizing, respecting, and reconsidering the emotions of conflict,* Ellen Hall and Alison Maher recast conflict as a metaphorical or interactional space, one that has the potential for positive outcomes and the building of nascent relationships among infants and toddlers. Traditionally, conflict among children is viewed as a threat to classroom life, with the potential to turn into aggression in such acts as biting. In this view, the emotions associated with conflict are fear and anger, and the cumulative impact is the creation of an atmosphere of distrust and uncertain safety. As a consequence, handling conflict effectively is treated as a critical behavior management issue for the adults of the classroom.

In contrast, Hall and Maher take the stance (and play it out in philosophy and practice) that conflict is a natural part of growth, that conflict is not necessarily bad, and that conflict situations do not have the same meanings for children as they do for adults. They speculate that when adults manage and short-circuit the natural process of social problem-solving of conflicts with arbitrary solutions or interventions, they may be contributing to raising adults who are and expect to be regulated and controlled by others.

Instead, they create an intimate space out of and for conflict, as teachers allow conflict to emerge and then work with it and those involved to resolution and to concomitant learning about others and self. Interestingly, this approach is one that is as much about faith in children as it is about the "in tune" behavior of the adults who listen to rather than discipline their youngest charges, and is as much about knowing when not to intervene as it is about when and how to mediate children's interactions. In this chapter, the authors describe the daily and over time work that transforms very young children's responses, initially based on fear, frustration, and anger, into responses based on trust, patience, and confidence. Children's perceived self-efficacy in handling social and emotional interactions emerges as very young children are supported in solving conflicts, deepening relationships, and becoming empowered social participants.

In Chapter 6, *How to hold a Hummingbird: Using stories to make space for the emotional lives of children in a public school classroom,* Melissa Tonachel goes well beyond the typical language- and literacy-related purposes for using story in the primary grades to embrace its possibilities for nurturing her urban first graders' identity development, emotional expression and growth, and widening of their real and imagined worlds.

With a collection of personal stories from the year she lived alone in a rustic cabin in the Maine woods as her departure point, Tonachel connects to her first graders' very different lives by sharing the wonder of this solitary experience with nature, the struggles she was challenged by, and the "scary" feelings she encountered there, such as fear of the woods and of being alone. Through stories that on the surface seem topically and culturally distant from her urban first graders' experience, she nevertheless creates a dialogic space full of universal feelings, co-constructed reimaginings, and human vulnerabilities and courage to be shared by all in collective safety. She creates the daily storytelling time as a place for teachers and children to be in community with each other, and where adventurous and frightening things can be considered in safety and co-constructed through conversation to "successful" outcomes. As she notes, "the narrative holds us because we know we can determine its ending; but when in it, we can experiment with danger, uncertainty, and thrill" (pp. 99–100).

Tonachel, of course, is not the first to connect emotion and story, with the classic work of Bruno Bettelheim on fairy tales as a prime example (Bettelheim, 1976). But in her classroom, the children follow her lead, learning to tell stories to confront emotions, connect to others, explore the self, and take on the deeper task of inventing the self through developing facility with emotions. Telling stories becomes a centerpiece of her classroom culture, a way to project more expansive opportunities for those children who do not imagine or feel that all doors are open for them to go through. Her point is to help children to imagine themselves beyond what they know and to help them envision meeting the problems they encounter in life.

In Chapter 7, *The woods as a toddler classroom: The emotional experience of challenge, connection, and caring,* Dee Smith and Jeanne Goldhaber reframe the woods, not as a place to remember or to visit, but as a school for toddlers and their teachers. The woods offer many challenges and present powerful and unique opportunities for the growth of these toddlers, their teachers, and even their parents. In this chapter, the authors extend beyond their past interests in the woods as a context that challenged and promoted children's physical strength, coordination, stamina, and shared play scripts to "the more serious consideration of the children's social-emotional life in the natural world" (p. 113). They reveal the woods to be a place that engenders in children deep emotions; connections to others and to the natural world; and caring for the people, fauna, and flora they interact with there. In line with the traditions of Rousseau and Thoreau, children experience many moments of joy, wonder, and serenity in the woods. But, as is true in other chapters in this volume, emotional experience is revealed to be more complex, mixed, and nuanced, as children also experience fears and what the authors call "a tension of emotion."

Reminiscent of how the Reggio Emilia Approach embraces "childish" thinking as powerful and creative, Smith and Goldhaber demonstrate how, with the sensitive scaffolding of their teachers, the anthropomorphic and animistic thinking of young children translates into actions of caring for the flora and fauna of the woods. Over time, children develop with the woods another meaning of intimacy: "A close association with or detailed knowledge of deep understanding of a place, subject, period of history, etc." (http://dictionary.com). At the same time, social intimacy is built too, as the children support one other physically and emotionally and, the authors suggest, develop an early form of empathy at an age when the traditional literature says that this is not possible.

Making the woods a school for toddlers is an ambitious undertaking, one bringing mixed emotions for adults as well; for the teachers, who knew both the woods and the children well and took the risk of responsibility for the sake of the anticipated rewards, and for the family members, who had to overcome their own concerns to trust the teachers, their young children, and the powerful potential of this educational experience. For the reader, this chapter poses the promising possibility that the woods can provoke significant emotional and interactional accomplishments in young children and helps us to reflect on the necessary conditions of support and preparation that make such an (ad)venture successful.

Understanding Emotion within Roles and Relationships

Just as a social justice perspective and places and spaces can be intentionally constructed with an explicit consideration of emotional life and emotional consequences, so, too, can educators reconsider and reconstruct the traditional social categories of roles and relationships. While much has been acknowledged and written about the roles and relationships of early childhood teachers and children in classrooms, many concurrent roles and relationships remain largely unexamined.

Chapters 8, 9, and 10 hold in common a questioning of the definitions of traditional roles and explorations of new ones by their authors. Earlier in this chapter, we noted how professionalism has come to mean a detachment from the very emotions that are often at the center of why and how early childhood educators wish to teach. Imagine if being a "professional" teacher or administrator didn't have to mean the absence of emotional displays, discomfort, and vulnerability. In today's climate of accountability, the transition to teaching for novice teachers is likely to feel isolating and to be filled with emotional discomfort. But what if induction-year practices and mentoring networks for novice teachers were extended to include familiar higher education mentors and the support of familiar peers experiencing this same perplexing transition? The supervision relationship often carries with it a detached professionalism and an implicit hierarchy of power and knowledge in favor of the mentor. Imagine if supervisors and administrators could reveal their human qualities, feelings, uncertainties, and vulnerabilities: Would this make it harder or easier to respect his or her authority and experience? Often, researchers of children, and especially of children with disabilities, do research and intervention on classroom participants rather than directly with them and for their benefit. Imagine if an expert's skills could be shared with the parents and peers of a child with autism. These are the kinds of wonderings, questions, and possibilities explored in these final chapters.

One unexamined opportunity for re-imagining roles and relationships for educators is the transitional time between preparation programs and entry to first jobs. The stress of that transition is assumed, and many veteran teachers will tell stories about their first year as a time of survival; but missing from the conversation is the possibility that children "lose time" with inexperienced teachers making their way alone in their first professional year. With many states adopting high-stakes yearly growth models, neither children nor teachers can afford an awkward year of diminished returns. Novice teachers might be under the most emotional stress of all. How do they work through this stressful transition and come to feel differently about their new roles?

In Chapter 8, *Critical friends work through the emotions of beginning teaching together,* David Fernie explores this stressful transition with a collaborating group of new early childhood teachers and their unique opportunity as novice teachers to continue to provide peer support to each other after they leave their institution of higher education and enter the professional world. As readers "listen in" on the Critical Friends group reflections of their first months of professional work, their angst initially is much more emotion filled than it is question filled about skills and pedagogies. Gardiner and Robinson (2010) have written about an "emotional zone of development" that teacher candidates and novice teachers can construct for and with each other. Their notion is that the mentors often provided for novice teachers are too distant from their level of skill and experience to emulate directly, which often creates additional anxiety for the novice. Instead, their peers can provide the much-needed support and the critical dialogue that can help bolster their confidence and shape their pedagogy. This dynamic can be seen in the group who shares its transition with each other and with their campus mentor.

In another arena, the emotional complexities and demands of the early childhood center administrator's role also have increased, with new accountability for early childhood learning outcomes, greater pressure to be accountable for children's readiness for school, and stagnant levels of resources. In Chapter 9, *Emotional intersections in early childhood leadership*, Nikki Baldwin documents how three directors from very different early childhood contexts manage the emotional dimensions of their work. She illustrates how their professional identities were strongly influenced by "emotional intersections" that were linked to the micro- and macro-level discourses unique to the personal and political aspects of their programs. To cite one example, Baldwin writes of a director who takes the risk to reveal her emotions in a moment of frustration and distress in front of a member of her staff and then spends a lot of time repairing that relationship. Her staff member cannot cope with her administrator being emotional, being a "real" person, any more than a young child can handle seeing her parent "lose it." But does it have to be this way? Must we dichotomize power/authority versus feelings/humanity? Can a leader be a "real person" and still lead? How is being emotional related to the policies and practices of early care programs? These are the questions provoked and taken up by Nikki Baldwin.

In Chapter 10, *Promoting peer relations for young children with autism spectrum disorder: The LEAP preschool experience*, Phil Strain and Ted Bovey write about their program for children with autism and the many years of research they have conducted to demonstrate the efficacy of their program. Their central concern is similar to that of most professionals who work with children with autism; that is, the social roles children take up in these early years are very challenging for children with autism, and their emotional connections with parents, family members, teachers, and peers are very limited at best. Parents mourn the distance they feel from their children and their inability to "be in the social world" with them. Most interventions for children with autism are aimed at the individual child—bit by bit, expert therapists work to help children build a repertoire of social skills and appropriate emotional reactions. Emerging skills are taken from the intervention room to the classroom and applied. Strain and his colleagues, however, have created a program that changes the role of expert and in doing so extends the reach of the expert's skills. In this alternative approach, the focus is shifted from the individual child to the social ecology of the child; that is, they work with the child, his adults, and his peers in the child's home and classroom so that they all change and learn to adapt and respond to each other. The expertise of the specialist is shared with the significant others in the child's social world and, as Strain and Bovey show us, with greater impact and efficacy.

In reading this volume, it is the co-editors' hope that readers will gain a new perspective on the emotional worlds of the early childhood classroom through the diversity of voices represented and authenticity of the experiences retold herein. More ambitiously, we hope you will join us and the collective of talented individuals represented in the volume by embracing a commitment to better understand emotional life in the early childhood setting and to support its critical role in the growth and well-being of all participants.

References

Ahmed, S. (2004). *The cultural politics of emotion.* New York: Routledge.

Bettelheim, B. (1976). *The uses of enchantment: The meaning and importance of fairy tales.* New York: Random House.

Boler, M. (1999). *Feeling power: Emotions and education.* New York: Routledge.

Bronson, M. B. (2000). *Self-regulation in early childhood.* NY: Guilford Press.

Bullough, Jr., R. V. (2009). Seeking eudaimonia: The emotions in learning. In P. A. Schutz & M. Zembylas (Eds.), *Advances in teacher emotion research: The impact on teachers' lives* (pp. 33–53). Dordrecht: Springer.

Colley, H. (2006). Learning to labour with feeling: Class, gender, and emotion in childcare education and training. *Contemporary Issues in Early Childhood, 7*(1): 15–29.

Copple, C., & Bredekamp, S. (2009). *Developmentally appropriate practice in early childhood programs.* Washington, DC: National Association for the Education of Young Children.

Day, C., & Lee, J. C. (2011). *New understandings of teacher's work: Emotions and educational change.* Dordrecht; New York: Springer.

Day, C., & Qing, G. (2009). Teacher emotions: Well-being and effectiveness. In P. A. Schutz & M. Zembylas (Eds.), *Advances in teacher emotion research: The impact on teachers' lives.* Dordrecht: Springer.

Elfer P., & Dearnley, K. (2007). Nurseries and emotional well-being: Evaluating an emotionally containing model of professional development. *Early Years, 27*(3): 267–279.

Epstein, A. S. (2009). *Me, you, us: Social-emotional learning in preschool.* Ypsilanti, MI: Highscope Press.

Gardiner, W., & Robinson, K. (2010). Partnered field placements: Collaboration "in the real world." *The Teacher Educator, 44*(3): 202–215.

Goldstein, L. (1997). *Teaching with love: A feminist approach to early childhood education.* New York: Peter Lang.

Hargreaves, A. (1994). *Changing teachers, changing times: Teachers' work and culture in the postmodern age.* New York: Teachers College Press.

Hargreaves, A. (1998). The emotional practice of teaching. *Teaching and Teacher Education, 14*(8): 835–854.

Hyson, M. (2004). *The emotional development of young children: Building an emotion-centered curriculum.* New York: Teachers College Press.

Immordino-Yang, M. H. (2011). Musings on the neurobiological and evolutionary origins of creativity via a developmental analysis of one child's poetry. *LEARNing Landscapes, 5*(1): 133–139.

Immordino-Yang, M. H., & Damasio, A. R. (2007). We feel, therefore we learn: The relevance of affective and social neuroscience to education. *Mind, Brain and Education, 1*(1): 3–10.

Jacobson, T. (2003). *Confronting our discomfort: Clearing the way for anti-bias in early childhood.* Portsmouth, NH: Heinemann.

Jacobson, T. (2008). *"Don't get so upset!" Help young children manage their feelings by understanding your own.* Saint Paul, MN: Redleaf Press.

Jalongo, M. R. (2013). *Teaching compassion: Humane education in early childhood.* New York: Springer.

Larrivee, B. (2012). *Cultivating teacher renewal: guarding against stress and burnout.* Lanham, MD: Rowman & Littlefield Education.

Liston, D., & Garrison, J. (2004). *Teaching, learning, and loving: Reclaiming passion in educational practice.* New York: RoutledgeFalmer.

Mackenzie, C. (2002). Critical reflection, self-knowledge, and the emotions. *Philosophical Explorations, 5*(3): 186–206.

Madrid, S., & Dunn-Kenney, M. (2010). Persecutory guilt, surveillance and resistance: The emotional themes of early childhood educators. *Contemporary Issues in Early Childhood, 11*(4): 388–401.

Madrid, S., Baldwin, N., & Frye, E. (2013). Professional feeling: One early childhood educator's emotional discomfort as a teacher and learner. *Journal of Early Childhood Research, 11*(3): 274–291.

Malaguzzi, L. (1994). Your image of the child: Where teaching begins. *Child Care Information Exchange, 96*: 52–56.

Markus, H., & Kitiyama, S. (1994). Introduction to cultural psychology and emotions research. In H. Markus & S. Kitiyama (Eds.), *Emotion and culture.* Washington, DC: American Psychological Association.

Meyer, D. (2009). Entering the emotional practices of teaching. In P. Schultz & M. Zembylas (Eds.), *Advances in teacher emotion research* (pp. 73–91). New York: Springer.

Moyles, J. (2001). Passion, paradox and professionalism in early years education. *Early Years, 21*(2): 81–95.

Nias, J. (1999). *Primary teaching as a culture of care.* London: Paul Chapman.

Noddings, N. (1984). *Caring, a feminine approach to ethics & moral education.* Berkeley, CA: University of California Press.

Noddings, N. (1993). Caring: A feminine perspective. In K. A. Strike & P. L. Ternasky (Eds.), *Ethics for professionals in education: Perspectives in preparation and practice* (pp. 43–53). New York: Teachers College Press.

Noddings, N. (2011). Stories and affect in teacher education. In C. Day & J. C. Lee (Eds.), *New understandings of teacher's work: Emotions and educational change.* Dordrecht: New York: Springer.

Osgood, J. (2006). Professionalism and performativity: The feminist challenge facing early years practitioners. *Early Years, 26*(2): 189–199.

Osgood, J. (2010). Reconstructing professionalism in ECEC: The case for the critically reflective emotional professional. *Early Years, 30*(2): 119–133.

Page, J. (2011). Do mothers want professional careers to love their babies? *Journal of Early Childhood Research, 9*(3): 310–323.

Salovey, P., & Sluyter, D. J. (1997). *Emotional development and emotional intelligence: Educational implications.* New York, NY: BasicBooks.

Schutz, P. A., & Pekrun, R. (2007). *Emotion in education.* Boston; Amsterdam: Academic Press.

Schutz, P. A., & Zembylas, M. (2009). *Advances in teacher emotion research: The impact on teachers' lives.* Dordrecht: Springer.

Shields, S. (2002). *Speaking from the heart: Gender and the social meaning of emotion*. Cambridge, MA: Cambridge University Press.

Taggart, G. (2011). Don't we care? The ethics and emotional labour of early years professionalism. *Early Years, 31*(1): 85–95.

Thompson, R. A. (2002). The roots of school readiness in social and emotional development. *Set for success: Building a strong foundation for school readiness based on the social-emotional development of young children, 1*(1): 8–29. Kansas City, MO: The Ewing Marion Kauffman Foundation.

Troman, G. (2000). Teacher stress in the low-trust society. *British Journal of Sociology of Education, 21*(3): 331–352.

Tucker, S. (2010). An investigation of the stresses, pressures and challenges faced by primary school head teachers in a context of organizational change in schools. *Journal of Social Work Practice 24*(1): 63–74.

Webster-Stratton, C. (1999). *How to promote children's social and emotional competence*. London: Sage.

Zembylas, M. (2005). *Teaching with emotion: A postmodern enactment*. Greenwich, CT: Information Age Publishing.

Zembylas, M. (2007). *Five pedagogies, a thousand possibilities: Struggling for hope and transformation in education*. Rotterdam: Sense.

Zembylas, M. (2008). Engaging with issues of cultural diversity and discrimination through critical emotional reflexivity in online learning. *Adult Education Quarterly, 59*(1): 61–82.

PART I

Just Practices and Emotional Discomfort

2

A FAMILY, A FIRE, AND A FRAMEWORK

Emotions in an Anti-Bias School Community

Caryn Park, Debbie LeeKeenan, and Heidi Given

UNIVERSITY OF WASHINGTON TACOMA, LESLEY UNIVERSITY, FAYERWEATHER STREET SCHOOL

> "I have learned that there are so many ways we can include all children and families in our educational community. Children are naturally inclined to be inclusive of one another, and as educators we have the responsibility to foster that generous spirit."
>
> —*EPCS community member*

> "An anti-bias community has the capacity to hold what is difficult."
>
> —*Hannah*

This chapter advocates anti-bias education as a framework for creating a supportive environment for social-emotional learning within a school community. It describes a traumatic event that occurred for a family and the role the school community played in helping the family process their emotions and cope with the hardship. We illustrate how the school's anti-bias stance provided a means for one teacher, her students, their families, and eventually the larger community to engage in emotional work around a traumatic incident. We aim to explore the relationship between social-emotional learning and anti-bias education through an account of actual events, and in this telling, demonstrate how emotions and the anti-bias commitment are closely intertwined and mutually reinforcing, binding our school community together.

This piece is the result of collaboration between three authors: Caryn Park, postdoctoral fellow at the Eliot-Pearson Children's School 2010–2012; Debbie Lee-Keenan, its director; and kindergarten teacher Heidi Given. We begin our chapter by providing a brief discussion of the literature at the intersection of social-emotional learning and anti-bias education. Debbie then introduces the school and its core anti-bias commitment. Caryn, drawing on conversations with the family at the center of our story, describes the fire that occurred at the family's home in the winter of 2012 and the events that followed. Next, Heidi provides a firsthand account of how she and her kindergarten class responded. The following section refocuses on the family and includes Caryn's reflections on how individual members framed their experiences and processed emotions in different ways, demonstrating the complexities of emotional recovery. We discuss the mutually reinforcing connection between anti-bias education and social-emotional learning within our school and call for further examination of and theorizing on this vital relationship.

Literature Exploring the Intersections of Social-Emotional Learning and Anti-Bias Education

In situating our work within larger conversations regarding social-emotional learning and anti-bias education, we first sought to gain a picture of how authors framed the connections between the two domains. Finding few direct examples, we selected prominent samples from each domain, including texts on social-emotional learning (Epstein, 2009; Hyson, 1994; Riley, San Juan, Klinkner, & Ramminger, 2008), and anti-bias education (Derman-Sparks & Edwards, 2010).

In the authoritative text by Derman-Sparks and Edwards (2010), some social-emotional learning goals are referred to specifically, but beyond the general sense that anti-bias education supports children's social-emotional growth, the emotional piece is generally seen as a by-product of the work. Pang (2001) and Pang, Rivera, and Mora (1999) emphasize caring-centered multicultural education as the key to supporting students from diverse cultural communities, but focus primarily on understanding students' cultures (rather than emotions) as the vehicle for achieving educational equity. The connections between emotions and anti-bias education are largely implicit and assumed in the literature, calling for a closer examination of the specific relationships between the domains.

We broadened our search and found several examples of educators reflecting on their own emotions in their engagement with anti-bias and multicultural education (Gay, 2003; Jacobson, 2003; Paley, 1979, 2000). Jacobson (2003) offers a personal exploration of bias and oppression as a vehicle for becoming an intentional and effective anti-bias educator for young children. She conceptualizes bias as part of a set of "survival skills" that we acquire as we negotiate painful experiences growing up. In order to serve children and families through powerful anti-bias work, educators must confront deeply rooted biases, emotions, and personal histories by "engaging with our inner child and confronting our fears" (p. 68).

Another example is from esteemed kindergarten teacher and author Vivian Paley (1979, 2000). Although all of Paley's work reflects anti-bias thinking and practice, in her book *White Teacher* she examines her beliefs, language, and childhood experiences of feeling different with emotional candor and a spirit of inquiry. In her attempts to create a classroom that is inclusive of Black children during a period of school desegregation, she discovers a class community that, through play, allows everyone to have a role, to feel understood, valued, and emotionally connected.

We aim to contribute to the literature connecting emotions with anti-bias work by further exploring the relationship between these two aspects of early childhood education. We believe our work is unique in that we do this in a way that encompasses not just teachers or children, but the whole school community.

Anti-Bias Education at Eliot-Pearson Children's School

In this section, Debbie describes how anti-bias education looks in our particular setting. The Eliot-Pearson Children's School (EPCS) is a laboratory school for the Department of Child Study and Human Development at Tufts University in Medford, Massachusetts. The school serves 80 children and families, from 3–8 years of age in five classrooms. Our community reflects a wide range of abilities and learning styles, as well as different economic, cultural, racial, linguistic backgrounds, and family structures. The school's longstanding commitment to anti-bias education is part of the core values and mission of the school.

Anti-bias education is a stance that supports children and their families as they develop a sense of personal and group identity within a complex and multicultural society. This approach helps teach children to be proud of themselves and their families, to respect a range of human differences, to recognize unfairness and bias, and to stand up for what is right (Derman-Sparks & Edwards, 2010). At EPCS, this means working to create an inclusive community that encourages conversations among children and adults about all types of human differences in the context of classroom life. Curriculum topics come from the children, families, and teachers, as well as historical or current events, and can include culture, race, language, abilities, ethnicity, family structure, religion, sexual orientation, gender, age, economic differences, and our many ways of being. Children learn about similarities and differences in individuals and communities. The anti-bias stance is integrated into classroom activities, in both planned curriculum and "teachable moments" based on children's social interactions, conversations, and play. When children ask questions about differences, adults listen in order to facilitate conversations and responses.

The anti-bias stance is woven into the fabric of the school, including its policies and structures, physical environment, classroom curriculum, and interactions among children, teachers, administrators, and families. Staff meeting time is dedicated to sharing anti-bias education dilemmas and reflections. Teachers set anti-bias professional goals each year. The physical environment of the school reflects the community at large, with photos of families and books and images that portray all types of diversity. Being able to answer "yes" to the question, "Do I see who I am, who my child is, and who my family is?" in the daily school environment and curriculum is fundamental. This is how trust and belonging are fostered.

Families must feel accepted and respected in order to actively engage with anti-bias issues. Each family is unique in their life experiences, expectations of school, and parenting approaches. Families also belong to various subgroups (ethnic, economic class, religious), which affect how they live. Our work with families begins with getting to know them, both informally and formally, from initial intakes and home visits to potluck socials and an open-door policy where families are welcomed to visit anytime. Learning about families is a process, not a one-time event. It continues as families develop more familiarity, comfort, and trust with the teachers and director.

Anti-bias work creates a climate for dialogue, reflection, and risk-taking on diversity issues. Our goal is to be a place where people can disagree and discuss conflicting values and ideas and work to find common ground. Over the years, I noted new families' many questions about anti-bias education. What does anti-bias education look like at EPCS? Is it appropriate for young children? What is my role as a parent? What if I disagree with the school? During 2010–2011, we invited families to collaborate with staff to develop a Frequently Asked Questions document about anti-bias education. The process took nearly the entire school year to complete and became a form of professional development for the staff and an empowering experience for parents. The final document became part of the school's handbook. From this process, we all learned more about each other. It is within this school culture that our story takes place.

The Family's Story: "Our House Is Burning . . . Can I Come Back to School with the Kids?"

Ten Alarm

She told us they watched the thread
of fire go down the bedside table
across the floor, under the double doors
& into her daughter's room. Then they
were running, down & out, onto the street.
It was too early for stillness or sorrow.

My phone rang in another town.
Your house is on fire, said the neighbor
across the street & soon all the neighbors
were calling, curtained by fire trucks
& the Red Cross.

It was just our house. We were preserved
in a rental in another town, but the water
broke the floors, went pouring to the beds below,
the cribs & books, the pictures hung on the wall.

Before long, there were videos posted
of our house burning—the whole world could
watch it disappearing, helpless until
the shiny trucks came bearing heroes, used to this
routine. They used pick axes to knock down
all the walls just to make sure there were no more
burning embers hiding. They did not stop until

there was no doubt. Then they drove away
& men came in the dark with business cards —
insurance adjustors, contractors, even photographers.

This is how it happens, the unattended candle,
the end of one life, the way it gets traded for
another one, in the middle of the night, without
warning.

—Hannah

I (Caryn) first met Cooper's parents, Hannah and Toby, through the Diverse Families Group, one of our school's many Parent-Teacher Learning Groups. Before we began working together on this project, I knew them as strong advocates of anti-bias education, as kind, gracious, generous members of our school community, and as loving, gentle parents to their two children, Cooper (age 6) and Hailey (4).

In 2011, the family lost their condominium to a fire (see poem above). They were not living in the building at the time but had tenants and friends who were. Toby went to the scene of the fire in the middle of the night, but neither Hannah nor the children were present. Still, it was a source of emotional and financial trauma for the family.

Almost a year later, on January 4, 2012, the children came home from school with their grandfather. When Hannah came home, she saw that Cooper had drawn a picture of the fire. He had been drawing these all year. She gently said to him, "We already have about 30 of these pictures, so do you want to give this one to Grandpa?" A few minutes later, they left the house and were getting into the car when her father said he smelled something burning. Hannah looked up. Smoke was pouring off the second floor deck (which belonged to neighbors in their multifamily house). It was an icy day in January, and neighbors brought blankets as Hannah stood with her children, waiting for the firefighters as they watched their home burn.

Having secured everyone's physical safety, Hannah intuited what her children needed emotionally. She recounts:

> I didn't feel like it would be fair to just whisk them away; I didn't know what their heads would do with just picturing our house going up in flames. So we stayed and we watched the firemen with their axes and stuff break into the roof and let the heat out, and we watched them put the fire out.

Although Toby and Hannah's memories of the fire and cleanup are vivid, it was difficult during our conversations for them to remember how the children reacted. Hannah tried to respond to my questions about the children's emotional states during the fire:

> I don't feel like I was doing a good job of tuning into how they were in the moment. I was shell-shocked myself so I was making sure to be close to them physically and I kept saying to them we're okay, everyone is out of the

house, no one's going to get hurt. But in terms of more than that, it was a traumatic experience in that I think we were all just frozen and waiting to see what was gonna happen next . . . I just felt like, all I can do right now is just know that they're physically safe.

Even though she may not have felt "tuned in" to Cooper's emotions, she knew with some clarity two things he needed emotionally. First, to see the fire put out. Then:

My very first thought as soon as the flames were gone was, we have to go to school . . .

I just felt like from the very beginning there was no question that I was gonna call the school right away and there was no question that they were just gonna kind of hold us up. And that's what happened . . . I felt like, I need to bring my children right now to a safe place, where emotionally they are safe. I need to remind them even right now that life is going to continue and that their school is still safe. We could have gone to a friend's house too, but I just partly felt like I wanted to be with professionals in a way.

Toby added:

And school is this big community, it's like this ocean of support, all these people doing their thing, this big institution full of support . . . and so full of all these amazing adults who are focused on all the kids.

As a newer member of the EPCS community, I found Hannah's choice to bring the children to the school remarkable. It made me want to better understand what it is about this school that creates such deep trust. In the following section, Heidi, Cooper's kindergarten teacher, describes how she initially responded to the family's crisis and gradually guided Cooper and his class toward social-emotional growth. Through Heidi's account, we begin to see how the anti-bias stance offers a framework for supporting individual children, families, and the larger community.

Heidi's Story: This Is What Being in a Community Looks Like

The Day of the Fire

It was early afternoon, about an hour after kindergarten dismissal. Suddenly, Cooper's mother was on the phone. "Heidi, our house is burning," she said. "We're outside on the sidewalk. I don't know what to do. Can I come back to school with the kids?"

My heart began to race, my mind remembering that just nine months earlier Cooper's family had lost another home to a fire. Though the children had not

FIGURE 2.1 An example of Cooper's fire drawings

witnessed the first fire, it had taken a toll on the family and fully captured Cooper's imagination. He was still drawing the same scene—a man walking down a tree-lined path, when suddenly a fire appears in front of him (see Figure 2.1). What would it mean now that there had been a second fire—one the children had seen and that would necessitate moving?

I had four minutes of panic and wondering what to do and say. I spent another four minutes running to the director, associate director, and Hailey's teacher until Cooper, Hailey, and Hannah walked through the door. You could smell the smoke on their bodies. My heart tightened. *Oh my God, this is so real.* I stepped into teacher mode, ready to listen and support. Hannah needed to figure out what to do and who to call. Toby was at the house, and her mother was on her way. Could we stay with the three of them until she arrived? The answer was so clear—of course we could; this is what being in a community looks like.

The children appeared to need very different things. Hailey needed to have a snack and be comforted. Cooper needed to verbally process what had happened. This was true to his learning style and needs. Cooper was wonderfully insightful, observant, sensitive, and a bit challenging to have in a group. He exhibited a range of sensory needs. He fidgeted, crashed into others and furniture, and made sounds during meetings and as he worked. He thought deeply about all sorts of things and verbalized his thoughts with more descriptive detail than most 5- and 6-year-olds.

Though fully engaging to adults, it was hard for peers to stay focused long enough to engage with all his ideas.

Cooper recounted his experience multiple times in great detail. I wondered and worried, was this productive, therapeutic, or was the telling and retelling too much? Should I try to distract him for a while? I decided to follow his lead.

Classroom Discussions, Children's Questions

I was concerned about what Cooper's needs would be in class the next morning and how he would tell the story to his peers. How would I support him? Would his friends listen? I tried to imagine the kinds of questions and fears that might arise. I consider myself a brave teacher who is a fan of telling the whole story, but in this instance, I found myself wondering how much was too much. I felt the need to balance aspects that might be scary for some and ones that could be interesting or even exciting.

I told the group Cooper had a serious and sad story to tell. He told every detail in a matter-of-fact way. He explained that the fire started on the porch of the apartment upstairs when a grill was left unattended (I was grateful that we knew how the fire actually started, as it was a cause that could be controlled and avoided). The children were riveted. With great enthusiasm and admiration, Cooper talked about how four fire engines came and blocked all the roads. The firefighters smashed windows and cut holes in the roof using axes and chainsaws. I explained that this releases the smoke and pressure and allows water in to extinguish the fire. Another child who lived nearby said that an ambulance came. I made the point that there was no one in the house and nobody was hurt. The ambulance was just in case there was a need as firefighters sometimes, although rarely, get hurt while putting out a fire. Children asked how Cooper and his family discovered the fire, where they were, and what they did. We also discussed the importance of getting out of a house or building if there is a fire and how to do that safely. Children knew a lot.

That day I sent an e-mail to the class parents to inform them about the fire and alert them to our conversation. I wrote:

> Overall, the discussion was calm, informed, and very engaging. The children asked great questions and shared their own experiences and knowledge about fire . . . Your child may want to share her/his understanding of what happened with you, as well as discuss your family plan for what to do if there were ever a fire in your house. When discussing this potentially scary topic, it is often best to give short, matter-of-fact answers. Reassuring your child that you, and if needed firefighters, would do whatever it takes to keep him/her safe is important.
>
> The children also expressed strong empathy for Cooper, immediately offering to share some of their toys and belongings with him. Other families

have also expressed an interest in helping. For now, it is a bit early to know exactly what is needed. What would be most supportive at this time is for people to sign up to prepare/donate a meal.

My letter elicited immediate responses, and many families throughout the school were eager to help.

Supporting Cooper's Process of Healing

Given the amount of stress and turmoil in Cooper's life, it was clear that his sensory and motor needs would escalate. My goal was for the whole class to support Cooper. For the other children, that meant more than just giving him toys or clothing. It would mean that they would need to step outside their own needs as well, which is harder for children than making grandiose yet simplistic suggestions such as, "We'll just build a new house!"

We'd done a lot of work around understanding the distinct strengths and needs of the children in our group and what accommodations each needed to do his or her best work. The children understood that Cooper might bump into them more and would certainly need to zoom around the bike path at full speed during outdoor time. Some children even offered supports to Cooper that they thought might help.

The children were attentive and engaged in revisiting the story of the fire the first few times. After that, teachers took on the role of attentive audience. In his oral storytelling and drawings, Cooper seemed to be finding resolution through narrative. During the first month, Cooper's drawings began to shift from the typical "man in a path encountering a fire" drawings that he had been "stuck" on for so many months, to drawings of the second fire, to drawings of adventures he was having with his grandparents, to eventual drawings of his new garden and house.

Cooper's story inspired several curriculum strands, including an exploration of volcanoes and a study of homelessness. During the past few years, I have been engaging with the constructs that kindergartners demonstrate and develop about social class. Cooper's experience gave life and depth to anti-bias concepts—about who are the people who make or receive donations, the differences between wants and needs, how we can truly be helpers in the community—challenging me, the children, and their families to articulate our core values and beliefs and to consider and respect the needs of others.

"Leaning into the Discomfort": Emotional Work as a Teacher

My goal as a teacher was to help develop children's awareness and empathy without making them worry. I pushed against the boundaries of my comfort zone when considering the potential risks in allowing Cooper to tell his story uncensored, how some children might become frightened about their own family's safety and home. I wondered: Is it okay to protect one group of children from stressors, while other groups live in emotionally hostile environments? Should we expose the "protected" to the truth, so that they may grow into fuller human beings who advocate for all?

Madrid (2013) emphasizes the importance of a teacher's ability to "*lean into the discomfort*" (p. 86), even when it disrupts his or her familiar ways of knowing and feeling. At EPCS, I have been supported in developing these abilities, and I hope to cultivate this in my kindergarteners by scaffolding difficult conversations and allowing them to take risks and respond to one another with authentic emotions.

Engaging in the Emotional Labor of Recovery

Shifting the focus back to the family, in this section, we dig deeper into the experiences of Hannah, Toby, and the children in the aftermath of the fire. As I (Caryn) learned through my conversations with Cooper's parents, each family member's journey toward healing was unique, with different emotional responses, processes, and needs.[1]

Toby was at work when he received the call from Hannah about the fire and remembers shifting immediately into "protective mode," accompanied by a kind of "stoicism." He describes these as emotional states, ones that carried him through the following week of going through each room of their home hauling out belongings for storage or the dumpster, and through months of assuring his anxious children that he and Hannah were very careful about fire, that when everyone is extremely careful, they would all be safe. He describes how he and Hannah felt "a general sense of wanting to wrap ourselves around our kids and say, it's okay, this is a terrible thing but it's gonna be okay," even when they weren't feeling so secure themselves.

As Toby described his stoicism, he simultaneously reflected on it:

TOBY: It's almost like I wasn't gonna let myself feel bad about it. Which is actually kind of maybe an unhealthy kind of stoicism, honestly, and here I am a year later looking at that again and wondering if that was actually so wise, but that was what I felt at the time, it's just, I'm not gonna let myself feel bad about this because I just can't.

CARYN: What emotions would you have felt?

TOBY: Just the sadness, and the loss and all the things you might naturally expect. The frustration with the neighbors and the sadness about having to leave our home, and the frustration with having to commute now and so much less time to do the things we wanted to do . . . so many negative emotions that would have been natural, they were there, they certainly crept in from various angles. I think partly it was a self-defense mechanism because I felt like—maybe not even consciously—if I allowed myself to feel how I really was feeling I would have been completely overwhelmed because we were doing everything we could just to hold it together . . . just the logistical work took everything we had, so to make any room for actually feeling the emotions that I naturally would otherwise have been feeling—I felt like I just didn't have time for it. Even though it probably would have been wise to make the time because it built up and then it takes more time to kind of unpack and deal with later, but that's just where I was at that time.

Although Toby begins by describing his stoicism as an emotional state, it seems he also recognizes through our conversation that there were emotions that seemed to be "naturally" surfacing, and stoicism was more of an action/reaction he was using to respond to and manage the emotions. With all the logistics and the physical work to be done, Toby felt he could not take the time or space to put emotions at the center of his response. He needed to bracket negative emotions that might interfere with handling so many practical issues. However, he recognizes that keeping his emotions at bay would not serve him in the long run.

One strategy for dealing with the trauma of the fire has been to maintain the family's core "big picture perspective that we're so lucky." Hannah explained that she told herself and others again and again, "This is not a tragedy." This idea was important to hold onto even as they assessed their many material and emotional losses as a result of not one but two fires. Hannah noted that the greatest loss affected her children, in that they no longer "just assume that you wake up in the morning and you go to school and everything's fine." She continued, "So that is a huge loss, but besides that, it was just stuff that was lost." They knew they had many places they could go and people to turn to, and they were able to find a new home in a few weeks. Two house fires in a year would have been enough to devastate many families, but Cooper's family seemed truly to be surrounded by a community of love and support, which helped them rebound quickly.

However, I wondered whether the insistence that they were a "lucky" family— and that the fire was not a tragedy—might be preventing Toby from allowing himself to feel the full range of emotions he knew were looming close. Hannah, too, wavered at times between describing her family as incredibly fortunate and feeling the "desperation" of their situation as their financial goals and dream home slipped away.

The children had their share of emotional work, too. They had to say good-bye to their house (see Figure 2.2) and nearly all of their belongings. In the early days, Cooper had nightmares about accidentally setting fire to the house himself. He felt the need to monitor and worry about things far beyond a 5-year-old's responsibilities. Hannah shared that even months later, during the summer, he came home and told her, "If there was another fire at our house, I would carry all of you out of the house."

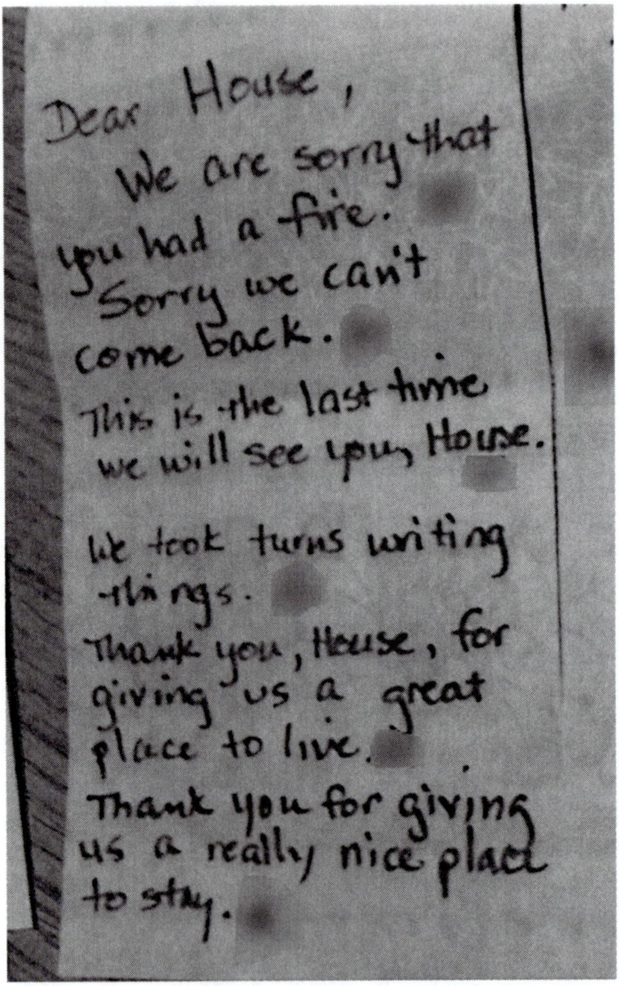

FIGURE 2.2 Cooper and Hailey's goodbye letter to the house

The fact that Cooper eventually stopped making the same drawings of fire shows significant progress. His parents and teachers, who allowed him to show them hundreds of fire pictures day after day, and his class peers, who listened and asked questions and were there with him as he relived the details of the fire, all played a vital role in Cooper's healing. Madrid (2013) writes that "being able to reveal our stories and concealed emotional pain is the path to reclaiming our spirit in and out of the classroom. Witnessing is the other side of vulnerability as it makes demands on the teacher to hear and hold the stories of students who have experienced injustices and emotional pain" (p. 87). Cooper's family, teachers, and classmates participated emotionally in his process, bearing witness to his story and allowing it to gradually achieve closure. Hannah and Toby credit the school for the way Cooper is now able to relate his own family's hardships to other things and people in the world. They describe how he seems to have more empathy for victims of natural disasters and other challenges. Hannah said, "Even though it is a kind of sensitivity, it's a positive kind of sensitivity."

Cooper's sister Hailey was only three when the fire occurred, yet her process was painful and lasting. Partly due to her age, she was not as clear in articulating her responses to the fire, and adults around her felt it was more prudent to allow her to initiate conversations than to take a more active approach such as Heidi did. She did not have the same opportunities to process her experiences and emotions with the type of classroom supports that were offered to Cooper.

Hailey's response to the fire manifested in several ways. For months, she suffered from daily stomachaches. Her imaginative play became stuck on scenes of emergency and hardship. Two dollhouses were donated to them after the fire, and Hailey would want Hannah to sit with her while she moved all the people and furniture from one dollhouse to the other. Hannah remembers, "It would feel like a desperate concentration." Erickson viewed repetitive play as a way for young children to "gain control over upsetting experiences" (Hyson, 1994, p. 33). Hailey needed to process her emotions through repetitive play, just as Cooper needed to draw the same scene or tell the story repeatedly. However, as a mother, it was difficult and painful for Hannah to accompany Hailey each time she engaged in these (re)enactments of trauma and loss.

Erikson's theory posits that individuals develop psychosocially through each resolution of conflict and achieve a greater sense of strength, autonomy, and trust (Hyson, 1994). In this sense, the family's loss might be seen as an opportunity to develop emotionally as individuals and as a collective. Such narratives of overcoming hardships to reap the rewards on the other side are the stuff of classic moral tales. However, when asked about the positive outcomes that she saw as a result of this experience, Hannah did not offer a simple happy ending:

> With me and Hailey, where we're at in our own process is that we've learned we can't count on life. There's nothing that's guaranteed. I still am working through my own hyper-vigilance about trying to protect everybody . . . Hailey and I still have to move past our PTSD [post-traumatic stress disorder] a little bit more before I'll be able to talk about what else we learned from it.

Hannah's awareness of where she is in her process gives her a perspective about where she may eventually be, which her young daughter lacks. Whereas for Hailey the present pain might feel like the only and permanent outcome of the fire, Hannah understands that this story is not over yet, and some day they may look back and recognize that it changed them for the better.

According to Ahmed (as cited in Madrid, 2013), "Healing does not cover over, but exposes the wounds to others: *The recovery is a form of exposure*" (p. 87). As authors of this chapter, we wonder how the parents' desire to protect their children (and themselves) from the extent of their emotional and material losses may have delayed the emotional work that had to take place before they could move on. Do they need to allow room to grieve their losses by releasing the family from the narrative of being "lucky"? Would it now be helpful to expose each family member's deepest fears about what this loss means to them now and in the future? Might their participation in this writing project have played a role in the process of recovering through un-covering?

Further Reflections

A Community Response

Hannah and Toby both felt grateful to Heidi and the school community for the care and support they received. They noted "how happy and excited people were to come pitch in and help out." Over 40 people helped them on their "move out" day. One of the kindergarten families came and removed 12 bags of smoky wet laundry from their basement floor. "They just came and put it all in their car, and said, 'We'll let you know when it's ready.'" They remembered with appreciation how they ate meals cooked for them by EPCS families "every night for a whole month."

Toby referred to the bonding and interactions that were made possible by the fire as a "nice side effect of this otherwise terrible event." He concluded, "I think it's easy to say that both our sense of place and strong sense of community with the school, which was already strong, was cemented without a doubt."

The school-wide anti-bias culture encourages all its members to come into the community fully and as they are. Racial, ethnic, and cultural identities are not the only forms of difference recognized. The fundamental spirit of acceptance and respect for the whole child and the work of the community in exploring what it means to be accepting and respectful of difference allowed Cooper to be himself and move through his unique process of healing with love and support.

Kindergarten families welcomed the chance to aid a family in need. They felt generous and empowered. Heidi's goals for working with parents became to support them as they grappled with topics they might not feel comfortable discussing with children and with personal values about economic inequality that may not previously have been articulated. She felt that the families responded more positively toward the anti-bias curriculum focus than in previous years. Cooper's family's experiences provided the community with an opportunity to explore the topic of economic hardship in a way that was concrete and personally connected to them. There is a danger of reinforcing stereotypes when we try to talk about groups and communities that feel socially and emotionally distant (Derman-Sparks, 1989). But children's emotional connection and empathy with Cooper strengthened the anti-bias curriculum. One possible indicator of the lessons learned by children is that during the course of the curriculum, Cooper was told by a friend that if he had another fire, "you can come home with us."

Our story illustrates the mutually reinforcing relationship between cultivating a school-wide anti-bias stance and fostering social-emotional learning. When a community member's emotional well-being became the focus of the whole class, this deepened and personalized the anti-bias messages of the curriculum.

Caveat: Tensions between the Need to Feel and the Need to Act

In anti-bias work, we encourage children to become active participants in the world, to stand for what they believe in, and to oppose injustice. This work is ongoing, and not without some perils. Heidi has observed children's gut reaction to hearing about Cooper's loss as wanting to see things get all better as quickly as possible. That sense of finding instant relief can feel comforting and supportive, but as anti-bias educators, we also must step back and wonder how much fixing is really possible, how important it is for the children to at least get a glimpse of the complexity of the issues. Recognizing the ongoing reality of injustice and inequality and learning to sit with the pain of unfairness are the hardest aspects of this work. There is a risk involved in moving children to action too quickly with little reflection, or missing the emotional aspect of the work—just feeling how it feels to encounter unfairness or suffering. Just as Madrid (2011) argues that emotional discomfort—more so than comfort—can push or motivate teachers to engage in social justice work, the same goes for children.

Theorizing the Relationship between Anti-Bias Education and Social-Emotional Learning

In Table 2.1, we list the four core goals of anti-bias education, as set forth by Derman-Sparks and Edwards (2010), alongside six of the 13 social-emotional learning topics covered by Epstein (2009) that are closely aligned with the anti-bias goals. The reader may notice significant overlaps in the goals for children's development.

TABLE 2.1 Comparison of Anti-bias Goals and Related Social-emotional Topics

Anti-bias goals (Derman-Sparks & Edwards, 2010)	Social-emotional learning topics (Epstein, 2009)
Awareness of self and pride in one's family and social identities	Developing a positive self-identity Developing a sense of community
Appreciation and knowledge of human differences and deep, caring connections	Valuing diversity Feeling empathy
Recognition of unfairness, language to describe it, and understanding that it hurts	Developing a framework for moral behavior
Empowerment and action against prejudice and discrimination	Creating and participating in a democracy

Are social-emotional learning and anti-bias education simply different ways of talking about the same goals for children's development? Could anti-bias work be understood as a collective version of individual social-emotional development? We propose a mutually reinforcing relationship: An anti-bias stance creates the conditions for every member's social-emotional learning by focusing on equity as a framework and foundation. When a school community recognizes and actively resists bias and oppression, the culture created enables members to explore their individual and group identities, emotions, and functioning in society. A school-wide anti-bias culture supports the emotional work of individuals and groups by serving as a framework, a language, and a provocation for this work to come to the fore of the learning experience.

Ongoing Emotional Work in an Anti-Bias School Community

> I think that if we hadn't had this experience in an anti-bias community, there is no way I would have shared so much vulnerability with the teachers, staff, and parents. An anti-bias community fosters a deeper kind of honesty, a "take me as I am" kind of honesty. That was why I felt comfortable calling the school that day to say, "This is what is happening for us right now."
>
> —*Hannah*

The narrative offered in this chapter shows how anti-bias education can provide a framework for social-emotional learning across a whole school community. The school-wide anti-bias education framework allowed individuals and families to experience learning around issues, identities, and emotions that might otherwise be considered outside the realm of school and classroom conversations. The framework functioned as a catalyst for the emotional work of the community, opening up numerous entry points for engaging with Cooper's family's loss, supporting him and his peers, and guiding the direction of the curriculum. It also moved and empowered the community to take their learning beyond school grounds to attend to the wider community.

Yet the work is never done. In preparing this chapter, as each of us reflected on the events, conversations, and curriculum, we noticed missed opportunities, unanswered questions, and emotional work left to revisit. What might we do differently next time, or even tomorrow? Are there limits to how much schools can support families through difficult events?

Scholarship is needed to further theorize and explicate the relationship between emotions and an anti-bias framework. In particular, we need a better understanding of how emotions operate in anti-bias work in early childhood education, not only for children, but also for teachers and families. In addition, scholarly work on emotions in early childhood education needs to be grounded in deeper understandings of diversity, equity, and justice. When schools engage in fostering cultures of recognition and appreciation of all of our differences, strengths, and challenges, they can become the first place of sanctuary for a family in a time of need.

Acknowledgment

The authors wish to thank Cooper's family for their story, their trust, and the privilege of working with their children. Special gratitude goes out to "Hannah," who shared her poetry and her heart with us for this project.

Note

1. The adults involved in writing this chapter agreed that we would make our best attempts to describe the children's experiences without approaching them directly to gather "data" for this project.

References

Derman-Sparks, L., & ABC Task Force. (1989). *Anti-bias curriculum: Tools for empowering young children.* Washington, DC: NAEYC.

Derman-Sparks, L., & Edwards, J. O. (2010). *Anti-bias education for young children and ourselves.* Washington, DC: NAEYC.

Epstein, A. S. (2009). *Me, you, us: Social-emotional learning in preschool.* Ypsilanti, MI: Highscope Press.

Gay, G. (2003). *Becoming multicultural educators: Personal journey toward professional agency.* San Francisco, CA: Jossey-Bass.

Hyson, M. C. (1994). *The emotional development of young children: Building an emotion-centered curriculum.* New York: Teachers College Press.

Jacobson, T. (2003) *Confronting our discomfort: Clearing the way for anti-bias in early childhood.* Portsmouth, NH: Heinemann.

Madrid, S. (2011). Emotional intersections: Learning how to feel as a social advocate. *The Voice: The Journal for Campus Children's Centers, 6*(3): 5–7.

Madrid, S. (2013). Care as a racialized, critical and spiritual emotion. In C. Dillard & C. Okpalaoka (Eds.), *Engaging culture, race, and spirituality in education* (pp. 81–88). New York: Peter Lang.

Paley, V. G. (1979, 2000). *White teacher.* Cambridge, MA: Harvard University Press.

Pang, V. O. (2001). *Multicultural education: A caring-centered, reflective approach.* Boston: McGraw Hill.

Pang, V. O., Rivera, J., & Mora, J. K. (1999). The ethic of caring: Clarifying the foundation of multicultural education. *The Educational Forum, 64*(1): 25–32.

Riley, D., San Juan, R. R., Klinkner, J., & Ramminger, A. (2008). *Social and emotional development: Connecting science and practice in early childhood settings.* St. Paul, MN: Redleaf Press.

COMMENTARY

Patricia G. Ramsey

MOUNT HOLYOKE COLLEGE

This chapter is a vivid and heartfelt story of how anti-bias work prepares teachers, children, and families to work together as a community to meet emotional needs. It provides a concrete and compelling example of how caring and community underlie anti-bias work and vice versa. This account is particularly powerful, as it includes voices of children and parents as well as teachers. For instance, the examples of Cooper's drawings and narratives over time show how, with skilled support, children can grasp and rise above personal disasters and gain the insight and courage to move on in their lives. Toby's honest discussion with Caryn about how he suppressed his feelings in order to appear strong for his family highlights the advantages of a community where teachers and parents talk openly and honestly about issues and roles—in this case, gender roles. Heidi's ruminations about whether or not she should protect the children from the harsh realities of the fire and how she can balance the needs of one child with the interests of the whole group show us how teachers can sensitively and astutely embrace competing priorities and the widely ranging emotional capacities of children.

This story also prompts us to think further about related issues and questions, for example: Why is emotional growth viewed as a "by-product" rather than a central focus of anti-bias work? In our society, we tend to polarize individualism versus collectivism, private versus public lives, and personal connections versus conflict; and these divisions may affect our views of social justice work. Often, the media show militaristic images of protest groups here and abroad. Stern angry faces, upraised fists, or displays of weapons collectively imply that advocacy is confrontational and does not allow for gentler feelings and personal attachments. These portrayals also suggest that true activists have to forsake families and friends and commit themselves to following group dictates and perhaps live for long periods in treetops or tents in city parks. In fact, some people shy away from being involved in social justice work because they assume that the personal and emotional costs are too great.

Social justice work *does* require a degree of discomfort—putting oneself into unfamiliar and challenging situations, taking risks, confronting authorities, and, at times, distancing oneself from family and friends. Conflict is also inevitable because individuals and institutions that hold power are not going to voluntarily give up their privilege and control. Furthermore, any movement requires a certain amount of conformity and adherence to particular values and strategies, because unity is necessary to send clear messages in our sound-bite society. Balancing conformity and coherence with the variety and richness of individual views, talents, and needs is always a tension in any collaborative effort, and especially one that evokes passions as does social justice work.

These polemics are reflected in our personal lives. We stress self-sufficiency and go to lengths to present a public image of successful lives and well-being. Often, we mask our pain and vulnerabilities, as so poignantly illustrated in the chapter by Toby's assertions about needing to be strong. Ironically, and perhaps as some type of compensation, the social media and many television shows vividly display the lurid details of personal tragedies and fraught relationships. Likewise, the media are saturated with violent images, but we often avoid conflict because we fear it will disrupt our personal connections.

These polemics also can undermine anti-bias work in early childhood settings. Teachers of young children, by nature and training, highly value nurturance, community, and the safety and comfort of children. Furthermore, many families with young children are protective of their youngsters and resistant to any risks or unpleasantness. Thus, teachers and parents often collude to avoid exposing children to the disturbing realities and controversies that are inherent in anti-bias work. Furthermore, many teachers see conflict among children as threatening and, as a result, children do not learn how to productively disagree with others. In his comparison among preschools in different cultures, Bill Corsaro (2003) observed that teachers in middle-class preschools in the United States often went to great lengths to prevent or mitigate conflicts. Not surprisingly, the children perceived themselves as vulnerable and their relationships as fragile and often turned to adults for help when disputes arose. In contrast, the Italian teachers Corsaro observed generally ignored children's *discussioni*, vigorous arguments about many topics, and their playful physical fights. Rather than rely on their teachers, the children themselves usually moderated or resolved conflicts in ways that affirmed their sense of collective identity and connections.

The authors of this chapter, however, show us that these polemics are false and that we can find our way through tensions and conflicting pressures that arise. They remind us that what is lacking in popularized images of people working for social justice is the camaraderie and support among activists and the love and caring that both motivate and emanate from doing this work. As Valerie Pang (2001) asserts, "Caring and social justice in a democracy are intimately connected. When we care, we act . . . social justice flow[s] directly from what we care about" (p. 63). Audrey Thompson (1998), speaking from a black feminist perspective, points out that for poor people and people of color, caring can never be confined to the personal realm; loving and caring *must* be about confronting and transforming inequities. Rather than motivating us to protect children's innocence, caring energizes us to embrace those who suffer and to challenge the inequities that cause pain to individuals and groups.

As I read this chapter, one particular question came to mind. This account illustrates the advantages of teachers, administrators, and families having had time to reflect and talk with each other, before a crisis occurs. It is a testament to the sense of community that the school was the first place the family turned to after the fire. Also, it is noteworthy that the teachers and administrators were able to drop everything and be at the center when the family arrived. I wondered about places with fewer resources. Would these connections and availability be possible in centers where teachers are working 8 hours a day at minimum wages and often have to rush home to pick up children or get to their second job? What advice can we provide centers and staff that may not have time and resources to be responsive at this level?

While musing on this inspiring story, a lovely and surprising image of anti-bias work came unbidden to my mind: A big, boldly colored pillow that provides a soft landing for individuals in crisis; a place where they can share their experiences and feelings honestly and openly; a place that honors vulnerability as much as strength; a place where individuals and community mutually support each other. At the same time, the pillow has a lot of bounce to it, and people cannot just sink into it. Rather, when the time is right, it gives them the momentum and courage to rise up and regain their footing, to embrace all who suffer, to expand the depth and breadth of their awareness and caring, and to recommit to social justice.

References

Corsaro, W. A. (2003). *We're friends, right? Inside kids' culture.* Washington, DC: Joseph Henry Press.

Pang, V. O. (2001). *Multicultural education: A caring-centered, reflective approach.* Boston, MA: McGraw-Hill.

Thompson, A. (1998). Not the color purple: Black feminist lessons for educational caring. *Harvard Educational Review, 68*(4): 522–554.

3

GUINEA PIGS, ASPERGER'S SYNDROME, AND MY SON

When Teachers Struggle to Recognize Humanity[1]

Steve Bialostok

UNIVERSITY OF WYOMING

Introduction

Only after our visit to the home of my friend, Mary, did I understand neurologist Oliver Sacks' (1993) description of a patient with Asperger's syndrome as an "anthropologist on Mars." My then 5-year-old son Ethan had been diagnosed with Asperger's at age 3. Mary's son, Jacob, was the same age. Mary and I knew each other from our social theory class and were better friends than Ethan and Jacob. Ethan didn't have any friends, and though Ethan's play tended toward internalized fantasy, we encouraged the boys to play together. But access to Ethan's inner world required conscious effort, far beyond the expectation of the average 5-year-old. Jacob quickly shifted his attention to gently roughhousing with his mother. While wrestling, Mary suddenly pushed Jacob away and yelled, "Jacob! That really hurt." Jacob burst into tears. "I'm sorry, Mommy. I didn't mean to hurt you." As Mary comforted Jacob, I watched Ethan silently studying them, wondering what was going on. Was he trying to figure out why Jacob was so upset, or why Mary's pain caused Jacob to respond so emotionally? The social theory that Mary and I had been reading no longer mattered. But Oliver Sacks did.

Not until later that evening did I recall Sack's *New Yorker* article, the title taken from Temple Grandin's statement: "Much of the time I feel like an anthropologist on Mars." Yet Grandin has become a professor of animal science at Colorado State University and authored several books. Parents with children on "the continuum" refer to Grandin's success as their source of inspiration. But more than inspiration, her rare success in entering a professional life provides enormous comfort. Of other successful people, such as Einstein, Newton, Warhol, Nietzsche, Jung, and Gates, we speculate they, too, could be located somewhere on the autism disorder spectrum.

This chapter chronicles a deeply personal account about my now adult son, diagnosed at 3 years old with Asperger's, and his experiences in school through fifth grade. I describe his emotional experiences as well as my own as we both interacted with teachers, all of whom deeply cared but were confused by how Ethan expressed his emotions. Emotions are entangled in a complex social framework, integrated into our other forms of life, based upon mutual agreement. But those on the autism spectrum offer distinctive styles of communication not always understood. Frequently, neither are the emotions of parents, who see our children's wonderfulness lost to a world that none of us ever anticipated.

Denial Isn't a River in Egypt

Recognizing and accepting Ethan's symptoms crept up on me. Even as an inexperienced parent, I intuitively recognized children's "normal behavior." Once Ethan's idiosyncratic characteristics appeared, I dismissed these as little more than the quirkiness I had appreciated in former kindergarten students. After all, I explained away formulaically, every child is different. Because so many of Ethan's other behaviors seemed perfectly ordinary, what need was there to add the Asperger's diagnosis? After all, *I* was a quirky kid without a diagnosis.

But just as the progression of a cough to a runny nose to a sore throat makes it impossible to ignore or deny a cold, the time came when I could no longer deny Ethan's nascent symptoms. His periodic hand flapping never really looked like attempts at pretending to be a bird. At first, his ability to identify the make and model of virtually every parked car before he was 3 was remarkable, but my pride turned to bewilderment when at 4, he wanted only to identify them repeatedly.

Ethan's early language was as remarkable as his knowledge of cars. He spoke intelligibly before 1 year, and his language grew exponentially by 2. "He's a genius," friends enthusiastically claimed. But Ethan seemed less linguistically gifted when he spoke in lengthy monologues instead of the give and take of everyday conversation. There were limited interactions with his peers. Whereas other children played and talked together, Ethan remained isolated and spoke to himself. Sometimes at home he spoke to them when they weren't there: "Oh, Luke, did you see that big truck? Oh yes, Luke, it was a really big fire truck." "Taylor, I can do a cartwheel. Watch, Taylor." He occasionally referred to himself in the third person: "Daddy. Get off the couch. Ethan wants to jump."

In retrospect, it's difficult for me to understand how I tried so hard to ignore his symptoms. But diagnostic labels are so culturally powerful that even following Ethan's official diagnosis, I didn't want to look through the Asperger's prism. I had adopted Ethan from Brazil as a single parent; seeing him as someone other than a normal child terrified me.

In the Beginning

Ethan turned 3 months just after we relocated to Arizona for me to begin a doctoral program. Until then, Ethan had stayed at home with a full-time nanny or with me when I was able to work at home. When the fall semester opened, Ethan began his first formal daycare. "Just leave," the teacher and administrator said when he'd start crying. "He'll stop the moment you leave." But Ethan rarely stopped crying even while napping.

What became particularly disconcerting was Ethan's aggression, never previously demonstrated. He would abruptly hit or push other children. The director, Jill, wasn't initially concerned: "It seems to be his way of saying 'hello.'" A month later, Jill said "goodbye" after Ethan awakened from a nap, picked up a Fisher-Price farmhouse, and dropped it on the head of a sleeping child. This was the final act in an ongoing saga of aggression. Neither Ethan, his teachers, nor I could explain his actions. I began avoiding his teachers by waiting in the car for Ethan to emerge. "What did you do today?" I'd ask strapping Ethan into the car seat. "Sit in Jill's office" was his repeated answer.

Ethan's aggression proved problematic for reasons beyond the obvious. I had started a doctoral program at this time because Ethan was seemingly brilliant, easygoing, and even-tempered to the point of being nearly tearless. At two-and-a-half years old, he was my gift, my joy. My friends encouraged me to pursue a doctoral degree: "Go now, while Ethan is young!" I sold my large home in the suburbs to begin our new life in a tiny two-bedroom graduate student apartment. But now, Ethan's unprecedented behaviors affected my ability to attend classes and do the work. Ethan seemed to be falling apart.

Another doctoral student referred me to her child's home day care. April, the provider, was a kind and intelligent Christian with her own young daughter and had been running a home day care for years. She agreed to take him, even after knowing about his history. Her only heads-up (knowing that we were Jewish) was that all the children were required to thank Jesus for their lunch. "Who cares?" I thought. Ethan's aggression continued, although with a handful of children, it diminished. April kept him, good days and bad. But eventually, it was time to move on.

I took out a student loan to send Ethan to a preschool with teachers described in the school's brochure as understanding of "the social and emotional needs of young children." *Child-centered* and *humanistic* experts inspired the school's philosophy. The director told me 6 months later that Ethan had to leave. It was the same story. Ethan would normally play alone, but when he played parallel to another child, there was a reasonably good chance that he would hit him. But the straw that broke *this* camel's back occurred the day his teacher brought her dog to school. The children stood around petting it. Suddenly, Ethan kicked its belly. The director tried to word it kindly: "We don't feel qualified to best help Ethan." *Ethan?* Was there anyone who felt qualified to help *me?* Who would help me through the frustration and anger I felt toward the humanistic teachers at that school? Who was qualified to diffuse the rage I felt toward my son for ruining my life? Who was qualified to help me with the guilt I felt for feeling such rage? He is, after all, my 4-year-old son.

When it was just the two of us, Ethan was a delight, especially during the many field trips to local car shows. Ethan's passion and knowledge of restored automobiles always impressed the owners. But when Ethan was in the company of peers without me, it was hit or miss, more frequently hit.

I met with Ethan's pediatrician to discuss my various concerns: Random aggression, nonstop monologues that went on whether or not someone was there to listen, eyes facing the sky while speaking, interest in nothing but cars, toilet training indifference. Ethan played with his cars on the office floor, indifferent to our conversation. Ethan was so delightful, verbal, and charming that the pediatrician looked confused when I said, "It's like he's got autism but not autism. Autism-*lite*." Only after I happened to watch a news report about a local Asperger's conference did I seek an evaluation from a psychiatrist specializing in autism. This was in 1995, and I had never heard the term *Asperger's*.

Preschool

Ethan's official diagnosis opened up the opportunity to attend a free public preschool that mainstreamed special-needs children. The school district did not recognize Asperger's in 1997, so he had to be diagnosed with autism. After 3 years of doctoral coursework and more French social theory under my belt, I recognized his Individualized Education Program (IEP) meeting as a poster for governmental forms of social control through the kindness of experts and their positive production of knowledge. Power was asserted through knowledge operating in the form of networks. The psychologist tested his cognitive and other developmental levels; the occupational therapist assessed his motor skills and worked on his ability to hold a pencil; the speech therapist developed a behavior program and periodically helped Ethan make transitions from one activity to the next.

The action that made the biggest difference was Ethan's teacher's intervention with *me*. I was an emotional wreck, and Kathy became the first person to try to reassure me and calm my anxiety. We spoke almost daily, sometimes Kathy consoling me as I cried, profoundly filled with guilt. What had I done wrong? Was it our relocation? Day care? The adoption itself? My inexperience as a parent? What would be Ethan's future? *My* future? *Our* future? Kathy remained positive and optimistic, countering my pessimism. Kathy developed a plan to help manage my emotions after learning about Ethan's aggression. Each day, just prior to pick-up time, Kathy called to inform me about Ethan's behavior. This way, in the worst-case scenario, I would have 20 minutes to calm down.

It was "water day" on the afternoon of the last day of preschool in June. Ethan's teacher called before she left for the day to say goodbye and to tell me that today had gone well. I arrived, feeling happy and relieved and approached the running hoses, sprinklers, and other water play toys. The aide in charge walked up and said sternly, "Ethan urinated on a child." "What do you mean?" I asked. "Just what I said. He walked up to a child, pulled down his pants, and urinated on her."

Noticing that I was speaking with the aide, Ethan ran up to me and confessed, "I peed on Katie." "I heard," I said, feeling more disappointed than angry. "Let's go," I told Ethan, and he turned around and jetted toward the car. As I turned to follow him, the aide called, "Is that all you're going to do? He urinated on a little girl. Why would he do that?" I paused, turned, and looked directly at her: "It's water day. He just wanted to participate."

Self-Management

No longer under the therapeutic care of Ethan's preschool teacher, I developed my own emotional self-management strategies. First, since knowledge was supposedly power, I spent the summer reading everything I could about Asperger's. But my search for information was intended for the sole purpose of finding hope, a kernel of optimism that wasn't available anywhere else. I left my Asperger support groups terrified after hearing parents chronicle the disastrous lives of their adult children. Ethan's psychiatrist suggested that I encourage him to get involved with computers so that he could work alone.

Such pessimism led to a second self-management strategy, which was to deny the accuracy of Ethan's initial diagnosis. His affect didn't resemble the other children I observed in the support group, which appeared to me as far more autistic. Even if the diagnosis was inaccurate, I decided, there were no medications, no programs at the time for students with Asperger's. Albeit irrational, thinking of Ethan as unusual rather than as having Asperger's helped me emotionally cope.

But I ultimately began to second-guess my own self-management strategies. An Asperger's diagnosis might provide Ethan's future teachers with an explanation for some of his seemingly irrational acts, especially with no other emotional or psychological explanation. Teachers are motivated by the folk model that characterizes emotions as private experiences and possessions: Individuals *have* emotions, are *driven* by emotions, express emotions properly or improperly. These mental states are believed to serve as a causal nexus for observable sequences of behaviors directed toward an object/person. Educators frequently seek or assume causes for student behaviors that do not align with classroom standards. Familiar teacher-expressions attribute behavior to mental states: "Were you feeling angry when you hit him?" "Jacob is quiet today because he's feeling sad about having to move." "I know you're running around because you're excited about your birthday, but settle down." These diagnoses serve as normalizing devices for summing up children's mental states in relation to behaviors.

I felt confident that Ethan's kindergarten teacher, a board member of National Association for the Education of Young Children (NAEYC) with 30 years of experience in play-based teaching, would be a match for Ethan. She seemed to understand and appreciate young children's reasoning and actions. But this play-based environment could not highlight Ethan's intellectual capacities, and her expectation that children interact and cooperate put Ethan's social weaknesses and aggression on full display. The class took naps after lunch, and because Ethan tended to sleep through the entire afternoon, I heard only about his negative morning behaviors. Once the teacher allowed the children opportunities to write, the teacher was amazed at the sophistication of Ethan's writing, which Ethan had taught himself to do at home. He couldn't hold a pencil very well, and his hand-writing was difficult to read. But later in first grade when other children wrote stories, Ethan wanted to write articles ("Like my dad").

When I began my first university position, Ethan attended second grade in an "open" school that embraced a progressive philosophy, one that I hoped would provide opportunities to demonstrate his academic strengths. But the difference between an educational vision described on a website and the execution of that vision proved enormous. In this environment, children isolated and mocked Ethan. His teacher refused to help him integrate with others on the playground: "There are yard duty teachers out there. You can ask them." When Ethan turned 7 in January, I managed to assemble half a dozen boys from the classroom to attend his bowling birthday party. They all had fun, treated Ethan like a peer, and Ethan never looked happier. He had friends, as he referred to the boys who normally did not play with him. I hoped that getting to know Ethan in his party context would open up friendship possibilities. But no "friend" ever reciprocated, not even Jared, the other adopted boy being raised by a single mother, a kindergarten teacher at the school. With my orchestration, Jared regularly joined us at our home, parks, museums, restaurants, and movies. After discovering Jared had a birthday party but hadn't invited Ethan, I asked his mother why. Awkwardly, she responded, "I wanted Jared to have the choice of who he wanted to invite. Sorry." "Seriously?" I walked away.

Depression Kicks In

Halfway through the school year, a perfect storm coalesced with devastating con-sequences. It became evident from the beginning of the semester that accepting this university position had been a mistake. I despised the job, loathed going to work, and felt angry about having spent so many years wasting so much money on a PhD. The daily commute compounded my hatred. I drove nearly an hour each morning to drop Ethan off at school. I'd drive another 45 minutes to the univer-sity. I supervised student teachers all around the city. Wherever I was at 3:00 p.m., I would leave to pick up Ethan by 3:30. On the two nights a week I taught classes, I'd bring him to day care halfway between the school and the university, drive 30 to 45 minutes to the university and teach, and return to the day care 3 hours later to pick him up and drive home. Then I heard Ethan's stories about his miserable day, how he was excluded, and/or how he got in trouble. Day care stories were not usually pleasant either.

Beyond this collection of angst, I shared with Ethan the challenge of social isolation. I had no friends. Neither of us had any. We were both lonely. Even if I wanted to just do something by myself on a weekend, I had no one to leave Ethan with for even a few hours. I blamed Ethan for what he had done to my life, for making me live alone, for the adoption in the first place, for having Asperger's. Most of all, I blamed him for my emerging depression. When spring break arrived, I didn't want to leave the house. The sun became too bright; I couldn't filter out noise. My body felt inside-out, and the anxiety I felt about virtually everything left me short of breath. I cried a lot. I was unable to sleep. I didn't want to hear his sadness about not having friends. I felt the same way.

For the previous 5 years, despite frustrations and desperation, I remained competent as a father. Now I no longer felt even remotely capable in that role. I could barely get up in the morning.

The More Things Change . . .

My depression lifted significantly immediately after being offered a position at another university. I promised Ethan a better school and a smaller, easier place to live. He would attend a school with a teacher whom my colleague said was "great." She had taught for many years, and I felt lucky that her retirement was still a few years away.

The geography and climate changed, but little else did, and in some ways, they got worse. Now I fought with his new teacher *and* the building principal. We were living in snow for the first time, and the first snowfall occurred in early fall. During recess, Ethan playfully threw snowballs and ice at some other children with no sense that snowballs can hurt (especially when flung 3 feet away from the target child) and he was nearly suspended. "He did this and he doesn't even care," the principal said. "He's never lived in the snow," I responded. "He didn't mean to hurt anybody." The principal was unmoved. He knew nothing about Asperger's.

The teacher was a little more sympathetic, but had different concerns. "We're reading *Sarah Plain and Tall*," she said. "He refuses to read it. I don't know why he doesn't want to read it. It's a great book." In spite of all the children's books at home, Ethan's greatest pleasure was reading the glossy automobile brochures that I'd gather from dealerships. Ethan wasn't interested in reading about a 19th-century family's loneliness, abandonment, and need to cope with change; he wanted to read about the luxurious interior of a Mercury Villager. I explained his unique interests and asked if he could bring the brochures to school. "Yes," she responded, "but he's not going to read them for Reader's Workshop."

The Monday after Thanksgiving, the entire district turned to Christmas. I had never witnessed this holiday celebrated with such intensity, far more than in any of Ethan's previous schools. It was not necessarily explicitly religious, but the extent to which the holiday had colonized the schools took me by surprise, so much so that I expressed bewilderment to my colleagues. We weren't particularly religious Jews, and I was not against some Christmas celebration in schools. But Ethan would talk about the daily Christmas routines in class and assemblies. This was not a matter that I wanted to deal with. I wanted to get to the winter (Christmas!) break with as little conflict as possible. The principal and teacher already didn't like me. Christmas would not be my battle. But it became Ethan's. Although Ethan had no real sense of what being a religious Jew meant, his Asperger-like rigid thinking led him to respond to the onslaught of school Christmas activities as if he had just emerged from a Chasidic community in Brooklyn.

A week before vacation, I was called in again. Ethan had gone on and on about "We're Jews and we don't celebrate Christmas and I'm not going to do this," whatever "this" was at the time. That particular day, Ethan refused to listen to Christmas tales from around the world. The teacher showed me the book, a collection of stories so old that I wasn't sure if Ethan refused on the basis of religion or because the stories were so boring. I explained that he had never before experienced so much Christmas in school and was—in that black and white way— asserting his religious identity. She responded: "I've had other Jewish children in my class, and they have never responded in this way." She punctuated her view by showing me the Hanukkah story she had read to the class.

"Has Ethan done *anything* positive in this class?" I was angry. She was visibly startled by the sound of my voice and said, "Well, of course." "What, then?" I asked, giving her only a few seconds of "wait time." She was unable to recall anything— not even the positive actions she had reported to me at previous conferences. But my outrage now sealed her construction of Ethan as an incompetent member of her classroom culture. Ethan simply could not be recognized as good. "You can't even think of a single thing," I said, my voice beginning to shift toward rage. She invoked Ethan's agency and choice: "He is choosing to be oppositional and defiant. And he is making the wrong choice."

Until that year, I had expressed appreciation for Ethan's teachers, no matter what I thought or believed. His previous teachers had *tried* to understand him; Kathy, his last preschool teacher, and Karen, his first grade teacher, both liked him a lot, in spite of the challenges he presented. They also liked me. But now, I could only depreciate this teacher, criticizing her teaching, and, probably, her beloved holiday. I continued: "You have done nothing to try to understand him. You don't even know what he's good at. The principal here doesn't even like him. *You* don't even like him. I heard you were such a great teacher." Her face turned red: "Take him out," she responded with anger. "You won't let me do my job. I refuse to teach him."

She kicked Ethan out of the school. She kicked *me* out. Good parents don't interfere with teachers. Ethan was temporarily placed in another school to finish third grade until a permanent placement was found for the following year.

The Panopticon Comes Home

Ethan was not the only one under scrutiny. Now I became the object of the gaze in this small town. I had been sharing Ethan's experiences with my undergraduates. My point was to make real the abstract concept of starting with where the child is, the needs of children that extend beyond an IEP, the importance of friendship, and the challenges of having children on the autism spectrum in one's classroom. I shared Ethan's experiences and my concerns cautiously, if only because some of these students would be placed in that particular school. I tried not to turn his teacher or principal into villains and to provide examples of the ways that schools are constructed. One morning during the spring semester, the dean came unannounced to my office. My comments about Ethan's experiences had come to his attention, not directly from students, but from an administrator in the school district. Details of who said what to whom and how my words were interpreted remain unknown. But I had been an agenda item at the monthly principals' meeting.

My dean was not angry but concerned. I tried to assure him that my intent was not to criticize anyone, but to provide lessons to my students about how important teachers are to the lives of children as well as to their parents. I told him that at times I had been emotional, but not angry. On the last day of the semester, I told my class, "Sometimes teachers feel so much pressure, they forget how important they are to both the academic lives of children and to their emotional lives." My voiced cracked when I ended with a decided, "You matter. You matter." Tears had rolled down my face. My dean was satisfied, and we never discussed the matter again.

Later that spring, I received a phone call from the principal of the school where Ethan would enroll in the fall. The principal asked to meet with me. We had met on several previous occasions, and I appreciated what she believed in philosophically and what she wanted for her school. On one of these occasions, she had told me Ethan would be placed with a teacher so warm and motherly that she nearly bled emotions. She had the compassion of George Orwell, Florence Nightingale, and Gandhi all rolled into one. Ethan would love her. I liked this principal and left that meeting with optimism.

But that conversation had taken place earlier. Now what followed was the revelation that the principal was not sure she would allow Ethan to enroll in her school. Once again, it was not about Ethan. It was about me. She reported hearing me yell at Ethan in public. She considered reporting my actions so that Ethan could be removed from me and placed in a safe place. She continued: "There are people who have heard you yelling at him at Wal-Mart and have expressed their concerns. I have also been told that you leave Ethan home by himself for long periods."

Rarely have I been left speechless. "What?" was nearly all that I was capable of saying. "What are you talking about?" She repeated the accusations. "Who told you this? When did you hear me?" Ethan and I had been walking by her school, and I was apparently screaming and yelling so loudly at him that my voice could be heard through her closed office window. She wouldn't disclose the sources of the other accusations. "You think I'm the only one in Wal-Mart who yells at their kid? And I leave him for one night a week when I teach a class. It's a 3-hour class, and it takes me five minutes to get home and check on him during my break." "It is illegal to leave a child Ethan's age at home by himself." I responded, "He's 9 years old. You don't think that kids his age get home after school and no one is there? You don't like it? I'll leave him with *you* on Tuesdays." She calmed a bit but added, "Almost everyone in town knows who Ethan is." She emphasized her responsibility to provide a positive school experience for Ethan, and she needed to be assured that I was able to provide him with a positive and safe experience at home. I conceded—only because I wanted Ethan in this school and wanted to get the hell out—that Ethan was exasperating at times, and I did occasionally lose my temper. I then lied about being in therapy to work on this issue. That seemed to satisfy her.

I left her office feeling like a story in Foucault's discussion of the Panopticon, no longer certain whether or not I was being observed, policed by everybody or no one, any time or any place. I would now police myself. But this event would be only the beginning of the breakdown of our private lives.

Guinea Pigs and Sociopathy

I would fly out for my conference on Thursday and return by Sunday. My former student would stay with Ethan. An honors student, Chris felt a sense of über-responsibility toward everything, but especially toward watching Ethan, which he had done on previous occasions. Sunday morning, just before leaving to fly home, Chris called. Much to my surprise, Zack, a boy who occasionally came to our home to visit, had spent the night. This was the first time that *anyone* had ever spent the night with Ethan, and had Chris called to ask, I would have said no. Chris was a great sitter, but he thought about Ethan in the way that most anyone would think about a typical young boy who had a friend come over. Chris explained that unbeknownst to him, after the two boys had gone to bed, they began playing with our two guinea pigs in such a rough manner that the next morning they were dead. I didn't ask questions, planning to deal with the issue later.

My arrival home, typically greeted with fanfare, was unusually somber. Ethan was noticeably upset, a combination of the loss of his beloved guinea pigs and the anticipated fear of my response. I remained calm, even as Ethan described quite honestly the horrifying events that led to their deaths. They were having a circus and the main event involved using Legos as weapons and submerging the animals in water. I decided to have a funeral. Zack came over, dug the hole, put the dead guinea pigs in the hole, and buried them. Each of us said a brief eulogy. I mentioned how cute their squeals sounded whenever I brought them lettuce. Ethan talked about how much he liked petting them. Zack had brought a small American flag and placed it on the mound of dirt. Pop-psychology's "closure" was complete. It was over, or so I thought.

On Monday morning, I dropped off Ethan at school, taught a class, returned to my office, and listened to a voice message from Ethan's principal. "As you might imagine, the events surrounding the death of the guinea pigs have been very disturbing. Ethan is now torturing and killing little animals. Please come by my office as soon as possible." I was there within minutes. Ethan had told his teacher, the supposed Gandhi of education, about the guinea pigs. She immediately removed him from class, claiming that he was now a danger to himself and to others. "This is a family matter and I dealt with it," I told the principal. She apparently knew no boundaries between home and school. "It is now a matter of the safety of the child and of other children." She repeated the phrase "torturing and killing little animals." The teacher refused to let him back into the classroom. "He is not taking animals out and secretly torturing them," I told her. "But there is history," she responded, meaning that his previous aggression was now being reinterpreted as having elevated into something far worse. "He shows no remorse. No empathy."

The following day, the school district "SWAT" team members convened— teacher, principal, speech therapist, psychologist, special education teacher, case manager, Ethan's counselor, and me. The teacher framed a sympathetic opening: "If the other children heard about what he did to the guinea pigs, they would never forgive him." But this was clearly not the real issue. Why would the class have to know at all, and if it had been some kind of necessity, couldn't she possibly explain it as an accident that Ethan felt very sad about? No, of course not. She went on to describe another boy in the classroom whose mouse had recently died. "He was inconsolable," she went on. "He couldn't stop crying. This is the kind of emotion I would expect from someone who lost an animal. Ethan demonstrated none of it."

The remaining comments from the "team" could only have been uttered because his teacher had established an emotional rubric in which Ethan fell below expectations. The speech therapist said: "There is something much deeper here. This is much deeper than Asperger's." The psychologist referred to a possible *sociopathy*, a nominalization new to me.

The case manager presented two options that had undoubtedly already been determined. Ethan could either be placed full time in a behavior disorder classroom at a different school, or "experts" could evaluate him at an inpatient state psychiatric facility. There he would spend up to a month going through a "thorough psychiatric diagnosis" that would determine "his problems" and the degree to which he was "a danger to himself and to others." Based on the discharge evaluation, the district would determine where he would attend school.

The meeting was Kafkaesque in the team's seeming lack of empathy and fervent need to pathologize Ethan and me as his parent. The irony struck me that a group who claimed Ethan had no empathy exhibited none toward either Ethan or me. Neither humanity nor empathy surfaced in a room of self-ascribed guiltless "Pontius Pilates" eager to wash their hands of responsibility.

The district presented me with two unacceptable options and little choice. Our life stories had spread through the few schools available. Ethan didn't belong in a behavior disorder classroom, so I opted for what I hoped was the lesser of two unsatisfactory options.

Ethan wanted to know when he would return to school. I tried to be simple: "Your teacher wants to figure out the best way to help you. You are going to stay somewhere where people can talk with you every day and figure out the best way to help you in school." "Are you coming?" "I'll come along, but I can't stay with you. I'll see you as much as I can."

He had more questions. How long? Would I be there? What was this place like? But most important, why? "It's just strange," I said not knowing exactly why myself. "It has to do with the guinea pigs." "I told Mrs. Smith what happened." "I know, honey." I shook my head and moved my hands to signify disbelief. I tried to explain that sometimes teachers get worried about things they hear happen at home and don't understand. I wanted to be reassuring. But the truth was that I was terrified. No teacher—no school—had ever responded in such a reactionary way.

"I told her the truth." "I know you did," I said, knowing that he was incapable of manufacturing a persona. "And I'm proud of you for that. But sometimes, and this is hard to explain, it's sometimes better not to tell people some things." Or, if you tell people "some things," you must also either demonstrate the proper affect or falsify an impression. Ethan was capable of neither.

Ethan never attempted to control the flow of information so that his teacher would think of him favorably. To do so called for a self-reflexive process he was incapable of—the ongoing monitoring of thoughts and feelings to ensure that they fall within the codes of deference and demeanor outlined by cultural scripts. Making that determination inevitably requires inferring the state of mind of others. Ethan wanted his teacher to view him favorably; he liked her in spite of their challenging relationship. Ethan only told her what had happened—unabashedly, shamelessly, and without equivocation or fear.

Ethan conveyed the information about the death of the guinea pigs through a personal story. But narratives accomplish more than recounting past events. Speakers convey their moral stance toward an event. Did she or he behave poorly or well; should he or she be praised or blamed; can the behavior predict future events? An interlocutor evaluates the morality of the protagonist's actions based upon explicit statements made in the story, a single word or phrase, and/or emotional affect, such as remorse, displayed in the narration itself. His teacher used these criteria to judge Ethan's moral stance toward the deaths of guinea pigs, but especially through an explicit demonstration of emotions, similar to those exhibited by the boy whose rat died. Individuals with Asperger's syndrome tend to express less remorse, but not because they don't feel remorse. Yet for Ethan, he had acknowledged to his dad a mistake in judgment. Then, like many children, he told his teacher about this significant event. But Ethan's social naïveté and immaturity were ultimately misinterpreted as a lack of remorse and as evidence of sociopathy. None of those assembled to determine what to do with Ethan could distinguish what they saw as a human predator from a little boy responding as an anthropologist from Mars.

Inpatient and Locked

We both remained silent for most of the drive. Ethan took my hand as we entered the building. After admission, we waited for the first locked door to open to enter the nurse's room. Unable to walk further because of the second locked door, we both stood at the station. The room had lots of people, but it was eerily silent, and no one seemed particularly friendly. I wondered who was mixing the Haldol cocktail. I asked about scheduling and especially times for visitation. I pulled out a bag of Hot Wheels and was grateful that Ethan could bring them. The second locked door opened. We hugged tighter than ever. Ethan saw my tears and tried to reassure me with, "Dad, I'll be all right."

I left, checked into a motel, went to my room, and wept.

I'd visit Ethan every morning and evening for an hour. Sometimes I brought him new Hot Wheels, and he'd roll them down the hallway. Ethan would tell me about others in his unit: The suicidal girl; the boy who tried to kill his parents; the runaway. He'd describe the details of his day, such as the group meeting where everyone sat in a circle and shared why they were there. "What did you say?" I asked. "I said that I didn't *know* why I was here." He described exchanging positive points for prizes. We'd end each visit by singing our favorite song, Sublime's "Lovin' Is What I Got." I'd always pick Ethan up while we sang and toss him in the air when we came to the last word. Spring break coincided with Passover. I brought our Passover items from home, and found next to the Passover section in the grocery store an 8-ounce box of dehydrated boxed matzah ball soup mix. Just add hot water. I bought two. The hospital made an exception and allowed Ethan a 2-hour furlough. We drove to my hotel room and set everything on a small, round table. The Passover theme of freedom took on an entirely new meaning when we got to the part in the Seder when the youngest child asks: "Why is this night different from all other nights?"

I attended regular meetings at the hospital. The chief psychiatrist described medications; the psychologist interpreted the Rorschach he administered, but he felt unsure because "I gave it to him late at night, and he was tired." The social worker asked about Ethan's birth family's history. The counselor advised me not to visit often so that Ethan could grow more independent.

The discharge meeting included several hospital staff members, the school district's special education director, and me. The diagnosis? Asperger's and attention deficit hyperactivity disorder (ADHD). Written recommendations included everything I had been begging for, but no one would listen, especially his teacher. A letter from her was read aloud at the meeting: "I'm a humanistic teacher," she wrote.

Back to School

Our drive home was nearly as silent as our drive there. In his bedroom, Ethan would normally crash his cars into each other and other objects, loudly vocalizing the collision. But for 3 days he sat quietly with his cars. I had never seen him like this before. I didn't wonder what Ethan might be thinking. I worried about what he was feeling.

The same team that had sent Ethan to the hospital for diagnosis reconvened to determine what would become of Ethan. That meeting went no better than the last one. The same players sat around the lengthy boardroom table, with me at one end, the principal and teacher at the other, and the remaining stakeholders on both sides. The district's special education coordinator summarized the discharge report. Ethan was no danger to himself and to others. His diagnosis remained Asperger's now layered with ADHD.

His teacher refused to believe the report's conclusions: "I've seen children with ADHD. This is far more than ADHD. I don't care what they say. I know Ethan killed the guinea pigs deliberately." No one challenged her. She refused to take him back. The other fourth/fifth grade teacher, who had joined this meeting, spoke: "I'll take him," she said. She liked Ethan and wanted to teach him yoga so he could relax.

I refused to attend his final IEP. In a letter to the principal, I complimented his new teacher for attempting all sorts of strategies that were generally successful. For the rest of the school year, I received no phone calls, no complaints. Ethan no longer attended the twice-weekly social skills pullout program where he filled out social skills workbook pages and learned to say, "Please pass the juice" during meals. I also expressed appreciation for her desire to establish a positive relationship with me. But I went on:

> "Nothing that I have asked to be included in either Ethan's 504 or IEP has ever been included or seriously considered, even after Ethan's institutionalization. It has become abundantly clear that the 'team' does not feel that either I or anyone outside the culture of the school and district has anything to contribute. The principal said that my reputation in the district is as an 'unappreciative and difficult parent.' On that matter, she is accurate."

Conclusion

I write this chapter a decade later, my first effort to account for Ethan's school experiences. Going through my many notes, e-mails, and other forms of documentation and putting these events into a sequence has been extraordinarily difficult and emotionally draining. I expect that some readers will claim there is another side (or many sides) of the story. They may well posit that Ethan's teachers provided reasonable responses, that he was a difficult child for a regular classroom, that teachers have so many children that he couldn't have been treated differently, that I'm still filled with anger, that my memory is distorted, that writing this is therapy, that this is my need to process.

One side benefit of a diagnosis, especially with children in school, is its ability to get everyone off the hook. This has long been true with more familiar diagnoses such as attention deficit disorder (ADD) and dyslexia. Educators suggest to parents that children's attention/behavior problems or reading difficulties may be the result of neurobiological disorders. Rarely do teachers reimagine their classroom structure and pedagogical approach. Similarly, the diagnosis of Asperger's invariably leads to a series of school interventions intended to modify student behavior, but never the teacher's. I remember the special education teacher coming to Ethan's IEP, clutching a manual about teaching students "on the spectrum" about self-control. "I've found it," she enthusiastically told the team even before sitting down. "This is what we need to control Ethan's behavior." Ethan's diagnosis may have enabled him to secure services, but his educators used that diagnosis to avoid the responsibility of trying to understand how Ethan understood his world. Ethan, of all people, faced for himself this issue head-on in preschool. His teacher, Kathy, pulled me aside one day: "Steve, I have to tell you what Ethan said today." She had a smile on her face, so my stomach didn't become queasy. "Ethan came up to me and said, 'Kathy, I think different than the other kids.'"

Ludwig Wittgenstein (1984)—a likely Asperger's candidate—wrote, "We tend to take the speech of a Chinese for inarticulate gurgling. Someone who understands Chinese will recognize language in what he hears. Similarly, I often cannot recognize the humanity of another human being" (p. 1). Wittgenstein introduced the question of what it is to understand the thoughts, feelings, and intentions of others. The task, Wittgenstein tells us, is to find humanity in the gurgling of others.

More than any other responsibility, teachers must find humanity in their students' gurgling. Literacy, math, social studies, and science are only important if they help our students become more human. Ethan never wanted be an anthropologist from Mars. He wanted his teachers to see his humanity. He wanted—and wants—to be human.

Note

1. Dedicated to Shirley Brice Heath, who always tells me the truth.

References

Sacks, O. (1993, December 27). An anthropologist on mars: A neurologist's notebook. *New Yorker*, 106–125.

Wittgenstein, L. (1984). *Culture and value*. (P. Winch, Translated). Chicago: University of Chicago Press.

COMMENTARY

Margarita Bianco

UNIVERSITY OF COLORADO, DENVER

Steve Bialostok provides the reader with a glimpse of the range of emotions he experienced as the parent of a child with Asperger's syndrome. Bialostok invites the reader into his home, to accompany him at school meetings, and most importantly, he gives the reader permission to hear his deeply private thoughts as he struggled with disappointment, anger, guilt, frustration, loneliness, and his own depression over the challenges of parenting Ethan.

I am grateful to Steve Bialostok for giving voice to his emotional journey as a parent of a child with special needs. Unfortunately, his story is a common one. Parents of children with disabilities describe similar emotions as they grapple with accepting that their children's needs are different from typically developing children (Friend & Cook, 2013) and, like Bialostok, parents also struggle while navigating educational systems that seem unresponsive to their child's unique academic, social, and emotional needs (Friend & Cook, 2013). By sharing his story, Bialostok provides an opportunity to reflect on the cycle and intensity of emotions parents experience as they raise a child with a disability and the roles teachers can play in mitigating these negative emotions by instilling a sense of hope. In this commentary, I draw from my years of classroom experience as a special educator, my research and scholarship in the field of special education, and my role as a teacher educator.

Disability Labels and the Emotional Impact for Parents

> "But diagnostic labels are so culturally powerful that even following Ethan's official diagnosis, I didn't want to look through the Asperger's prism."
>
> *(p. 40)*

Learning your child has a disability can have a crushing emotional effect on parents. Researchers have compared the range and cycle of emotions parents experience as similar to the stages of grief that are felt when a loved one dies (Friend & Cook, 2013). Although the array and intensity of emotions may vary depending on the severity of the child's disability, when and how the disability is identified, and the age of the child (Mansell & Morris, 2004), the emotional impact experienced by parents cannot be understated and should not be ignored—especially by teachers.

Mansell and Morris (2004) explored the cycle of emotions parents of children with autism spectrum disorder experience at various stages in the diagnostic process, from pre-diagnosis to acceptance and adaptation. Much like Bialostok's experience, the authors note that during the pre-diagnostic phase, parents already suspect that something is different. Doctor visits sometimes result in false reassurances or incorrect and misleading diagnoses, which further fuel frustrations and anxiety. Once an accurate diagnosis of autism or Asperger's syndrome is made, parents experience mixed emotions. On one hand, parents feel a sense of relief in having a "label" to explain their child's idiosyncratic behaviors. Conversely, the diagnosis also brings a sense of shock, disbelief, guilt, and fear as parents begin to imagine what this might mean for their child's future.

During the post-diagnosis phase, parents are again flooded with emotion, new concerns, and many questions. As Bialostok shared, searching for information about his child's disability and advocating for appropriate school supports became primary concerns. Many parents also begin the grieving process at the loss of their "hoped-for child" and lost dreams they once had for their child's future (Mansell & Morris, p. 389).

As typical young adults approach high school graduation and begin to make plans for the future, their parents share in the excitement, enthusiasm, and the sadness in leaving home. Parent involvement gradually diminishes as the adult child takes on more responsibility and control over their own life. In my research (Bianco, Garrison-Wade, Tobin, & Lehmann, 2009), I learned that for parents of young adults with disabilities, these experiences are markedly different—especially when their adult child has more intense support needs. For these parents, their involvement in their child's life does not diminish as their child ages. In reality, their level of involvement increases in intensity for an extended and somewhat uncertain amount of time—something many parents report feeling inadequately prepared to deal with (Bianco, Garrison-Wade, Tobin, & Lehmann, 2009; Lloyd, Wehmeyer, & Davis, 2004). Above all else, parents are concerned about their own mortality and how their adult child will be cared for after they die.

All teachers need to be aware of, and sensitive to, the range of emotions parents experience as they navigate through the school system in search of the best possible options and outcomes for their child with a disability. As I read Bialostok's chapter, I was struck by the absence of hope. What do parents experience when teachers greet them at the classroom door with a list of all the things their child did "wrong" that day? What happens when parent-teacher conferences or Individualized Education Program (IEP) meetings become opportunities to focus on everything your child *cannot* do? In these instances, teachers and school administrators strip away any level of hope for parents and for their children.

Disability labels also have a negative impact on teachers. Once a disability label is attached to a student, special education teachers, general education teachers, and even teachers with specialized training in gifted education tend to focus on what students can't do versus their identified strengths and talents (Bianco, 2005; Bianco & Leech, 2010). The negative effect of disability labels on teachers' expectations for what students are capable of and what they communicate to parents is very real.

Teacher educators can play a significant role in helping pre-service teachers understand parents' perspectives by regularly inviting parents as guest speakers to share their stories and help teachers understand what they needed at various stages of their child's school journey. It is also helpful to invite young adults with disabilities to guest speak in classes. Although most young adults with Asperger's syndrome will not necessarily become the next Temple Grandin, many young adults do go on to have very productive and satisfying lives. Helping teachers understand that focusing on students' strengths and talents rather than narrowly focusing on the disability can go a long way in building hope and preparing students to become self-determined young adults (Bianco, Carothers, & Smiley, 2009). A deeper understanding of the intense emotions parents and students with disabilities experience may foster more meaningful collaboration between parents, students, and teachers and ultimately bring about more positive outcomes for young adults with disabilities.

Bialostok's chapter serves as a good reminder for teachers and teacher educators. Our work must extend beyond the child to the family as much as possible. We must continuously reflect on the cycle of emotions parents experience as they deal with the loss of their "hoped-for child." By moving away from deficit perspectives of disability and focusing instead on students' strengths and interests, we will better serve our students and foster hope in their parents.

References

Bianco, M. (2005). The effects of disability labels on special education and general education teachers' referrals for gifted programs. *Learning Disability Quarterly, 28*(4): 285–293.

Bianco, M., Carothers, D. E., & Smiley, L. R. (2009). Gifted students with Asperger syndrome: Strategies for strength-based programming. *Intervention in School and Clinic, 44*(4): 206–215.

Bianco, M., & Leech, N. (2010). Twice-exceptional learners: Effects of teacher preparation and disability labels on gifted referrals. *Teacher Education and Special Education, 33*(4): 319–334.

Bianco, M., Garrison-Wade, D. F., Tobin, R., & Lehmann, J. P. (2009). Parents' perceptions of postschool years for young adults with developmental disabilities. *Intellectual and Developmental Disabilities, 47*(3): 186–196.

Friend, M. & Cook, L. (2013). *Interactions: Collaboration skills for school professionals* (7th ed.). Boston: Pearson Education, Inc.

Lloyd, R. J., Wehmeyer, M., & Davis, S. (2004). Family support. In D. E. Broli & R. J. Loyd (Eds.), *Career development and transition services* (4th ed., pp. 94–116). Upper Saddle River, NJ: Pearson Prentice Hall.

Mansell, W. & Morris, K. (2004). A survey of parents' reactions to the diagnosis of an autistic spectrum disorder by a local service: Access to information and use of services. *Autism: The International Journal of Research and Practice, 8*(4): 387–407.

4

FOOD FIGHT

Difficult Negotiations between Adults in an Early Childhood Center

Susan Twombly

INFANT TODDLER CHILDREN'S CENTER (ITC) OF ACTON, MASSACHUSETTS

"I believe that this center tries to do what is best for kids, so why allow store-bought cupcakes with preservatives and food coloring for birthday celebrations?"

—*A parent's comment*

"I will be really upset if this program bans sweets. Sending in cupcakes on my child's birthday is something I love doing. My mother didn't do that for me and I missed it. I'm going to do this for my kids."

—*A parent's comment*

"We don't want to be a part of this craziness, what's wrong with the way we've been doing things?

—*A teacher's comment*

"My mom says chips aren't good for you, why do you have them in your lunch?"

—*A comment from one child to another*

Feeding children in a group program provokes strong emotions and puts teachers in the center of conflicting beliefs about what is best for children, nutritional information, parents' feelings about how best to nurture their child, and a variety of cultural and family practices. I am the director of a private nonprofit early care and education center in a suburb of Boston. We serve 110 children and have a staff of 35 teachers and administrators. This is the story of an ongoing debate within our program centered on our program's food policies. In this chapter, I describe discussions, negotiations, and dilemmas that emerged among parents, teachers, and administrators, and the emotions evoked and expressed within our school community as we worked through this thorny issue.

As an organization, we are known for being flexible and individualized in our approach with children as well as with parents, and we pride ourselves on this reputation. Although our organization has strong shared values, our teaching teams have a fair amount of autonomy in how they choose to carry out the values and goals of our program. Most of our teachers have many years of experience and have good supervision and support from our program coordinators. As a leader, I am comfortable with considering multiple ways of doing things and I tend to dislike hard-and-fast rules.

In the past few years, we have been focusing on deepening our responsiveness to children and on being more intentional about our classroom practices by encouraging more reflection, primarily through the process of pedagogical documentation (Rinaldi, 2005; Guidici, Rinaldi, & Krechevsky, 2001). We have also been working on extending that reflection to policies and practices that affect parents and staff more directly. Our desire to respect family members and children as unique individuals and to allow for as much flexibility as possible can sometimes make things difficult, because finding a nuanced approach to policies and practice takes much more time and involves lots more discussion. In thinking about our food policies, I wanted any changes to come from an examination of our values and intentions, so I chose to take more time to explore this issue with staff.

The emphasis in this chapter is not so much on what is an appropriate food policy, but about the process of understanding our thoughts and feelings about this topic and balancing competing opinions and ideologies about what is best for children. In this chapter, I use as a framework the notion of emotional labor as defined by Artie Hochschild (1983). Working with parents and children involves a balancing act between one's own feelings and opinions and what actions will best serve the goal of supporting the growth and education of young children and families. The emotional work involved requires deconstructing the strong emotions that conflicting opinions engender in order to gain some clarity about what our role with children and parents is and what actions will best serve that role.

The topic of food in an early childhood program is emotionally charged. I discovered this as we started working on our policies. Feeding is one of the very first ways we nurture children and ourselves, is tied to notions about what is "best" and "right" for children, and is often used as a marker of "good" caregiving. For example, I recall that as a new mother, what and how much my child ate became a measure of how I was succeeding as a parent. I wanted my child to grow and thrive. Feeding my child was a way to express my profound love and fulfill an important responsibility as a nurturing parent. Moreover, the way we nurture a child through food is culturally bound—related to the beliefs, values, and customs of the diversity of families in a community (Kittler, Sucher, & Nelms, 2012).

In the first months of a child's life, parents often spend a great deal of time worrying about whether their child is getting enough nourishment and making choices about what and how they feed their baby. Later, this strong desire to make sure a baby is well fed can lead to struggles as the growing and maturing child begins to assert control over their own eating habits and is influenced in their food choices and desires by the media, peers, and their expanding contact with the world around them. Issues around feeding can be the first experience a parent has with coming to terms with a child's uniqueness and the subsequent loss of control over their child's everyday existence, sometimes resulting in tension and conflict between the parent and child.

When parents enroll their young one in a childcare program, this tension can be exacerbated as parents give up a measure of influence over the quality and nature of the food their child is offered. For many parents, particularly those who may be new to this country or whose culture may be in the minority in a particular community, this is a difficult transition. For instance, some of our parents have noted:

> "My child is a picky eater. At the center, I don't think that the teachers try hard enough to get her to eat. She needs a lot of encouragement to try certain foods."

> "In my country, we tend to just eat three meals a day. Everyone stops to eat together. The idea of snacking and eating little bits throughout the day isn't considered a good thing to do. Letting a child eat as much or as little as they want is very different."

As these comments demonstrate, food issues, rules, and patterns of eating are neither static nor universal. Families from different racial, ethnic, regional, and socioeconomic backgrounds adhere to and follow various customs around food, and when such customs are broken or challenged, emotional tension between the school and the family can result (Gonzalez–Mena & Eyer, 2004; Im, Pariakian, & Sanchez, 2007).

Within our program, children bring their own lunches from home and are served a snack provided by the program. As children become more verbal and interested in each other, lunchtime observations about each other's food and conversations about what foods they like and don't like are common. One day at lunchtime in a preschool classroom, I observed a little girl eating her vegetables and yogurt as she watched the girl next to her devour a big deli sandwich. She remarked to me, "I really would like to have a bite of that great big sandwich." Children often challenge one another's ideas as they comment on each other's lunches. "My mom says that chips aren't good for you." "That egg smells yukky." "We don't eat meat, why do you?" "I don't drink that kind of milk." Eating together in the center presents an opportunity to learn about respecting differences and can cause children to broaden their ideas about eating and food as they learn about a wider range of choices and diverse reasons for food selection. Parents may not welcome their child's increasing awareness of other children's food practices because it may challenge them to explain and evaluate their own beliefs and values about their family's eating habits. It causes the children to question and reflect on differences among families, and this is not always an easy conversation for parents to have with their child.

Teachers have their own feelings and traditions around food. They, too, desire to nurture the children in their care and draw on their own cultural assumptions about how best to feed a child. Some may be parents themselves, and all of them have childhood memories centered on food and eating. Since teachers work in teams, they must not only take into consideration the desires of the parents, but also the values and expectations around food of the other teachers they work with. For example, how much importance is placed on snack time and lunchtime in our Center varies from classroom to classroom, with some teachers wanting a "serve yourself" open snack and others wanting to control the timing and quantities eaten with a more traditional sit-down snack. Teachers also differ in their views about whether a child eats certain foods first or whether to allow a child to decide which foods to choose to eat from a packed lunch.

In addition, there are differences around whether to monitor what a child eats and whether to encourage a child to eat more or to eat certain foods first. For both parents and teachers, social and cultural expectations around the value of independence lead to differences in whether to feed children or let them feed themselves. Teachers find themselves having to do the emotional work of finding a balance between a parent's wishes and their own ideas of what seems right for a child. As one teacher commented, "I believe that children can be trusted to make choices about how much they eat. I am very uncomfortable when a parent asks me to make sure her child eats all of her lunch. I can gently encourage a child to eat, but actually feeding a child is not something I want to do." Because children bring their own food from home, teachers sometimes worry about the nutritional content of lunches or the appropriateness of the food sent in; however, they must balance a desire to respect each child's home culture with beliefs about what is an appropriate and nutritional lunch. While they are modeling respectful language around food for the children in their classrooms, they also need to decide whether and/or how to talk with parents about their choices for lunch foods.

Moreover, group programs, of necessity, have limitations and regulations that require certain practices. For example, in our program, we ban gum, candy, and foods that might pose a choking hazard to young children. Parents are often surprised that we won't serve some foods that a child easily handles at home. Banning peanut butter or other nut products when there are children with food allergies forces parents to make further adjustments to the foods they send in for lunch. Changing behavior for the sake of the larger community, especially when it involves food, is difficult for many parents.

So, we have parents, teachers, and regulators with varying expectations around food practices. For parents and teachers, these expectations are further complicated by strong emotions around nurturing children, individual cultural practices, memories of one's own childhood, and a desire to help children be kind and thoughtful to one another in a community that is respectful of diversity.

In the following sections, I describe the events and circumstances that made me realize that the time had come to take on this issue. I anticipated this with some trepidation, as I expected that our conversations around food policies and practices were going to be difficult.

The Food Fight Begins!

While reviewing our annual program evaluations from parents, the following comments drew my attention:

> "My only pet peeve is the snacks."

> "[W]ith parents bringing snacks in, things can get out of hand. I think additional clarity and reminders about when sweets are appropriate and when they are not would be helpful. My children eat far more sweets at the [c]enter than at home which I know is not the intention of the program at all."

> "The center seems like a progressive place that tries to truly do what is best for kids . . . So why serve artificially flavored hot cocoa mix to 18 mos. olds? Why allow store-bought cupcakes with preservatives and food coloring?"

> "I know this is a group setting, but we shouldn't have to set the bar low to be inclusive."

Reading these comments, I thought, "Ouch! Here we go; tackling this is not going to be easy." The annual program evaluation completed by parents is taken seriously. We pride ourselves on our responsiveness and strive to give children the very best of care. We are used to being complimented by parents and have a loyal and stable parent group. When I saw so many comments about our food program and recalled questions and conversations teachers reported having with parents, I realized that we had to pay attention to this. However, I did not look forward to sharing this feedback with teachers or to addressing it.

I had my own emotions to deal with as well. The tone of some of the parent comments triggered some anger for me because I felt that they were exaggerating or perhaps being provocative. I also found myself resisting the implication, for me personally, that we might not be providing healthy foods because of complicated changes I had already experienced in my own life. In the past few years, I have made enormous changes in my own eating habits. I have integrated a lot of the information about our American diet and its faults. I have two grown children who talk and think a lot about living a healthy lifestyle. In fact, my daughter has chosen to become a vegetarian based on her feelings about the way that animals are treated in the meat industry. This necessitated a big change in our entire family's eating habits. I am more comfortable with my diet now, but the tug from the past is still there. I grew up eating meat and potatoes at most every dinner; burgers and hot dogs, Jell-O salads, cakes and pies were always a part of family celebrations. Now, deciding what to eat and what to serve family and friends is more complicated (and more expensive). Would I now have to face this at the center too? I am fortunate to be able to afford fresh food and that I live in a part of the country where there are ample food choices; but applying this to our center is a different matter. Not everyone in our community has the same food choices or the income to afford alternatives. In fact, our program might not be able to stretch our limited resources to include more fresh healthy foods in the classroom snack program. All of these considerations, both personal and professional, affected my own emotional investment and reactions to this topic.

At the same time, I do believe that as a program, we should not ignore information about what constitutes a healthy diet and did believe that some practices might have to change. I also know that changing deeply ingrained behavior takes time and effort. If it was going to work, this was a process that teachers would have to buy into cognitively and emotionally. If teachers don't feel it is worthwhile, they may not follow through with change. Making a change was going to involve the deep emotional work of letting go of some feelings, beliefs, and practices in the interest of what is best for all of the children and for the program. For me, it was also going to mean I would have to resolve the tension between wanting to please everyone and the realization that this was probably not going to happen. If we were to "raise the bar" as one parent implied, would some families feel criticized for their well-meaning offers of food for the children? What about the children? Food from home is part of who they are. How far from the familiar do we want to take children in the interests of what we think is good nutrition? Who gets to decide what children eat at our program?

In an effort to bring some order to the potentially "dicey" task that was ahead, I formulated a number of questions:

- Are we meeting children's nutritional needs well?
- What is the role of food in classroom and center celebrations?
- Is it possible to really listen to parents' and teachers' various desires and ideas around food and make decisions that everyone can live with?
- Is it possible for families to contribute to our classroom snack-time foods and classroom celebrations if some families will be upset by what is offered?
- Can our program budget stretch to include more fresh and healthy foods?

Thus began a long and ongoing search for answers to these and other food-related questions, and eventually to some changes (for the good, we feel) in our practices. During this search, we would learn about the complex emotions and negotiations that teachers face as they attempt to meet children's needs. We would have to confront our own biases and unpack our emotional investment around food as we thought more deeply about our commitment to children and to partnering with parents. As a leader, I would also learn how much emotional and interactional work it takes for deep change to occur in the culture of a program. I discovered that the naming and tasting of a practice and belief is one thing, but fully digesting new behavior is quite another! Issues and negotiations unfolded at the series of meetings described next.

September, Meeting of the ITC Board: Experiencing the Emotional Tensions

My first inkling of the surprising complexity I was about to uncover came during a discussion with our board shortly after receiving the parent evaluations. I had listed the reexamination and possible revision of our practices around food and nutrition as one of my goals for the year. This sparked a remarkably lively conversation. Several board parents took this opportunity to chime in about a range of food-related practices, such as the timing and content of snacks, the choices of cooking projects, the differing ways in which teachers encourage or don't encourage children to eat what parents pack for their lunch, and the number of classroom celebrations at which sweets are served. The emotional energy in the room was high, and everyone seemed to have something to say. It was clear that among this small group of parents, opinions varied greatly and many beliefs were strongly held. Stated positions ranged from "there are far too many classroom celebrations at which sweets are served" to "If you are going to ban sweets for birthdays, I will be really upset. Sending in cupcakes on my child's birthday is something I love doing. My mother didn't do that for me and I missed it. I am going to do this for my kids."

I could sense the parents' deep concern over "doing the right thing" for their children. For some, this took the form of wanting their child's food to reflect the very best of what is known about current nutritional and health benefits. For others, the desire to replicate the sense of fun and celebration that they had enjoyed or were denied in their childhoods was strong. For all the parents, the emotions created by complicated and unique motivations for their particular parenting behavior made it difficult to listen to one another's perspectives.

October, Meeting of the Early Childhood Council: It's Not Just My Problem

Next, seeking some input from informed outside colleagues, I took the issue to a meeting of our local early childhood council. This council consists of area preschool directors and early childhood coordinators from public schools from four area towns. I knew that several of the public schools in our area had policies around food and I was curious to know more about them.

Again, the emotional reaction to the topic surprised me. The energy in the room was conspicuous. One of the public school representatives had served on a committee to revise their food policies. She warned that I had better be ready for some hot debates and to hear many strong opinions. I gathered from her emotional tone that serving on this committee had been a challenging task. Several representatives of the preschools said that they had not wanted to "go there" with parents and staff because of the many strong and competing sentiments this issue raises. I was astounded when the members of the council actively jumped into the debate. One suggested, "Why not just ban all sweets along with peanuts and tree nuts too?" Another countered, "Some of the public schools have done this, and I think it's just a shame." Someone lamented, "Kids need a little fun in their lives—can't they eat a treat once in a while?" Again, I wondered, what is this really about? We can't all care so much about a cupcake or two.

First Lead Teacher Meeting at ITC: No Progress!

Bringing the topic back to my program, I opened a discussion at our weekly meeting with lead teachers and program coordinators. I chose to start this discussion about our food policies with this group because we meet weekly and I believed this was going to take some time. I also thought that starting with a smaller group would give me an idea of what the issues were going to be. In addition, I knew that this group would begin some informal discussions with their teaching teams, thus planting seeds for change in the whole program. As I described the parents' comments on the program evaluations and at the recent board meeting, the reactions among staff were strong. The comments from the parents on the annual evaluation were hard for teachers to hear. Someone noted, "The squeaky wheel gets the grease. These few parents shouldn't get to determine what we do." Many teachers felt that the parent comments did not represent accurately the quality of most of the food served in classrooms. Some characterized those parents as "complainers" who were overly concerned about nutrition, could afford to shop for organic foods, and were expecting something at odds with the cultural norms of many of the parents and teachers in our program. Many of the teachers felt caught between the extremes of the competing notions around food among the parents. "We don't want to be a part of this craziness. What's wrong with the way we've been doing things?" one remarked. I felt caught in the middle of emotions that seemed to be provoked by questions of who gets to decide, which opinions we honor, and how far we should go to make changes without alienating people. I did not want to make teachers' lives in the classroom more complicated, but I also felt it was important that we pay attention to all parents' concerns and desires.

This discussion became so animated and emotionally charged that we couldn't move forward. The meeting spiraled out of control as teachers became more defensive, anxious and angry. Being criticized hurts, especially when your intentions are good; being asked to "police" the quality of food others bring to share with the class is hard; imagining a new way to create community and fun in the face of what feels like a loss is exhausting; paying attention to every family's unique food limitations and requests is confusing. In the end, all we could agree upon at this meeting was to try again at our next meeting: Clearly, we had a lot of work to do.

Second Lead Teacher Meeting: Beginning to Unpack the Issues

The next meeting was more productive. I divided the agenda into sections so we could organize our reactions and thoughts in a slower and more democratic way. For example, I wrote down teachers' comments as they spoke in order to slow the exchanges, and I asked that we go around the room to each have our say before commenting on one another's remarks. This proved to be a good technique to reduce the tension and to cause everyone to reflect critically. A number of persistent questions surfaced:

- How do we define a special celebration? If there are too many celebrations, children may eat a lot of sugary and nutritionally empty foods over time. What is the definition of a good snack for children? Some children come to the program having eaten little or no breakfast. By snack time, they are loading up on crackers and milk and then not eating lunch.
- Should we be serving fewer crackers and more fruits and vegetables? Can we afford to do this? Is it okay to ever serve cupcakes at morning snack? Will children be too full then to eat lunch?

There was also disagreement about appropriate serving sizes for children:

- For children who seem very hungry, should we continue to insist on limiting the number of crackers or glasses of milk consumed?

Another set of questions concerned parents and our responsibility and limits in "policing" and educating about good nutrition:

- What is the teacher's role if lunches seem inappropriate?
- What should teachers do when parents send in foods that are choking hazards according to the American Academy of Pediatrics?
- How much do we intervene when parents send dessert with lunch and children want to eat that first?
- How do we respond when a parent asks us to feed her 3- or 4-year-old and to make sure they eat everything? If we feed a child, it may hinder that child's movement toward independence (which is an important value in our culture) or we may be asked to feed a number of children. Is this feasible in a classroom setting? What is the role of teacher versus parent—does this feel too much like being a parent to a child?
- How should teachers address the conflicting food-related concerns of parents coming from very different cultural backgrounds? How can we have discussions with parents about the importance and meaning of feeding a child?
- Should we refuse the often-sugary or low-nutritional-value supplements to our regular snack foods that parents often send in? We understand that parents

are trying to offer the group a gift and we don't want them to feel rejected or unappreciated.

I was struck by the extraordinary array of competing pressures teachers must deal with every day, just around food, and wondered how they dealt with the conflicting emotions that such challenges must engender.

Third Lead Teacher Meeting: Realizing that Change Involves Letting Go

Prior to this meeting, we all read two articles: Erin Eliassen's piece in the March 2011 edition of *Young Children* entitled "The Impact of Teachers and Families on Young Children's Eating Behaviors" and Daniel Kessler's article entitled "Nurturing Healthy Eating Habits from the Start" published in *Zero to Three Journal* (2012). The staff agreed on the idea of fostering healthy eating habits in young children expressed in these articles. However, one statement in the Eliassen article made some of us uncomfortable:

> Food as reward or celebration is common in some early childhood settings. Such practices may be well intentioned but can have negative consequences and impact long-term eating behaviors. Food rewards or party treats are often sweets or other "desired" snack items. Giving a desired food as a reward enhances a child's preference for the food.
>
> *(Eliassen, 2011, p. 88)*

Debating this statement brought the group's discussion back to the issue of group snack and the role of food in celebrations. Some teachers felt that this statement applied to our program; others did not. Some proposed banning all sugary snacks. This suggestion elicited a number of expressions of loss:

"We shouldn't deny children a birthday cupcake."

"We don't want to be militant."

"We already have so many rules to follow."

"Saying 'you can't' gets people defensive, and the other teachers and parents won't like it."

"Restricting foods often results in an overreaction to these foods; we don't want to do this."

The teachers recognized that an all-or-nothing change in our practices might not be a practical or desirable solution. I sensed that banning all sugary foods, although it might move us more quickly to always offering a healthy choice, was not going to result in buy-in from all teachers, nor was it going to solve all the problems involved with parents' participation in our food program. Emotions were high among teachers as well as parents and dictated that an arbitrary or top-down solution not only contradicted my leadership style, but also was unlikely to be effective and accepted.

At this point, I realized that we did need to change some of the practices around snack time and celebrations and I was committed to moving our program in the direction of improving the nutritional value of the food offered. Part of me longed to just make change by dictating exactly what was to be served for snack and by requiring that celebrations no longer involve food. But, I remembered my struggles with changing eating patterns in my own family and realized that long-lasting change may take time and would require that all of us work through our own emotions to get there. My belief in the value of engaging our community in deep reflection and negotiation is strong, and I decided that this was going to have to be a longer and "messier" process if I was to honor that belief. My desire to put the issue to rest and settle my emotions would have to take a back seat for the moment to that strong leadership goal.

Fourth Lead Teacher Meeting: Coming to Some Agreement around Our Bigger Purpose

At this meeting, we focused on food in the context of celebrations, because there seemed to be considerable emotional energy and dissonance about this particular aspect of our food program and many of the parent comments seemed to be focused on this issue. We looked at the number of sugary snacks served by reviewing the food logs of the past six months. Although the situation might not have been as bad as the parent comments suggested, we did indeed find that in several classrooms, there were some months when the combination of sugary cooking projects and "cupcake-worthy" celebrations, birthdays, and other events resulted in a high frequency of sugary snacks.

When I asked if we should stop serving sugary snacks for celebrations, teachers strongly resisted, expressing the notion that most families and children would feel disappointed if we banned birthday cakes. In addition, they reasoned that most children don't eat much of the cake offered and noted the following benefits:

"Just having the treat makes their eyes sparkle."

"The kids notice when cupcakes don't come in for a birthday; they have come to expect these treats."

Many teachers were thinking about the potential losses in making a change like this. They were also identifying with positive nostalgic feelings connected to their own childhood memories of celebrations and special treats served at family gatherings. The discussion felt mired in defending current practice rather than considering alternatives.

Finally, we had a breakthrough when one of the teachers reframed the question, saying, "We do have knowledge about good nutrition for children. Isn't it our obligation to serve as a role model for cultural change around eating well?" This reframing led to a more nuanced discussion, with remarks such as:

> "Best practices around food include daily healthy choices and an occasional special treat—let's not deny treats but teach that they have their place."

> "A discussion of treats at celebrations is not the place to start this food conversation. It is more important to focus on the richness of daily offer- ings and our usual choices, not the occasional treat. Healthy food habits are largely based on what happens daily, not during celebrations, as long as we are attentive to the frequency and duration of these."

This discussion felt freeing. It was as if remembering our role as educators helped us to put our emotions about the parent criticisms and the work and losses involved in change in perspective. Hochschild (1983) refers to this as transmuta- tion of an emotional system. By reframing our emotions in relation to our role with children, we were able to focus on what a positive daily good nutrition pro- gram should be and define the teacher's role as a leader and model. There were other parts of this issue to work through, and now it felt like we had some energy to do that in a positive way.

Fifth Lead Teacher Meeting: Beginning to Come to a Consensus

At this meeting, we looked at a summary of the notes of our previous discus- sions. We were able to come to a consensus on several related issues: Celebrating with food seems to be strongly valued and is part of the culture here. If we were going to continue to have celebrations with food, we would need to reconcile that decision with our responsibility to help children to establish healthy eating habits. We were able to recognize that feeding children in groups is different from feeding children in a family. We realized that as teachers, we do have multiple obligations—to respect home cultures and to model good nutrition practices and policies that protect children's safety and are realistic for children (and teachers) in group care. Recognizing this, we were able to move forward with plans to change our practice.

Meeting of the Entire Program Staff: Beginning to Think in New Ways as a Whole Center

We ended the year with a meeting of the entire staff that focused on food and nutrition. Until this time, the discussions had been with lead teachers from every classroom as well as our program administrators. Although these discussions had been informally shared with the other teachers, we felt ready to open this topic up to the entire program and share what we had discovered in a more formal setting. When I looked at the comments that teachers wrote at the end of this meeting (a sample is included next), I realized that we were beginning to think more broadly about the complexity that is involved in making decisions for our food program:

> "How do we truly partner with parents around food issues? It's much more complex than I realized."

> "Maybe we should question why we do what we do more often—we can be rigid on this issue."

> "We need to realize and talk about our program's culture and limitations around food. Feeding children in groups is different than children eating at home."

> "I believe our program does have a role to set an example for parents and to be clearer about our role in teaching about healthy eating."

By reflecting on some of our dilemmas and emotional investments, we became more aware of the necessary balancing that must go on as we partner with parents and family members around our mutual desire to nurture and care for children.

We were finally able to add to and agree upon a statement of purpose, which is featured at the beginning of our newly revised food policy:

> At our program, we recognize that growing children thrive when their nutritional needs are met. Our staff is trained in USDA nutrition requirements annually. Children are fed taking into account parents' wishes, children's developmental needs, state regulations, and the dictates involved in feeding children in groups. Our goal is to serve a variety of nutritious foods and to encourage the development of healthy eating attitudes and behaviors that promote positive long-term health outcomes. We welcome your feedback and suggestions regarding food at the center.

Agreed-upon changes that strengthen this policy and help to resolve some of teachers' dilemmas include:

- A clearer statement that we will not serve foods that are listed as choking hazards by the American Academy of Pediatrics
- A statement that we will encourage children to eat the food that parents send and that we will offer uneaten lunch foods at afternoon snack, but we will not force a child to eat
- Creation of a uniform supplemental snack sign-up sheet for classrooms that requests only foods that offer good nutrition so that parents can still contribute to our snack program

- Agreement to a periodic review of our snack logs to be sure that sweets are only an occasional offering among many other healthy choices

The new goal statement at the beginning of our revised food policies provides the higher purpose that we hope to achieve. However, reaching our goal continues to involve extensive emotional work on the part of teachers and parents. The pull from the past, differences in cultural traditions that may conflict with good nutritional practices, the requirements of regulations, and limitations imposed by food allergies demand a complex balancing act for both parents and teachers. The burden of reframing emotions around this issue falls most heavily on the teachers because they must balance a wide diversity of parent requests, program needs, and customs.

As a leader, I have learned that strong emotional reactions to policy changes may signal a complexity of competing values that need to be unpacked. Initiating change requires both creativity and emotional effort. We live in a world where the necessity for change confronts us daily. We have more information available to us, and our crowded world is suffering from the impact of population growth and the excesses of overdevelopment. We are forced to adapt to technological advances and increasingly diverse communities. Our old habits are constantly challenged in order to live in a healthier and more sustainable manner. It's not surprising that resistance to change is so prevalent. This is especially true in a program dedicated to partnering with parents to support children's healthy growth. In reflecting on this process, I realize that this is not just about giving children cupcakes; it's about our capacity to change. I now appreciate the value of deep and active listening to all opinions. Most importantly, I learned how critical it is to recognize and honor the difficult emotional work teachers do in order to respond respectfully to diverse opinions and to model, for children and adults alike, tolerance and empathy.

References

Eliassen, E. (2011). The impact of teachers and families on young children's eating behaviors. *Young Children, 66*(1): 84–88.

Gonzalez-Mena, J., & Eyer, D. W. (2004). *Infants, toddlers and caregivers* (6th ed.). Mountain View, CA: Mayfield Publishing.

Guidici, C., Rinaldi, C., & Krechevsky, M. (Eds.). (2001). *Making learning visible: Children as individual and group learners.* Reggio Emilia, Italy: Reggio Children.

Hochschild, A. (1983). *The managed heart: Commercialization of human feeling.* Berkeley, CA: University of California Press.

Im, J., Pariakian, R., & Sanchez, S. (2007). Understanding the influence of culture on care giving practices from inside out. *Young Children on the Web.* Retrieved from www.naeyc.org

Kessler, D. (2012). Nurturing healthy eating habits from the start. *Zero to three Journal, 32*(3): 38–41.

Kittler, P. G., Sucher, K. P., & Nelms, N. M. (2012). *Food and culture* (6th ed.). Belmont, CA: Thomson Wadsworth.

Rinaldi, C. (2005). *In dialogue with Reggio Emilia: Listening, researching and learning.* London: Routledge Press.

COMMENTARY

Tamar Jacobson

RIDER UNIVERSITY

In the introductory paragraphs to this chapter, Susan Twombly describes a process of reflective practice that is critical for teachers (and administrators) who work with young children and families. As the entire center community considered revising their food policies, Susan, their director, wanted "changes to come from an examination of [their] values and intentions" (p. 59). Indeed, she emphasized that the food policy was not as important as the process of understanding their "thoughts and feelings" about the topic (p. 59). Twombly and her staff had the courage to extend their reflection through "pedagogical documentation to policies and practices that affected their staff and parents directly" (p. 59). She talked about how reflection has helped the center staff become more intentional about their classroom practices.

Most certainly, self-reflection is an important process that accompanies our teaching practice. In my work with teachers, I encourage them to reflect specifically about how their emotions or biases affect their relationships and interactions with children and families (Jacobson, 2003, 2008). Indeed, I recommend that teachers conduct an *internal ethnography* so that they can get to know themselves better (Jacobson, 2008). In order to have authentic relationships with children and families, it is important for teachers to understand what makes them *tick* emotionally, whether it is in understanding how they were disciplined or sought attention when they were children, or how they learned prejudice and bias from the significant adults in their lives.

I can only imagine how challenging it was for Twombly and her staff to come up with a food policy for their center, for, as she says, "The topic of food in an early childhood program is emotionally charged" (p. 59). With all the talk about their issues around food and food service, I found myself thinking of how my feelings about food affect me as well. Twombly shared a personal memory about how she, as a new mother, measured her success as a parent by how much or what her child ate. The best thing about people sharing personal stories is that it helps readers, or listeners, to jog their memories and make associations with their own life stories. At once, I began to reflect on my emotional triggers about gender issues related to body image and my relationship to food. For example, when my son was 15, I remember one morning walking into the kitchen to make him a sandwich for school just as I had always done for years. To my surprise, I found him spreading peanut butter and jam on a piece of bread. It was not unusual for him to be doing that, but somehow it seemed different and more significant on that particular morning. "What are you doing?" I asked, startling him and me with my question. "Making myself a sandwich for school," he replied. For a brief moment, I registered a slight emotional shock wave through my body because of the change that was transpiring within our family system. What became more interesting to me, however, was that for the rest of that week I noticed that on and off I felt mildly depressed, sad, as if something was missing.

By the week's end, I realized that I had been sensing a type of loss. One of the ways I showed love to my son was by feeding him; when he independently made that sandwich (and subsequent sandwiches going forward), I had lost a way to express my affection for him. For me, food represented the giving and receiving of love. It was a powerful moment of recognition for me about the connections between food and love. I identified with Twombly when she described how she felt she measured up as a successful parent by "what and how much [her] child ate" (p. 59). By understanding herself, she was able to become more understanding about how parents or guardians of children in their center might have emotional responses to formulating a food policy.

As they came together to reflect on thoughts and feelings related to the center's food policy, Twombly and her staff discovered that "[their] relationship to food [was] emotionally charged" (p. 59). For young children with parents who are able to love and want them, feeding time was a source of pleasure and comfort. Indeed, we still feel that old yearning as we reach for what we adults call "comfort foods." For me, it is a couple of soft-boiled eggs accompanied by toast spread generously with a type of yeast extract called Marmite that I learned to eat as a child growing up in British colonial Rhodesia (now Zimbabwe). My husband, on the other hand, finds comfort in a glass of warm milk and honey.

From the plethora of diet and self-help books about eating habits, disorders, and our body image, it is easy to see that *Fat is* [still] *a Feminist Issue* (Orbach, 1990)! In a profession that is populated predominantly by women, our relationship to food must be emotionally charged. For generations, women have been, and still are, shamed about what we should and should not eat (Orbach, 1990; Knapp, 2002; Roth, 2010; Koppelkam, 2013). Caroline Knapp, in her book, *Appetites,* writes painfully about "female hunger" (Knapp, 2002):

> There is a particular whir of agitation about female hunger, a low level thrumming of shoulds and shouldn'ts and can'ts and wants that can be so

chronic and familiar it becomes a kind of feminine muzak, easy to dismiss, or to tune out altogether, even if you're actively participating in it.

(p. 24)

I confess, I am one of those women who was shamed by family, friends, media, and society about body image and how my "female hunger" is considered "risky" or, even, "impermissible" (Knapp, 2002).

Just this past semester, I distributed to the undergraduate early childhood education students in my class a copy of an article printed in the *Parents* section of the *Huffington Post* (Koppelkam, 2013). In it, the author gives suggestions to mothers about how to talk to their daughters about their body, starting with: "Don't talk to your daughter about her body except to teach her how it works." I especially liked the following tip:

> Don't you dare talk about how much you hate your body in front of your daughter, or talk about your new diet. In fact, don't go on a diet in front of your daughter. Buy healthy food. Cook healthy meals. But don't say, "I'm not eating carbs right now." Your daughter should never think that carbs are evil, because shame over what you eat only leads to shame about yourself.

In class that evening, the students (all women) were silent after they read the article. After I asked what they thought about it, many expressed outrage about how they were made to feel about weight or how they looked. They wished people would notice them instead for their strength or intelligence.

We become more conscious and intentional in our interactions with children and families when we have the courage to face ourselves, whether it is about bias, emotions, or how we feel about food—for this type of internal ethnography is uncomfortable. Twombly's chapter shows us how a community of childcare staff was able to take on just such a challenge. As the author states in her conclusion, "This is not just about giving children cupcakes; it's about our capacity to change" (p. 71).

References

Jacobson, T. (2008). *"Don't get so upset!" Help young children manage their feelings by understanding your own.* Saint Paul, MN: Redleaf Press.

Jacobson, T. (2003) *Confronting our discomfort: Clearing the way for anti-bias in early childhood.* Portsmouth, NH: Heinemann.

Knapp, C. (2002). *Appetites: Why women want.* New York, NY: Counterpoint.

Koppelkam, S. (2013). How to talk to your daughter about her body. *Parents, Huffington Post.* Retrieved from www.huffingtonpost.com/sarah-koppelkam/body-image_b_3678534. html

Orbach, S. (1990). *Fat is a feminist issue: A self-help guide for compulsive eaters.* New York, NY: Berkley Books.

Roth, G. (2010). *Women, food and God: An unexpected path to almost everything.* New York, NY: Scribner.

PART II

Place and Spaces for Emotional Intimacy and Challenge

5

RECOGNIZING, RESPECTING, AND RECONSIDERING THE EMOTIONS OF CONFLICT

Ellen Hall and Alison Maher

BOULDER JOURNEY SCHOOL

It is early afternoon at Boulder Journey School, and all but two of the eight children in the infant classroom are asleep. The teacher places the two children who are awake on a large, soft carpet in the middle of the room (not in traditional pieces of infant equipment, such as bouncy chairs and sassy seats, that are intended to keep children contained, separated, and safe). The beige carpet is solid as opposed to one with a design or print, to call the children's attention to the materials that the teacher will place on it as an invitation for exploration. The teacher offers the children large materials—cardboard tubes, wads of cellophane, and rolls of paper—materials that are similar in size and shape but different in weight, texture, opacity, and sound. She anticipates that the children will discover ways they can use the materials collaboratively. The large size of the materials beckons many small hands, versus smaller sized materials intended for individual use.

George, 5 months of age, is seated with pillows behind him for support, and Sophia, 10 months of age, is seated beside George. Sophia is comfortable sitting on her own and can scoot, but is not yet crawling, whereas George is learning to sit upright. The teacher's placement of the children, side by side, is intentional. She trusts the children as socially competent, and thus is not fearful that they will unintentionally cause one another harm.

The teacher sits close by, confident in her ability to offer support and encouragement for what may be the children's first interaction. She feels a sense of excitement as she anticipates a budding relationship among two of her students, who will most likely be classmates for the next 5 years. The teacher is curious about the ways in which the children will interact. She decides to use her video camera to document this experience, hoping to learn more about these children, but also, more generally, about the initiation of relationships among infants.

Sophia lifts a cardboard tube. Its length is twice hers. Although she is able to lift the tube off the ground, she has trouble controlling it. Sophia starts to scoot around in a circle in what appears to be an attempt to master the tube's large size. Her movements, along with the sounds of delight she utters, capture George's attention, and the paper on his lap sits untouched. Sophia is the most intriguing object in view. As Sophia continues to wield the tube, it moves close to George's face several times. Given the circumstances, the teacher feels some tension. She wonders if she should either move the children farther apart or take the tube from Sophia. She decides, for the moment, to wait. She remains close, but does not intervene because the tube is made of light cardboard.

The children seem content—George is engrossed in Sophia, and Sophia is engrossed in the tube. Then, in a chance encounter, one end of the tube falls into George's immediate space, and he grabs onto it. Sophia is holding onto the other end. For a split second, both children are holding the tube. But, George is now focusing on the tube, not Sophia, and doesn't realize that when he lifts the tube up and over, it causes Sophia to lose her grip. George now holds the tube she was exploring. Sophia immediately cries out over the loss of her treasure. She waves her arms and kicks her feet. Her cries, although loud, are not those of distress, but rather cries of discontent. George is quiet and looks confused. This is clearly a conundrum for him. He turns to the teacher, who is videotaping, seemingly seeking clarity and guidance. Interestingly, Sophia does not look at the teacher, but continues to look at George, the person to whom she is communicating her displeasure. This is yet another moment of tension for the teacher, on several levels. Her instinct is to respond to George's request and Sophia's cries. She worries that the children might become increasingly confused and frustrated the longer the situation remains unresolved. She struggles, but ultimately makes the decision to wait before responding, seeking to communicate confidence in the children's ability to resolve this situation on their own.

The teacher's decision to wait offers George the time necessary to understand why Sophia is upset. Once he understands the situation, he returns the tube to Sophia, which is not an easy feat. It takes George several attempts to push the large cardboard tube over a big pile of paper in order to move it within Sophia's reach.

QR CODE 5.1 George and Sophia

The teacher is filled with emotion. She is pleased with herself for making a decision that was more difficult in the moment, but clearly more beneficial in the long run. Moments such as this one affect children's feelings of autonomy and self-efficacy. Although the teacher had exuded confidence in the children's social competence, she was at the same time still amazed, witnessing empathy in George, a child of only 5 months. She was also amazed by Sophia's ability to communicate effectively, using gesture and cries. This moment will affect every future interaction this teacher has with young children. Her memory of George and Sophia's social competence will help her to enter similar interactions with even more confidence, in herself and in the children.

But what if the teacher's fears rather than her curiosities and confidence had dominated the story? How would this experience have unfolded? More specifically, what if the teacher had been fearful of placing the children on the carpet beside one another? What if the teacher had been concerned about offering the children large, unwieldy materials, typically not found in infant classrooms? What if the children had to wait for a specified "project time" when all of the children were awake to play with the materials? What if Sophia, the older infant, were moving to another classroom in a few months, rather than remaining with the same group of peers throughout her early childhood years; would the teacher have invested this amount of time in supporting the beginning of a relationship with George? What if the teacher had taken the tube away as soon as Sophia began swinging it close to George's face? What if the teacher had reprimanded Sophia for not being careful with the tube? What if the teacher had shamed or reprimanded George when he ended up with the tube that Sophia was holding? What if the teacher had picked Sophia up when she was crying, interfering with her communication to George? What if Sophia had not protested? What if Sophia had not protested, and the teacher still intervened? What if George had not returned the tube? What if Sophia had not stopped protesting, even after George returned the tube? What if Sophia had grabbed the tube back from George, and George had cried? What if other children had been present? What if the teacher had been reluctant to videotape interactions not under her direct control? Would she have been able to study this interaction in depth and with colleagues? What if the teacher had been concerned about a colleague or parent entering the classroom in the midst of this interaction and possibly interpreting her interactions as neglectful? What if the teacher did not work at a school that values children's social-emotional development and devotes time and attention to this aspect of children's learning?

The story of George and Sophia demonstrates conflict, as well as the emotions surrounding conflict, when two individuals—in this case, two infants—hold differing perspectives. It also demonstrates the emotions that a teacher as an observer may feel when conflicts occur: The dismay that watching children engage in conflict naturally produces as well as discomfort in the knowledge that there are many strong and contradictory opinions surrounding how teachers should handle situations in which children disagree. The focus of this chapter is the recognition and reconsideration of conflict in a school for young children.

The narrative took place at Boulder Journey School (www.boulderjourney school.com), a full-day, year-round school located in Boulder, Colorado, that welcomes children ages 6 weeks to 6 years and their families. Woven into the school, the Boulder Journey School Teacher Education Program, in partnership with the University of Colorado, Denver and the Colorado Department of Education, offers up to 40 students an opportunity to earn a master's degree in educational psychology. Intern teachers participating in the year-long program join a permanent faculty of 25 mentor teachers. The philosophy of education and pedagogy of Boulder Journey School are inspired by the schools for young children in Reggio Emilia, Italy (www.reggiochildren.it) and the ideas of Frances and David Hawkins (www.hawkinscenters.org). The school's fundamental values reflect an image of children as competent and capable and as valuable citizens with inherent and irrefutable rights. These values are foundational to Boulder Journey School's Theory of Supportive Social Learning.

Supportive Social Learning is a way of thinking about social-emotional learning that supports the creation of caring school communities. Caring communities are characterized by a focus on empathy in daily interactions, collaboration among children and adults, and communication, both verbal and nonverbal. The defining features of Supportive Social Learning are: 1) community members value and seek to include everyone in creating a sense of community; 2) the nurturing of relationships among community members takes precedence over other agendas; 3) children are seen as capable of overcoming problems and succeeding socially as individuals and as a group; and 4) the teacher enters all classroom interactions with a questioning posture and commitment to conversation (Hall & Rudkin, 2003).

Boulder Journey School educators, beginning in 1989, developed this approach to social-emotional learning. The approach resonates strongly with the views of educators in Reggio Emilia, who consider the school as a system of relationships (Edwards, 1995), and of David Hawkins, who wrote of the importance of both love and respect in adult relationships with children (Hawkins, 1997).

Building upon Boulder Journey School's foundational image of children as competent and capable citizens, adults communicate to children that what they say and feel are important and that every individual must be respected for their unique contributions to the learning of the group. We invite children not only to share their ideas with one another, but also to elicit feedback from other children. In this way, children come to know the strengths of their peers and eventually seek their counsel without adult prompting. We believe that children have the following rights: 1) To initiate and maintain relationships with other children and adults; 2) to have a voice in the organization of the classroom and in the development of processes and procedures that take place there; 3) to identify and find solutions to issues; 4) to discuss and debate; 5) to negotiate and possibly resolve differing opinions, and; 6) to the time required to learn ways to share spaces and experiences with others. Adults support children's inherent rights by listening to their thoughts, feelings, and opinions; by offering words and gestures to facilitate their expression; and by encouraging them to make decisions that include rectifying mistakes. By exhibiting sensitivity to and respect for children's emotions and unique perspectives, adults model and promote children's natural empathy toward others, both children and adults.

As resources, adults offer environments replete with materials that are interesting and provocative, organized and accessible, comforting and aesthetically pleasing. Adults, with the support of children, design classroom spaces in which children can explore together, in large and small groups and on their own. In addition, adults offer children experiences within the classroom and in the larger community that encourage collaboration and the communication of their ideas and emotions.

Boulder Journey School educators are engaged in ongoing investigations, designed, documented, and reflected upon to better understand and support children's social-emotional learning, including *the aspect of conflict*.

Questions that have emerged with respect to conflict include:

1. What emotions arise for children and teachers during conflict?
2. When is conflict negative and when is it a necessary and productive aspect of building relationships in a community?

FIGURE 5.1

FIGURE 5.2

3. Do children and adults have similar or different perceptions about conflict?
4. What is the role of the teacher in children's conflict?

As an example, two 3-year-old children are building a tower with unit blocks. They are approaching the peak, when one of the children becomes frustrated while trying to balance a block at the top and knocks the tower over. The child who has destroyed the tower may feel remorse, but also defends his actions. He argues that the tower wasn't working and that he needed a fresh start. The other child may feel a sense of betrayal combined with sadness over the lost creation. Clearly, both children are sad. The teacher, recognizing the children's sadness and frustration, wants to offer support. Because she is removed from the situation, she is able to see both perspectives and wants to intervene without judgment. She views this event as an opportunity to support the children in taking the perspective of "the other." This is a life skill. Conflicts in personal and professional relationships are inevitable but can provide opportunities to strengthen relationships when addressed with compassion, commitment, and compromise. After the initial shock of the destroyed tower is absorbed, the teacher helps each child articulate his point of view and invites the children to brainstorm possible solutions to the problem they now face together—the possible reconstruction of the tower. The children decide to do this together the next day, using a sketch that one of the children created. The teacher videotapes the rebuilding as an example of how conflict and the process of resolving conflict can strengthen relationships.

Understanding the differences between adults' and children's perceptions about conflict is critical to supporting the development of classroom communities. Research indicates that adults tend to view children's conflicts as crises that threaten the social and emotional order of the classroom. Whereas adults see conflicts as crises, children see disagreements that are short lived, eliciting strong emotions that do not result in residual negative feelings (Hall & Rudkin, 2011). The differences in perception between children and adults are evident in the language each tends to use when describing conflict. It is not uncommon for a child to report that his friend is "being mean." Adults may term the child in question "aggressive." The former describes an emotion-filled moment in time; the latter labels a child's nature. Such notions on the part of adults tend to make them emotionally uncomfortable with conflict and often result in their entering a conflict too quickly and forcefully, seeking its end as an overriding goal (Hall & Rudkin, 2011).

We think that adults' discomfort with conflict is culturally situated. Contrary to other countries, in the United States there is an emphasis on safety, both physical and emotional, reflected in the high number of regulations imposed on educators in schools for young children. Conflict is seen as antithetical to safety, so teachers implement strategies to reduce potential conflicts. For example, teachers often predetermine how many children can play in a particular classroom space. This is intended to reduce conflict caused by overcrowding, but as a strategy it ignores the opportunity for children to express diverse opinions as they negotiate in a limited space. The negotiation of conflict encourages children with diverse opinions to express their feelings and ideas, while showing empathy for others' feelings. This is the foundation of the democracy we have established in the United States, which ironically is neglected in schools where children are asked to disregard their opinions and emotions and just play "nicely" in order to avoid conflict.

Conflict is typically defined as a serious disagreement or argument (www.merriam-webster.com/dictionary/conflict). This definition only includes the negative aspects of conflict. We propose a broader definition that includes the positive aspects that emerge when individuals and groups of individuals are supported in sharing conflicting ideas, opinions, perspectives, and emotions. As a result of our research, we realize that children understand this. Conflict, as typically defined, is an adult interpretation that negates and deprecates children's explorations of the social-emotional world. Expanding the definition of the word "conflict" supports the transformation of our thinking about "behavior management," moving from the idea of managing children's behavior to the idea of building communities that are socially and emotionally supportive. At Boulder Journey School, we have learned (along with the children) to think about social-emotional learning in an environment that values children's autonomy, empathy, and self-efficacy.

Based on our studies, educators at Boulder Journey School have found that what is often termed "conflict" is really a critical part of children's research about themselves and others. It involves the interactions—physical, social-emotional, and intellectual—between and among children and adults as they form and develop relationships within their communities. We recognize and appreciate the idea that children and adults bring diverse perspectives and differing opinions to their investigations, providing opportunities for ongoing disagreement and negotiation.

Children are born ready to engage with others through gazes, cries, smiles, giggles, etc. From the moment of birth, children are engaged in investigations surrounding the physical and relational world and their place in this world (Rinaldi, 2006). An infant encounters the world with all of his senses—looking, listening, smelling, tasting, and feeling with its entire body. Reaching out with hands and arms, legs and feet, and mouth to learn about objects is perceived as natural exploration to be encouraged. Infants also explore their own bodies and the bodies of the adults who are near. This, too, is encouraged.

But how is the reaching out of one infant to explore another perceived emotionally by the adult? Is a sense of potential danger or fear communicated? Do adults intentionally place children out of reach of one another to minimize the possibility that one child's "explorations" will harm the other? Do adults intercept physical interactions before they occur? What does this communicate to infants about the other children in their classroom? What does this communicate to infants about adult discomfort with these types of interactions?

Why not place children in proximity to one another and support their explorations, modeling "gentle touches"? The process of observation and documentation provides adults with an understanding of the competencies of infants. This understanding gives adults the confidence in children that moves us from intervention to nonintervention, as infants learn about one another from one another.

Regardless of precautions that prohibit interactions, as infants become increasingly mobile, they inevitably and naturally find one another. One infant's explorations of another's body might elicit a vocal response that brings the teacher to separate the two. Considering the lens of infant as researcher, the cause and effect response is ripe for study. If I touch you, you move and scream. If I touch you again, will the response be similar? No harm intended, just research. What if the teacher, rather than moving in and separating the two infants, supports the exploration with words and an alternative idea: "That's Carter's leg. He is not happy when you touch it, so he moves it away and screams. Maybe, we can bring him his favorite book to show him that we would like to be his friend and play with him." In this scenario, the teacher verbally frames the reactions and emotions experienced by Carter, bringing them to the child's attention. In this way, the teacher offers the child an opportunity to experience empathy, the understanding of another's emotions. Further, by suggesting that the child bring Carter his favorite book, the teacher offers the children an opportunity to come together in a new way.

Communications among preverbal and emerging verbal children are based on actions and gestures. The teacher's role is to "listen" to the children's movements and gestures and to give words to what their possible thoughts and intentions may be. Yet, hypotheses should not be made quickly. Is the child who approaches another child during lunch seeking a bite of her friend's dessert? Or is the object locked inside her closed hand actually an offering of food for her friend? Teachers must "listen" to their own actions, both verbal and nonverbal, and reflect on the emotions and opinions they hold that lead them to act and react as they do.

As children move from infancy into the toddler years, the sense of self as distinct from others becomes more clearly defined. "I am me, not you, and this toy is mine, not yours." The notion of ownership is complex and often evokes strong emotions, particularly in toddlers. At home, there are things that cannot be touched because they belong to mommy, daddy, or siblings, and there are things that belong solely to the toddler. At school, most everything is community property and must be shared. Toddlers must move from a mindset that says, "This is mine because I want to use it" to "I can use this because it is currently not being used by another child or adult." When disagreements surrounding the concept of shared objects occur, toddlers communicate through actions and expressions of emotion. Space is another commodity that must be shared. A toddler may push another toddler out of her space so that she can play uninterrupted. Teachers can refrain from assigning ownership to objects or space, instead offering suggestions that require collaboration. For example, the teacher might introduce a large ball or a long rope, objects that require two or more children to manipulate.

Infants and toddlers may also have different ideas or plans that evoke strong emotions. For example, one child may think that blocks are made for building up, while a second child may think that a tower of blocks is ideal for knocking down. Is it possible for these two children to work collaboratively? How can teachers support collaborations such as this one? Can the children first build together and then knock down together? Or, is it all right to decide that a solution that requires a sharing of blocks is not possible in this particular instance? Perhaps each child requires her own set of blocks to either build up or knock down in this space.

The movement from difference of opinion to negotiation and, in many but not all instances resolution, is a critical aspect of collaboration. In a socio-constructivist classroom, children can only be expected to learn if they are able to work collaboratively, sharing spaces and objects, and acknowledging and respecting the varied perspectives of the other children and adults in their classroom community.

At Boulder Journey School, we have found that offering children many opportunities to experience the process of negotiation results in a change in their emotional responses. Over time, responses based on fear, frustration, and anger are transformed into responses based on trust, patience, and confidence. Self-efficacy surrounding social and emotional interactions emerges. For example, we often observe 3- and 4-year-old children using phrases such as "I have another idea," "listen to my words," "we can take turns," and "what do you think?"

As children enter the preschool years and develop oral, written, and graphic languages, they have more sophisticated strategies for sharing space, objects, and perspectives with peers and adults. Although children have strong emotions and opinions and many ideas to contribute, their thinking is flexible. Loris Malaguzzi believed that children's flexibility "comes about because they have the privilege of not being excessively attached to their own ideas, which they construct and reinvent continuously" (Edwards, Gandini, & Forman, 1998, p. 75). Whereas children openly share their ideas and feelings, adults are often more concerned with protecting their ideas and emotional space. Children tend to critique one another's ideas freely and empathetically. They also receive critique without the strong and personal emotions that adults often feel when their opinions are critiqued. To a child, a critique of an idea is just that—not a judgment of their character or their value to the project. Further, when preschool children hold differing opinions, they are apt to argue until consensus is achieved.

Negotiation is a term that enters the conversation when moving from disagreement to agreement. We observe that children's negotiations involve dialogue versus bartering. Carlina Rinaldi (2006) highlights this difference in her interview with Gunilla Dahlberg and Peter Moss:

> Negotiation is not a matter of finding the middle or the in-between. Real negotiation, I think, for me goes directly to dialogue. There is no way to escape transformation. In negotiation the two subjects have to accept to change, partially at least, their own identities. I don't think that negotiation is simply a transaction, in which I get this and you get that.
>
> *(p. 187)*

It appears that whereas adults often find disagreement leads to feelings of embarrassment, children do not. When two children have exhausted their repertoire of strategies for negotiation, it is not uncommon for them to turn to another child who is an "expert" or to bring the problem to the entire group for reflection and support. If we incorporated the children's process of disagreement and negotiation more often, would it be possible to minimize true acts of aggression, conflict, and even war? What an amazing and hopeful thought!

Let's return to the story of George and Sophia. This story, and others that occur daily, are possible because of the value we place on social-emotional learning and the important role that this learning plays in both school and life. It is a hopeful story.

But, what if . . . What if we rushed children through social negotiations in order to have time to cover a planned daily curriculum? Would we be valuing the cognitive learning, but not the social-emotional learning embedded in this curriculum?

What if we created rules for children, as opposed to creating understandings with children? In our efforts to avoid potential problems, would we be robbing children of the opportunity to be active members of their community?

What if we only considered the relationship between the child and the adult and did not consider relationships among children?

What if our response to children's negotiations was to immediately identify the perpetrator and the victim? What would this communicate to the children about their capabilities to live together peacefully?

What if we always offered children individual learning experiences? What if we did not recognize the child's ability to blend ideas with those of others?

What if we were so fearful of disagreement that we hesitated to invite children to offer their perspectives to one another?

What if we viewed children as incapable of complex thought? Would we offer them the opportunity to solve complex social-emotional challenges?

Twelve 4-year-old children work in various spaces in a prekindergarten classroom. The children's voices permeate the classroom as they share ideas with one another. The two teachers observe and document, offering suggestions and supplies when needed, but they do not instruct the children to be quiet.

Caleb and Jordan work together in the classroom studio with paper, markers, and colored tape. They have been classmates since they were infants and have had a close relationship since they first met. When Jordan entered the classroom that morning, she was wearing a brace on her arm. Jordan lives with cerebral palsy as a result of a stroke experienced during birth. Her leg brace, worn from infancy, and her new arm brace help keep her muscles from contracting. Caleb had commented on the brace, calling it a "brace-e-let," and wanted to make one for himself, because in his words, "I really like it."

As Caleb begins the process of creating his brace-e-let, he consults Jordan's model. To facilitate the process, Jordan removes her brace and sets it on the table in front of Caleb. The brace is blue, green, yellow, and red, but Caleb can only find blue, green, and yellow tape on the studio shelves. His solution is to find the white masking tape and color it red. While he is looking for a red marker, he trips. Jordan calmly warns him to be careful. Other children, working in other parts of the classroom, enter the studio at various times to look for writing materials for their projects. They stop to ask Caleb what he is doing. He explains that he is making himself a brace-e-let like Jordan's, an object that he admires.

Once the long and arduous task of creating the brace-e-let on the studio table has been achieved, Jordan carefully wraps it around Caleb's arm, referencing her brace, still lying on the table when needed. When Caleb's brace-e-let is in place

QR CODE 5.2 Jordan and Caleb

and securely fastened, Jordan puts her brace back on her arm. By the end of the day, all of the children in the class have Caleb's idea, each creating arm brace-e-lets to wear.

This story fills our hearts with joy and provokes us to ask: Can we envision a school for young children or, in fact, a world for young children, in which the ideas and emotions associated with aggression and conflict have no meaning and are sources of growth, learning, and emotional satisfaction? How might we learn to feel differently about conflict? How might this begin? Our hope lies with young children, who have not yet been socialized to shy away from and fear differences, judging others to be "right or wrong," "fit or misfit," "able or disabled."

What if we trust children, beginning in infancy, to enter into social and emotional relationships—questioning, hypothesizing, testing, reflecting, and creating meaning? Rather than keeping children apart, what if we find myriad ways to bring them together, across boundaries of age, gender, race, culture, and ability and just let them discover one another? What if we stand back and observe their interactions, without interfering, without judging? What might we learn from the children about our own preconceived notions regarding relationships? What might we learn from the children about living with one another with love and respect and in peace?

References

Edwards, C. (1995). *Democratic participation in a community of learners: Loris Malaguzzi's philosophy of education as relationship.* Lecture prepared for "Nostalgia del futuro: Liberare speranze per uno nuova cultura dell'infanzia," an international seminar to consider the educational contributions of Loris Malaguzzi, Milan. Retrieved from http://digitalc ommons.unl.edu/cgi/viewcontent.cgi?article=1014&context=famconfacpub

Edwards, C., Gandini, L., & Forman, G. (1998). *The hundred languages of children: The Reggio Emilia approach – Advanced reflections.* Westport, CT: Ablex.

Hall, E., & Rudkin, J. K. (2003). Supportive social learning: Creating classroom communities that care. *Childcare Information Exchange, 149*: 12–16.

Hall, E. L., & Rudkin, J. K. (2011). Seen and heard: Children's rights in early childhood education. NY: Teachers College Press.

Hawkins, D. (1997). Afterword. In F.P.L. Hawkins, *Journey with children: The autobiography of a teacher.* Boulder, CO: University of Colorado Press.

Rinaldi, C. (2006). *In dialogue with Reggio Emilia: Listening, researching and learning.* London: Routledge.

COMMENTARY

Mary Jane Moran

THE UNIVERSITY OF TENNESSEE

> "To care for our children means we teach them how to receive care and give care."
> —*(Noddings, 1995, p. 139)*

In this rich description of two babies and their teacher, I am reminded of the many times I have witnessed and discussed the challenge felt by teachers regarding when to intervene and when to step aside (Moran, 2007; Caudle & Moran, 2012). Here, in the series of connected moments described by Hall and Maher, what comes alive is the emotional "push-pull" of the teacher as she positions and repositions herself between her fears and her curiosities and confidence about the competencies and rights of the babies. More often in the field of early childhood education, teachers' emotional tensions are not acknowledged. Yet, the authors help us get in touch with the fact that teaching is both an emotional and cognitive experience that draws upon an "ethic of care" and the tensions that may arise when deviating from a particular cultural norm of caring.

In the United States, the dominant culture of child *care* promulgates a belief that very young children are needy, fragile, and dependent, requiring teachers to hover closely and continually. However, this was not the case with the teacher and the babies in the preceding chapter. Instead, the teacher had an intention to create a context that was safe and intriguing, with the expectation that she and the babies might experience some feelings of discomfort or challenge. As a result, the teacher repositioned her affective orientation and physical proximity. What might this mean for the development of the babies' emotional selves, and what is the import of the teacher's watchful "emotions in check" stance for her own emotional growth and subsequent practice?

Most American childcare programs include the expectation that teachers provide sensitive and responsive caregiving as a hallmark of "best practice." Teachers often translate this practice as being poised for the possibility to: (1) interpret the perceived needs of children and rescue them from unhappy and potentially stress-ful moments; and (2) create contexts that prevent potential tensions and conflicts in the first place. As a result, an unintended message to babies may be that we, as teachers, do not trust that they can sort through conflicts and related emotions of frustration and unhappiness as they learn to read and respond to one another's emotional displays. Yet in the detailed description by Hall and Maher, when Sophia and George responded to one another's emotional displays, they learned how to read and respond to emotional cues and create processes for solving the prob-lem of how to alleviate a conflict and care for one another. Moreover, when the teacher resisted intervening (counter to what some may define as being responsive and sensitive), she commanded her own ethics and that of her local school culture in which teachers are encouraged to create authentic experiences for children that offer them the opportunity to access their emotional understandings as they build upon their knowledge about and relationships to others. As a result, the ethic of care operationalized by this teacher included the assurance of the babies' right to take charge of their emotional selves and resolve a conflict.

Intentionality

The classroom setting is counter to a more traditional approach by U.S. teachers who diligently "step in" to protect young children from harm by anticipating and removing potential risks. At times, this interruption creates tension for the teacher and frustration for the children. Here, the teacher made a commitment to act and think about when to intervene or remain on the sidelines. The teacher made deliberate decisions by first creating a setting filled with atypical objects for infant exploration, placing the babies close together, and removing herself from the immediate space. From Noddings' (2003, 2005) perspective, this orientation may ensure the teacher stays out of the way of the children's emotional acts to prevent giving the impression that they are not emotionally capable enough to handle the challenge of sharing the cardboard tube.

To be sure, the babies were not alone in experiencing both conflict-ridden and happy emotions. The teacher waited at least three different times to give the babies time and opportunity to work through their disagreements. The conflict of when to intervene and when to hold back is not a new dilemma in early childhood education, but here Hall and Maher make visible a series of moments emotionally laden with tension, uncertainty, and hope that the babies would solve their dilemma. This state of "conflict of caring" (Noddings, 1984, p. 13) required the teacher to "consider their natures, ways of life, needs, and desires. And, although [she] can never accomplish it entirely, [she tries] to apprehend the reality of the other" (Noddings, 2003, p. 14). Consequently, the teacher held back to prevent her interference and observed the babies reveal displeasure and uncertainty, "read" displeasure through cries and gestures, consider the cause of the displeasure, show empathy in resolving the unhappy moment, and reach a happy state once again.

Proximity

The teacher made two important proximal decisions. The first was to position the babies close to one another rather than giving them their "own space," and the second was to distance herself away from the pair. The teacher's repositioning was not passive or disengaged. More often, teachers of very young children position themselves close by so that they can intervene on behalf of the children. Yet, does close proximity to children help ensure or interfere with their autonomy and self-regulation? In this vignette, there is evidence that the teacher was highly engrossed visually but not physically, thus giving the space over to the babies, sending a message to them that, together, she thought they were capable of resolving their conflict.

As a social constructivist teacher, she drew upon her beliefs that children first construct knowledge on the social plane of development before they can appropriate it as their own. In this instance, had she been physically closer to swoop in and return the tube to Sophia, the babies' reconciliation likely would have been thwarted.

Temporality

Temporal considerations made by the teacher contributed to ensuring the babies were given opportunities to resolve conflicts even as it created conflict for the teacher. Before the babies were ever brought into the classroom, the teacher took the time to purposefully create a context that: (1) situated children close to one another; (2) provided single objects that would encourage exchanges; and (3) slowed her response time in order to give the babies time to resolve their differences on their own. She "sat" with the periodic emotional tensions that bubbled up inside her, believing that her action was not to move in physically but rather to think about what she must focus on during this "conflict of caring" (Noddings, 2003, p. 14). Her attention to her role slowed her tendency to intervene and gave the babies an opportunity to respond to one another and solve their dilemma. As a result of tolerating some discomfort, the teacher and the children were rewarded with Sophia using her languages to convey her needs and with George "reading" Sophia, making a concerted effort to respond to her—to care for her.

The contribution of this chapter brings home the importance of tapping into the emotions of teachers as they engage in pedagogical decision making. Too often, teacher educators ignore this aspect of teaching as we strive to guide teachers toward creating contexts that are more outcomes based and cognitive in nature, due to the shifting educational culture of moving further away from the emotional aspect of teaching and learning. For example, now are there rarely discussions about how teachers' emotional selves influence pedagogy. In this chapter, Hall and Maher bring to our attention the value and need to take explicit steps to help teachers focus on their emotions as they teach, to identify their emotions as they critique their practice and the learning of children, and to harness evolving understandings of how our emotions influence practice. Only then are teachers positioned to tolerate and make use of the emotional "push-pull" that is part of teaching to ensure children are given opportunities to enact their innate capabilities and capacities to resolve emotional issues for themselves.

References

Caudle, L., & Moran, M. J. (2013). Developing professional identities through participation within a hybrid community of practice: Illustrating the front-line experiences of four pre-k mentor teachers, *Action in Teacher Education, (35)*5–6, 387–404.

Moran, M. J. (2007). Collaborative action research and project work: Promising practices for developing collaborative inquiry among early childhood preservice teachers. *Teaching and Teacher Education, 23,* 418–431.

Noddings, N. (1984). *Caring: A feminine approach to ethics and moral education.* Berkeley, CA: University of California Press.

Noddings, N. (1995). Care and moral education. In W. Kohli (Ed.), *Critical conversations in philosophy of education* (pp. 137–148). New York, NY: Routledge.

Noddings, N. (2003). *Caring: A feminine approach to ethics and moral education* (2nd ed.). Berkeley, CA: University of California Press.

Noddings, N. (2005). Caring in education. *The Encyclopedia of Informal Education.* Retrieved from http://infed.org/mobi/caring-in-education/

6

HOW TO HOLD A HUMMINGBIRD: USING STORIES TO MAKE SPACE FOR THE EMOTIONAL LIVES OF CHILDREN IN A PUBLIC SCHOOL CLASSROOM

Melissa Tonachel

BOSTON PUBLIC SCHOOLS

> "The family stories you grow up with make you. They actually build you, they create you."
>
> —*Donald Hall in conversation with*
> *Jane Kenyon and Bill Moyers (1993)*

I tell a story:

A long time ago, when I was a grown-up but before I was a teacher, I lived in a house that looks like this:

The children and I are sitting on the rug in a semblance of a circle. I pick up a marker to make a sketch on large paper.

It has a round window right on the top and little triangle windows all around the sides.

This house is in the woods. I was living in a city, and I was curious about living in a very different place. My friend had a tiny house in the woods. I drove out of the city and into the country and into a little town, and then out of the little town. I parked the car at the edge of the woods and got out. You get to this house by walking down a long dirt path. There are trees all along this path and all around the house and flowers growing all over, scattered through the woods.

No one had lived in this house for a long time. It was empty. There was no furniture, the chimney had to be fixed, and it was dirty. It was fall, like now, and I decided to go live there.

How might this story, a teacher's particular personal narrative, be useful to the emotional and social life of young school children? Certainly, it opens an avenue for personal connection between teacher and students; what further possibilities does it suggest for children's emotional and social growth?

Reasons to Tell Stories

State and federal educational standards charge us with teaching specific rules of written and spoken language at given grade levels, and district curricula often chart a path for how to accomplish this. Almost any written story might be used as a tool for looking at conventions of print, character, setting and plot development, narrative structure, dialogue, and even the particulars of letter sounds. We recognize the power of using stories to foster oral language and vocabulary. Beyond literacy development, this chapter is about how stories can also nurture the emotional development of young children.

In classrooms across the country, teachers daily set aside time for children to relax and listen to a book read aloud. It is not a new idea to use stories to teach moral lessons and impart information. Moreover, this ritual links the members of a classroom in community and helps to define the affective environment in which ideas of how we can *be* in the world are contemplated together. Stories provide accounts about how elements of identity—our motivations, emotions, and values—are enacted: Love, fear, joy, greed, generosity, courage. What might these look like?

The Early Childhood Department of the Boston Public Schools has recognized the power of stories by launching Boston Listens, a storytelling/story acting program based on methods developed by Vivian Gussin Paley (Mardell & Boni, 2012). Children dictate and then act out stories of their imagination, and these experiences foster the development of literacy skills, creativity, and collaboration. The stories told reveal themes that are important to children and issues with which they are wrestling.

Heath (1983) has devoted significant study to the purposes and effects of storytelling across cultures, in part noting how personal storytelling might be adapted to relating true events or offer a possibility for self-invention. On the surface, we like to tell stories of our past adventures in part because it keeps those experiences alive. And the children are entertained; it's a lovely way to spend 20 minutes together. Of course, it's bigger than that; children are engaged, their minds at work with puzzles and connections and the beginnings of their own inventions. At the broadest level, we tell stories to instruct, to inform, to encourage, to warn, to humor, to console, and to show care. We tell stories to confront emotions and to make emotional connections with others.

Implicit in this chapter is the assumption that we are better teachers of young children when we know those children well: We respond meaningfully to their emotional, social, intellectual, academic, and physical selves when we appreciate their environments, experiences, passions, and fears. Although we are increasingly charged with knowing children narrowly as academic learners, "knowing" means finding ways into others' emotional, social, and aesthetic lives. It depends upon an exchange of ideas and identities. Knowing a child is not a one-way endeavor, but a reciprocal action.

Children will reveal themselves to us over weeks and months, as we are patiently *listening*, letting children know that we are paying attention. What if we set aside time in our schedules for listening and attending to children's emotional needs? Better yet, what if we made listening a habit that permeates our every action, an attitude palpable to the children so that it acts as an invitation, constantly issued, for children to open themselves to us? What does that attitude look like in action?

Telling stories is one way to build this attunement between and among the adult and child members of our classroom communities. Sharing my personal narratives sets up a context of candor and vulnerability and offers a model of telling about oneself. As I reveal who I am and how I come to understand my world, the children find the beginnings of this same exchange with each other and within themselves. We tell, we listen, we ask, we rework and redefine, and then we tell and listen some more. We create a culture of attending to each other.

How do children get to know and develop their emotional identities? If we accept the "self," as Eakin (1999) suggests, "less as an entity and more as a kind of awareness in process" (p. x), how do we help children become comfortable in their own skin? In turn, how do they approach being uncomfortable, meeting the task of changing their skins in response to new provocations?

In an early childhood classrooms, children continually bump up against surprises: A child has been working with determination on a block structure, and another bumps it. From a complicated menu of emotional responses, which does the builder access? Does she feel exasperated, irritated, woeful, discouraged, or does she find it hilarious? What she then does with any feeling sets a multitude of things in motion. She faces the immediate question, "Is this what I wanted to have happen?" More deeply, she is coming to understand something about herself. As a teacher, I ask, "What story might I tell to help her make sense of this moment?" More broadly, how might stories be useful in the children's elemental task of emotional development?

How Stories Become More than Stories

"What kind of nighttime story do you want to tell?" I ask a small group of children. They have been in my class for 2 years and have heard my woods stories multiple times. Jonathan offers this one:

> You were in there, in the house, but you was downstairs, and when I heard steps I thought that was me but it wasn't, and then Zora came up, and then Martin came, and then Soleil came and said that "I'm scared because I heard a loud noise." And then when they came, there was a big bat ["caw, caw!" from Martin, Jonathan's arms up like wings] and they were following you and when they opened—when you opened—when they o—when I opened the door they were all right behind me, and when I turned around [Zora turns her head to look behind herself], and then when they were on the floor the bats were crawling over them.

The Common Core State Standards (2012) now direct that first-grade writers "write narratives in which they recount two or more appropriately sequenced events, include some details regarding what happened, use temporal words to signal event order, and provide some sense of closure" (CCSS.ELA-Literacy.W.1.3) and that first-grade speakers "describe people, places, things, and events with relevant details, expressing ideas and feelings clearly" (CCSS.ELA-Literacy.SL.1.4). A child's story well told requires the meeting of these standards, and an adult's stories provide models on which the child builds her own model of story. More happens, too, besides what is written in the standards. When I tell a story, children are alit with wonder and a desire for more. They ask provocative questions and make connections that demonstrate how they access their own social and emotional experiences to understand new ones. Children listening to my stories know that there is another story to come and that together these episodes form a fuller picture of me, their teacher. I trust they also understand viscerally that my stories are connected to their own; that being in a story is about being in a life. Oliver Sacks (as cited in Eakin, 1999) claims, "This narrative *is* us, our identities" (p. 104). Not consciously but through experience, stories provide an avenue through which our emotional identities take form. Eakin defines narrative as "not merely a literary form but a mode of phenomenological and cognitive self-experience." Jerome Bruner and other "narrative psychologists" pursue critical connections between autobiography and identity (Eakin, 1999). Powered by emotional experience, stories are tools with which children can build their cognitive, social, and emotional selves.

For example, I tell a short story in which a mouse features. This follows from the children:

JONATHAN: Last time when I was sleeping, and this was a long time ago, when I was 5, I was sleeping in my sports bed, and I kept hearing squeak, squeak, and then a mouse climbed up my bed, and then the mouse came near my pillow, and then when my mom came upstairs, she saw the mouse, and then my cat started swallowing it.

SOLEIL: I have a cat, her name is Jasmine, and she's very old . . . She scratched me.

ZORA: Oh, I remember the last time my cat scratched me [she furrows her brow].

MELISSA: Were you mad at your cat?

ZORA: I was sad. And then I was bleeding.

Children are flexible in their storytelling, intermingling real and imagined experiences to reveal emotions, desires, and concerns that others then take up with passion and recognition. They connect with each other and discover paths from story to real life, back and forth. Think about when you ask a child to pretend to drink from a cup of cool water: *Ahh!* Don't they lick their lips with relief from their thirst! As Jonathan tells his bat story, he flaps his arms and ducks his head, eyes up, as the bat swoops closer. What do we read in his face? Bringing their bodies and facial gestures into a story encourages children to expand their emotional repertoire and vocabulary. Telling a story brings us into interaction—talking about, listening to, interpreting and evaluating feelings with and in relation to each other. According to Lev Vygotsky (1978):

> Every function in the child's cultural development appears twice: First, on a social level, and later, on the individual level; first, *between* people (interpsychological), and then *inside* the child (intrapsychological). This applies equally to voluntary attention, to logical memory, and [to] the formation of concepts. All the higher functions originate as actual relations between human individuals.
>
> *(p. 57)*

This proposal promotes storytelling as an ideal vehicle by which children encounter the experiences of others and then negotiate their developing internal (emotional) responses. Through their various interpretations of a story, children find opportunities for interaction; sharing ideas, disputing the merits of one approach or another, listening to nuances, enacting and reenacting, and jumping off into new stories. This, in turn, brings them back to themselves.

I haven't yet seen a lesson plan in which the primary goal is "an opening for exploration of the self." The standard requiring that children express feelings clearly hints at the importance of awareness of emotions, but does not suggest the deeper task of inventing the self through developing facility with emotions. Some of my stories feature unexpected encounters with wild animals in the nighttime, beginning on warm nights, when I am asleep. The porcupine story begins with a distressed yowl. My cat has been chased up a tree by a woodland animal, and my first problem (standing barefoot in my pajamas in the middle of the woods in the middle of the night) is how to get the cat out of the tree, knowing, as I do, that cats are much better at climbing up than at climbing down. Further along in this story, I discover the woodland animal inside my house, and the dilemma then is how to convince a porcupine to leave.

As the narrative unfolds, I make sure to include how I feel, details about what I think I know about each animal, what I do based on what I think I know, what I discover, and the puzzles I encounter. In a different story, I recall my mother's fear of bats and instead consider the animal with surprise and curiosity; I will call this the "meta-emotive self": What am I feeling here? There are many good moments to pause and let children do some of this feeling and thinking with me. So much is revealed as they share their emotions and ideas. "*I* wouldn't be scared!" one child insists, and he proceeds to explain how he would respond in my situation. He is contemplating his emotional response and playing out possibilities of action in relation to them. The children have different ideas about this:

> "Kill the porcupine."
> "Hit it on the head."
> "A bigger animal could chase it away."
> "Block the door."
> "Let it live with you."

Each Idea Illuminates Emotion and Reveals an Evolving Self

When I find myself in these precarious situations, bringing forward what I know and weighing questions and possibilities in my head and through my feelings, I offer an invitation to children to do the same. Inserting themselves into the new scenarios I provide for them, they imagine themselves more broadly, illuminating and exaggerating aspects of themselves. They learn to see themselves as complex, inventive, and flexible beings.

If we consider engagement with stories a kind of play—that is, play with ideas, emotions, responses, the work of imagination—then Vygotsky's stance about play reinforces stories' role in emotional and social development: "[A] child's greatest achievements are possible in play, achievements that tomorrow will become her basic level of real action and morality" (Vygotsky, 1978, p. 100). She will use her character self in a story to develop her sturdy, flexible emotional self. Children grapple with their capacity for problem-solving "as though he were a head taller than himself" (Vygotsky, 1978, p. 102), able to meet any variety of challenges. The children listen as I confront danger, but they are equally present as I conjure up courage. They accompany me as I access prior knowledge and resourcefulness. In these ways, stories turn real-life experiences into resources for self-creation. I tell my stories and then leave them as clay in children's hands for reimagining.

These particular stories also serve to reveal fear in a grown-up—in a teacher no less!—and this is instructive and comforting for children. They are not scary stories, but ones in which something unexpected happens and in which the protagonist has to think about things in new ways. Children regularly encounter events they don't understand, simply by virtue of being relatively young in the world. One gift of stories like these may be that the listeners have an opportunity to be generous with themselves and the feelings they experience.

I tell a new story:

It was a sunny day in the fall when I was walking along the road, enjoying the song of birds and the leaves just beginning to think about changing color. All of a sudden, I heard a growling noise coming from the trees at the side of the road.

"Oh!" Zora declares, "I would be so scared."

And what would you do, Zora?

In the stories she dictates, Zora's little girl character has adventures and returns home to find her mother waiting for her. Inserting herself into a story that demands a new kind of problem-solving, Zora's whole self must stretch. She considers herself frightened, yes, and then empowered to make a decision. What decision will that be? It's an uncomfortable place, but an exciting one because the narrative holds her. She knows this story has an ending and that the ending still brings its protagonist to this present moment, safe and able to tell the story again. This narrative is a hammock made of rope, swaying some distance off the ground, suspended between two tree trunks. The force of the swing is uncertain, but the suspension is secure. Fingers wrap through the holes, grabbing the rope. What if I lean this way? Will it flip me out? Will it wrap me tighter? The narrative holds us because we know we can determine its ending; but while we're in it, we can experiment with danger, uncertainty, and thrill.

The Purpose of Quiet Stories

Remember how I always left my door open just a little bit? Do you remember why I did that?
"So your cat could go in and out," one child offers.

Yes, my cat was accustomed to going in and out whenever she wanted, as you know. In this story, it's important to remember that I left my door open just a little bit.

One afternoon I'd been out for a walk in the hot sun. It was a hot day, the kind of hot day that's quiet. No wind to rustle the trees, even the birds taking a rest from chirping. It was a hot, quiet day. I came back from my walk and into my house. It was cool in the summer time because my house was shaded by tall trees. I came in and sat down to write about things I had noticed. As I was writing, I heard a squeaking sound. Squeak! Squeak!

"It was a mouse!" the children call out. They are remembering that mice live in the eaves of my house. Perhaps they are remembering the story of when I reached in my backpack for something and pulled out a live mouse. I nod in acknowledgement of their good guesses.

At first, I thought it was a mouse, and I looked around . . . I didn't see anything moving. The afternoon was so quiet and still. Then I realized that the squeaking sound was coming from up above me.

Again I pause, and I let my eyes drift up to the imagined window above.

You remember the big, round window up on the roof of my house? At first, I didn't see anything, but I heard it again. Squeak! Squeak! Squeak! Then I noticed, right at the edge of the window, a tiny bird. It was trying to get out through the window. You know, birds don't always know a window is a piece of glass. They see through it and it appears to be an open space. This tiny bird had a long, long beak, and as it was pushing itself to get out through the window, its beak kept scraping against the glass, Squeak! Squeak! How did this little bird get into my house?

"Through the door! You left the door open for your cat and it flew in!"

It must have come in through the open door while I was gone. I knew I had to help it, because it wasn't remembering the door (even though it was wide open now); it was just trying to get out through the window. I was afraid it was going to break its beak.

The window on the ceiling was too high for me to reach. So I got my chair—I had one chair, it was blue—and I moved it slowly to the place right under the little bird . . .

I get up and move a chair, slowly, to the middle of the circle of children.

. . . I moved very slowly, so I wouldn't scare the bird. It was still squeaking against the window, and I was getting more and more worried that it was hurting itself. Still, I moved slowly. I stepped up onto the chair, first one foot, then the other. I caught my balance. I stood still. Then slowly, slowly, I raised up my hands. I held them like this, in a little cup shape . . .

I move my hands up into the air, an inch at a time.

. . . I moved them slowly until I was just under the little bird, and then I closed my hands around the bird gently but quickly.

Do you remember our monarch butterflies? It was almost that small, this bird. It weighed just that much. I could hold it in my hands, just like this. At first, it was fluttering, and then it was still. Then I had to get back down off the chair.

Slowly, slowly, I back off the chair, one foot at a time, my hands holding the imaginary bird.

I walked to the door and stepped outside. Now I was out in the bright, hot sun. The day was still quiet, no wind, almost no noise at all. I held the bird in both my hands, and the long beak was poking through my fingers just a little bit. I almost didn't want to let it go, because I had never held a bird that tiny in my hands before, and I was feeling amazed. I held my breath and slowly opened my hands.

It stayed right there in the palm of my hand for a moment. I looked at it, 1 . . . 2 . . . 3 . . . and then Bzzz! It flew away like a flash, and it was gone between the trees into the bright blue sky.

When children's lives are loud and overscheduled, perhaps even chaotic and unpredictable, of what use is a quiet story? This moment must have lasted fewer than 5 minutes when it happened, and here it is, stretched into a story that leaves space for breathing, for the bright, hot sky and quiet air, for a big adventure with a tiny bird. Even the climax offers only the miniscule action of a hummingbird making its way back into the sky. Here is a quiet moment in a world where such things are rare. In the middle of a busy school day and busy lives, a story like this begs us to slow down to consider how we breathe and sit in these still spaces with ourselves and others.

How do we hold something delicate in our hands (in our minds, in our hearts)? What do we do next? How do we respond to others' fragility? What is our responsibility? I do not pursue questions explicitly with the children. Rather, I trust that the questions are hanging in the air with us. Children suggest that I keep the bird, even just to study it for a little while. They wonder: If I did, how would I feed it? I would need to bring it flowers, and if I did that, I'd have to put the flowers in water. In imagining himself in this story, the child is recognizing himself as very big and strong, capable of care or of harm. Each child is asking, "Could I hold a tiny bird in my hands without hurting it?" Am I the person who keeps the bird or lets it go? He is seeing himself in relation to the world: Small like the bird compared to the big, bright blue sky, large compared to the bird; shaky on the chair, uncertain in a world that brings constant surprises; empowered to act. When we find something tiny and delicate again, we have the opportunity to think about the bird. Perhaps children will cup their hands and move slowly toward it or simply stand in awe. Perhaps they will rush to it and scare it away, and they will remember then about delicate things. My job is not to instruct or decide how the story will be useful, but to make it available—just in case it is.

Colleagues tell me, "But I didn't live in the woods; I don't have stories like yours to tell." It doesn't matter. Tiny things happen to us every day. *I put my hand in the pocket of my spring jacket and found a smooth stone I put there the last time I went to the beach. The weather was so warm that day!* When we make space for quiet stories, the stories also make space for us to learn about the emotional core of who we are, both individually and collectively. They suggest that we stop and notice ourselves in our actions and thoughts. Lucy Calkins (2007) instructs children to catch and stretch out "small moments" from their lives in her lessons about writing personal narrative. While her writer's workshop is highly structured and pointed toward the production of writing on a page, this idea that we can find meaning in our daily lived moments matches the invitation of a quiet story told aloud.

Making Meaning

Throughout each school day, teachers help young children navigate the choppy waters of classroom interactions. The children come to these moments carrying habits developed at home and in their communities. We can predict, if we know the children even superficially, which ones will do most of the talking, walk away, apologize quickly, become defensive, make a generous offer, wiggle out of responsibility. Hopefully, we engage our compassion and creativity to help children find satisfying ways through seemingly impossible situations. Naturally, children respond to an opportunity to solve a problem out of their images of themselves: powerful or not, "good at" this or not, invested or not. Where are these images borne? We can impact the shape a child feels himself to be through his position in a story. We can give a child a notion of herself as powerful even if her world has told her otherwise, providing an avenue toward defining herself even as the bigger world has already begun to do this for her.

I have not found another way to draw children *in* (to engage their minds and hearts) and to draw them *out* (to bring them forward through themselves into other possibilities) as authentically as through stories. I have not experienced other ways to make transparent such a variety of possibilities in a single moment. Stories—as something we create and share—open us to our selves, to consideration of who we are in our lives, in relation to others, in the world. They are made of the endlessly malleable stuff of interaction, perception, and emotion.

Stories surprise even the storyteller: When I tell a story, I am not sure what the children will grab from it, where I will find myself stopping, or what will be the "point" of the story for the present listeners. The best moments happen when I invite children to participate in creating the life of that story. This is not about co-constructing a story (I'll tell one part and you tell another and so on), but saying to children . . . Here, consider this: What if you were here in this moment with me, or instead of me, what would that be like? Put yourself on the bicycle at the top of the hill; come stand in the cabin with this porcupine.

Stories are playthings. Like blocks, they can be built, reconsidered, rebuilt. They can be considered from various angles and adjusted—take this part out, and what if this happened instead? Identities, too, are constructed, reconsidered, adapted as children (and we) experience and grow. The stories we tell might just provide the children with new materials out of which to construct understanding of who they are and who they might be. A child takes a turn down a wooded path, watches an owl swoop silently overhead, and in the moment of a breathless "oh!" has a new vocabulary for how we can move through our environment. Carlina Rinaldi (2004) speaks to the need for children to actively entertain a multiplicity of possibilities as they develop:

> Observe and listen to children because when they ask "why?" they are not simply asking for the answer from you. They are requesting the courage to find a collection of possible answers. This attitude of the child means that the child is a real researcher. As human beings, we are all researchers of the meaning of life . . . How can we support and sustain this attitude of children to construct explanations?
>
> *(p. 2)*

As teachers, we meet many adults who involve children in conversation about big ideas and current events, who ask children for their opinions. Some children receive this wonderful message: The world is before you to explore, and I am here to explore it with you. Of course, all children benefit from an ever-expanding world. I hold particular concern for those who do not experience in their early years consistent opportunities to entertain expansive possibilities and in turn to tune their selves to our wide world. These children do not imagine that all doors are open for them. These are children who see themselves reflected in our broader society in ways that are limited or, worse, negative. I am a white, middle-class teacher. I enjoy all the privileges that led me to believe in the first place that I could toss security to the wind and move to a dilapidated cabin in the woods. I teach in an urban public school, and most of the children with whom I spend my days are children of color, many from economically stressed families, many with special needs or histories of trauma. For me, making stories matter, making them available for children to make meaning of, does not mean making them "culturally relevant" in simple terms. Stories are both culturally bound and culturally limitless. The purpose of sharing personal narrative is not, in my examples, to reflect a child back to himself, but to reflect elements of self and experience as playthings.

My stories about the woods are joyful, quiet, scary, difficult, loud, still or full of movement, embracing or punishing; "the woods" is offered in a complicated context, recognizing the richness and complexity of children's own contexts. *Home* can embody all these same characteristics for children. We know this because children talk about their parents as loving and conflicted, about their weekends as dull and exciting, about nighttime as cozy and scary. Children have real and regular experiences with fear, pain, disregulation of hunger and sleep, and, for some, scarcity of resources. When my story includes a focus on or even hints of these, children find the familiar. In the wintertime, I have to break the ice to get to water. I run out of wood for my stove. A hurricane blows through.

The better I tell a story, the more entry points it has for more children in the room. And if I tell that story a second or third time, I can shift the emphasis and suggest a different way of thinking about the problem, the wonder, the event. The house where I lived in the woods, remember, had one large round window at the top, a ring of small, triangular windows circling the perimeter, and a tall, rectangular window in the side wall. Which window you use to peer into this space reveals something particular, a point of view. A story isn't singular; teller and listeners look through one window or another, maybe in, maybe out, making of the story an understanding fitted to what we see and need.

Whether a story is remembered or imagined (and we can wonder about just where that line is drawn) does not matter so much. Often, the children ask me, "Did this really happen?" The stories are true, or as precisely true as I remember them. Sometimes, I pause my own story to let children play it out and then resume the story because the children do ultimately want a resolution to the problem I've posed. Their own imagining takes it from there, in the block or dramatic play or writing area. Then it is my opportunity and responsibility to listen: What is this child making of this story? What is important in how she tells and retells it? The research of Peggy Miller and her colleagues suggests that when children move between stories that are real and imagined (as they do in putting themselves fantastically inside my personal narrative), they create new ideas about themselves in the world:

> Through this continual interanimation of genres, not only do children make stories meaningful by personalizing them, but also new hybrid ways of envisioning reality are created—ones that stretch the child's personal perspective to encompass the parameters of multiple social worlds, real and imagined.
>
> *(Miller, Hengst, Alexander, & Sperry, 2000, p. 240)*

Here is where the self forms, through consideration and reconsideration, shaping and reshaping of narrative so that the unknown becomes possible and our worlds grow larger.

Conclusion

The point of my telling these stories is not to convince children that they, too, should grow up to do something seemingly outlandish. The point is to insist that creativity is nonetheless ours—that we have the possibility of imagining ourselves beyond what we already know, and that we can meet the problems we encounter. I am insisting on children having experiences that promote emotional awareness, flexibility, and sturdiness. I am communicating: I felt this way, and I didn't know what to do, and in the end, it was (or will be) okay. Children need experiences of confronting feelings that are hard to have—fear, confusion, desperation—in the context of safety, with people who will accompany them and help them develop solid interpretations. A cozy storytelling circle is just the place for facing these feelings, with friends to offer possibilities of new perspectives. Children grow into a story; literally, they cower in fear and then straighten their spines in confidence. They dare and surprise themselves while they encourage each other. These stories may be far, far removed from most children's daily lives and experiences, but perhaps the power of the stories lies right in that fact. The gift of my personal narrative is the place where my real life and their imaginations intersect: The message is that this can really happen because it happened to me. What might happen to you? How will that feel? What will you do?

The questions and feelings currently percolating inside a particular child are those that surface with most relevance as he listens to a story, and those may be quite different from those bubbling up in the child next to him. In a classroom, we are concerned not with a single child's emotional development, but with that of many children of diverse experience. Like every lesson we offer throughout the school day, we find ways to make a story accessible—and more, to make it *matter* —to as many children as possible. A story well told offers novel points of view, new ways of thinking something through. Perhaps I am the person in the woods, or perhaps I am the porcupine or the bat or the hummingbird.

Children use these stories as touchstones as they contemplate their own experiences: "Is this what it was like when you were in the woods and . . .?" and I can reassure her, *Yes, it was a little scary, like this. But I knew I would be safe, just like you are now.* Or, "How did you know what to do?" *I didn't,* I reply, *but I decided to try to figure it out.* "Was your mom there? Was anyone else there with you?" *No, just me. But I was okay.* Children need bravery all the time. It is my responsibility to let them know it is accessible to them, along with joy and surprise and the chance to try something new.

When I first planned to tell the stories of my life in the woods, I was primarily interested in promoting the value of oral storytelling. I wanted to move children away from screens and closer to people, to see the adults around them as essential resources for connection, identity, and information about the world. I wanted children to experience delight in listening to stories and to appreciate this resource of history and culture that travels through people. I wanted children to begin to see themselves as storytellers.

As I have begun telling the stories, I identify a longing to make my authentic self available to the children as a *resource* for the exploration of emotion, identity, and connection. Young children greet these stories with the wide eyes that signal wonder. They ask me to tell another. They emit gasps and sighs; they ask questions. The telling embodies those abstract values I'd first identified. More importantly, the stories themselves offer connection in an intense way I hadn't anticipated. The children want to be with me inside the stories with the sounds of wind and rain and animals, in the hot sun (a child moves her hand across her forehead as if wiping off sweat), with bare feet on the woodsy earth, arms lugging a heavy bucket of water from the stream (they groan). They eagerly suggest solutions for dilemmas and tell me what I might do next time. How full of possibility they are! How ready with their feelings! How willing to ponder new questions and embark on adventures in uncertain places. In some way, the children become *me* in these stories; in so doing, they expand their very notions of themselves.

References

Calkins, L. (2007). *Units of study for teaching primary writing: A yearlong curriculum (Grades K-2)*. Portsmouth, NH: Heinemann.

Common Core State Standards Initiative (2012). *English language arts standards*. Retrieved from www.corestandards.org/ELA-Literacy

Eakin, J. P. (1999). *How our lives become stories: Making selves*. Ithaca, NY: Cornell University Press.

Hall, D., Kenyon, J., & Moyers, B. (1993, December 17). *A Life Together: Donald Hall and Jane Kenyon*. [Audio podcast]. Retrieved from http://billmoyers.com/content/423/

Heath, S. (1983). *Ways with words: Language, life, and work in communities and classrooms*. New York and Cambridge: Cambridge University Press.

Mardell, B., & Boni, M. (2012). *Boston listens: Storytelling/story acting in the Boston public schools*. Retrieved from http://bpsearlychildhood.weebly.com/guides.html

Miller, P. J., Hengst, J., Alexander, K., & Sperry, L. L. (2000). Versions of personal storytelling/versions of experience: Genres as tools for creating alternate realities. In K. Rosengren, C. Johnson, & P. Harris (Eds.), *Imagining the impossible: magical, scientific and religious thinking in children* (pp. 212–246). New York, NY: Cambridge University Press.

Rinaldi, C. (2004). The relationship between documentation and assessment. *Innovations in Early Education: The International Reggio Exchange, 11*(1): 2.

Vygotsky, L. S. (1978). *Mind in society: The development of higher psychological processes*. Cambridge, MA: Harvard University Press.

COMMENTARY

Laurie Katz

THE OHIO STATE UNIVERSITY

As I read Melissa Tonachel's chapter, I wanted to be a "fly on the wall" and observe her telling a personal story about her experiences living in the woods during a period of her life, to see how she so adeptly mediates the children's responses to her story; whether to help them construct their own meaning-making, develop their emotional lives, and/or connect to others. In this commentary, I discuss Tonachel's storytelling practices in her first-grade classroom and the importance of these practices in connecting with the emotional lives of the children she teaches.

When Tonachel shares personal stories, it sets a context for her children to share their own stories. When she shares her stories, children respond from their own real or imagined experiences. Tonachel doesn't expect her first graders to have a specific or correct response; rather, by sharing a story about her experiences of being alone in the woods, children are provoked to share their own emotions, whether from their own experiences in the woods, from a TV show or a movie about a similar experience, or from other experiences of feeling "alone" or "scared." By sharing personal experiences, children construct their understanding that there are different ways to be "alone" or "scared," as well as different ways to express and manage these universal emotions and to problem-solve the everyday and hypothetical situations that can cause them.

Tonachel's examples of how she and her children tell stories are not simply narratives of what they have experienced or imagine, but storytelling events in which people act and react to each other while producing the narrative. Solsken and Bloome (1992) make a distinction between story, narrative, and storytelling event, although they view the three as interrelated:

> A story is an abstraction of history realized in narrative within a storytelling event . . . A story is a chronological sequence of events abstracted from

experience. That is, experiences are not inherently packaged as stories with beginnings, middles, and ends nor do experiences necessarily provide coherent relations between events. Rather, story transforms experience into events and imposes boundaries, a chronology, and a set of coherent relationships on experiences . . . When people construct a story they are constructing an abstraction that, by itself, has no realization. Rather it is realized in narrative. A narrative is the text of the story . . . Narratives do not exist by themselves. They exist only in storytelling events.

(pp. 5–6)

Given these definitions, a teacher may find a child's story unclear, unstructured, invented, or even nonsensical, because the narrative does not follow a prescribed sequence. Tonachel didn't interpret her children's narratives through these lenses, but utilized storytelling to allow her children broad degrees of freedom to signal and shape their meanings. Her emphasis on knowing her children or "finding ways into their emotional, social, and aesthetic lives" resulted from listening to their stories in these storytelling events. Similarly, Bloome, Champion, Katz, Morton, and Muldrow (2001) found in their storytelling project from oral and written narratives of African American preschoolers that the children experimented with narrative style, structure, and content to create and re-create social relations, affiliations, and social identities.

Tonachel's emphasis on knowing her children's emotional lives is an example of identifying the *funds of knowledge* held by the children and their families (Moll, Amanti, Neff, & Gonzalez, 2005), defined as "the historically accumulated and culturally developed bodies of knowledge essential for household or individual functioning and well-being" (p. 72). By learning about what's important in her children's home and community lives through their stories and their contributions to hers, Tonachel integrates these experiences into her classroom practices and creates a welcoming place where children's diverse ways of experiencing the world are respected.

These ways of feeling, when respected, enhance children's identities and further connects them to responsive school practices. McDermott's (1993) assertion that classroom practices "crucially influence what students can learn and *who they can become*" (italics added, p. 303) relates to how Tonachel uses storytelling to enhance children's constructions of their social identities. Her use of stories stretches the worlds of her children's possibilities. Tonachel writes, "Stories are both culturally bound and culturally limitless. The purpose of sharing personal narrative is not, in my examples, to reflect a child back to herself, but to reflect elements of self and experience as playthings" (p. 103).

In other words, Tonachel's practices create spaces for children's (and their families') voices to be expressed and valued. In her classroom, children actively negotiate multiple selves, integrating both home and school identities, a favorable condition advocated by DaSilva Iddings and Katz (2007) that was missing in their study of second-grade Hispanic English language learners (ELLs) in an English-dominant classroom. In that study, the teacher negatively evaluates ELLs because she considers only their school identities, whereas their home identities (which consisted of strengths and responsibilities) were unknown and, thus, not brought into the classroom curriculum.

The relationships Tonachel and her children have developed are quite different from many of the relationships between early childhood educators and their students. In these relationships, Tonachel has provided opportunities for her children to express themselves, which in turn serves her valued and critical role as a learner in "knowing" her children and their families. Too often, teachers only present themselves as authority figures to their children or as transmitters of disciplinary knowledge. As authority figures, it's difficult for teachers to develop these meaningful relationships beyond children's academic profiles. Yet, Tonachel does not ignore academic or cognitive outcomes in favor of social and emotional goals. Instead, she demonstrates the importance of connecting the nurturance of children's socio-emotional development with their academic development as she addresses the Common Core Standards (CCS) through her storytelling. And, to her credit, she moves her children beyond the CCS by writing that "stories also make space for us to learn about the emotional core of who we are, both individually and collectively" (p. 102).

The idea of addressing children's emotional core builds on Noddings's work in caring and education, and there is a strong sense of caring that develops between Tonachel and her children in this chapter. Noddings writes (as cited in Bergman, 2004):

> The need to be cared for is a human universal. We are absolutely dependent on the caring of others. If our life is to be preserved, if we are to grow, if we are to arrive at some level of acceptability in our culture and community, we must be cared for constantly from the moment of our birth.
>
> *(p. 150)*

When children experience a caring relationship with their teacher, a type of trust is developed that encourages children to express themselves. "We have to show in our own behavior what it means to care . . ." (Noddings, as cited in Bergman, 2004, p. 154). Noddings calls for teachers such as Tonachel to educate the caring response by providing the conditions under which caring is possible and by engaging children in responding as "carers" to others. Tonachel demonstrates these conditions by modeling through her storytelling. Her storytelling creates a culture of (teacher and children) attending to one another where important dialogues take place. Noddings highlights the essence of these dialogues by writing "Dialogue allows us to receive the other in a 'common search for understanding, empathy, or appreciation' and 'builds up a substantial knowledge of one another that serves to guide our [caring] responses' (Noddings, as cited in Bergman, 2004, p. 155).

In summary, Tonachel's listening and learning about her children through storytelling captures and edifies their emotional lives. In the process, she perceives each child as unique and as developing their moral selves in a manner that is distinct for him or her, and refrains from attempts to inculcate the same virtues or to posit a single ideal for everyone. According to Noddings (as cited in Bergman, 2004), through this type of confirmation, a better self is identified and its development is encouraged. As educators and as caring people, may we all learn from Tonachel's teachings and start sharing our own personal stories.

References

Bergman, R. (2004). Caring for the ethical ideal: Nel Noddings on moral education. *Journal of Moral Education, 33*(2): 149–162.

Bloome, D., Champion, T., Katz, L., Morton, M. B., & Muldrow, R. (2001). Spoken and written narrative development: African American preschoolers as storytellers and storymakers. *Literacy in African American Communities* (pp. 45–76). Mahwah, NJ: Lawrence Erlbaum.

DaSilva Iddings, A. C., & Katz, L. (2007). Integrating home and school identities of recent-immigrant Hispanic English language learners through classroom practices. *Journal of Language, Identity, and Education, 6*(4): 299–314.

McDermott, R. (1993). The acquisition of a child by a learning disability. In J. Lave & S. Chaiklin (Eds.), *Understanding practice: Perspectives on activity and context* (pp. 269–305). NY: Cambridge University Press.

Moll, L., Amanti, C., Neff, D., & Gonzalez, N. (2005). Funds of knowledge for teaching: Using a qualitative approach to connect homes and classrooms. *Funds of knowledge: Theorizing practices in households, communities, and classrooms* (pp. 71–87). Mahwah, NJ: Lawrence Erlbaum Associates.

Solsken, J., & Bloome, D. (1992, April). *Beyond poststructuralism: Story and narrative in the study of literacy in the everyday world.* Paper presented at the meeting of the American Education Research Association, San Francisco.

7

THE WOODS AS A TODDLER CLASSROOM

The Emotional Experience of Challenge, Connection, and Caring

Dee Smith and Jeanne Goldhaber

UNIVERSITY OF VERMONT

"We had previously talked about trying to spend all day in the woods so we sat down and wrote out a list of all of the things that would need to happen and that we would need to physically bring . . . it was a BIG list!"

—*Emily, teacher*

"We were ecstatic, impressed at the undertaking from a logistic and learning perspective and the richness/multilevel learning that can happen in a natural place."

—*Charles, parent*

"We had hesitations around sleeping in the woods, eating in the woods, sun exposure, poison ivy exposure, injuries, and potty training. But our #1 concern was around mosquito and tick-borne illness."

—*Tracy, parent*

Daniel, Mason, and Sarina come across a small tree that has partially fallen over. Together they try to lift the tree back up to a standing position. "We're fixin' the trees!" they announce.

Introduction

This is a story about two teachers and seven toddlers who spend 2 full days a week in the woods over the course of a Vermont summer and of the emotions and relationships they experience together. This story is also about their parents, who despite concerns about ticks, mosquitoes, and other possible risks, agree to drop their children off at the entrance to the woods in the morning, knowing that their 2- or almost 2-year-olds will spend the day hiking rocky, sometimes muddy, terrain; climbing trees and scrambling over boulders; and navigating rocky streambeds. They give their children kisses good-bye with the knowledge that the children will be eating their morning and afternoon snacks and packed lunches on a blanket situated in a clearing by a stream, napping in a large communal tent, and getting their diapers changed on a mat placed on the forest floor or using a child-sized camping potty.

This experience was a first in our school. Although we have been observing and reflecting on young children's experiences in the natural world since the year 2000, no group of children had ever spent full days outdoors over an extended period. But teachers Emily, a native Vermonter who spent her childhood playing in the woods, and Spencer, an undergraduate at the University of Vermont who was an environmental studies major, had a dream. In their letter to families, they explained their hope that spending full days in the woods will "provide the children the opportunity for extended exploration and investigation in the natural world and [the development of] a responsive curriculum that reflects the importance of a connection to nature."

Dee and Jeanne followed the teachers' experiences with great interest as documenters who often participated in the experience. They, too, had memories of childhood filled with outdoor play. Like Emily and Spencer, they were intrigued by how the children would spend long uninterrupted hours in the natural world. What would interest them? What would they do? How would they play together?

For over 10 years we have been documenting our youngest children's almost-daily outings as they explored the properties of lichen, fallen pinecones, and rock-covered surfaces with their hands, feet, and even tongues (Goldhaber & Smith, 2008). We noted the attention they paid to the terrain of our university's grounds and considered the possibility that place had unique and contextualized meaning to children. For example, whereas we adults "mapped" the campus primarily in terms of its buildings and walkways, the children's cognitive maps included places like the "fake hill" where they would release themselves joyfully to the pull of gravity to run or roll down the incline. Their "maps" also seemed to reflect invented rituals such as games of peek-a-boo around a particular trash receptacle where they always stopped to play on their walk across campus (Goldhaber, 2010).

When observing the children on campus outings, we also noted that their interactions seemed qualitatively different from those in the confines of the classroom. Given that our classrooms are quite small, we expected the children to spread out and take full advantage of the expansive space of the outdoors. Instead, we observed the children clustering in small spaces with natural boundaries where they happily jostled and bumped into each other, forms of physical contact that often resulted in cries of protest in the classroom. We wondered whether the element of choice allowed the children to experience the physical contact of confined space because they had the option of both joining *and* leaving it.

We also looked beyond our own experiences to research findings related to the natural world. Sebba (1991) describes the multiple ways in which nature engages the senses. This supported our view of the open-ended quality of materials that one encounters in the natural world (Norris, Smith, & Gandini, 2009). Moser and Martinsen (2010) identify the characteristics of the outdoor environment and examine how children relate to wild natural spaces as opposed to planned nature playgrounds. Of particular interest for our study is Little, Wyver, and Gibson's (2011) investigation of the opportunities that the natural world offers that involve risk, as opposed to outdoor play yards that often limit risk-taking. Melhuus (2012) looks at the potential educational practice that nature offers, while Clay (2001); Kaplan, Kaplan, and Ryan (1998); and Taylor, Kuo, and Sullivan (2001, 2001) look at the role nature plays in the formation of the brain. Kellert (1997), Kellert and Wilson (1993), and Wilson (1984) raised our awareness of the psychological benefits of nature. Crain (2001) states that nature "instills a sense of peace and being at one with the world" (p. 23), whereas Hart (1979) describes a sense of quiet and calm that children experience in the natural world. Although not referring to specific research findings, Olds (1985) writes about nature as a powerful influence on the quality of wellness in life.

Research such as the mentioned cases and our own previous experiences in the woods contributed to our excitement about how the children would respond to long uninterrupted blocks of time in the woods. Our expectations that the children would fully immerse themselves in the rich diversity of the natural world were confirmed. We observed them touching, smelling, examining, and even kissing both living and nonliving natural objects and incorporating them into their play. We also noted that the children had clear preferences for areas where particular activities would take place. And they continued to congregate as a group, both spontaneously and by invitation.

But there were surprises as well. In fact, this chapter is an opportunity to reexamine and reflect on those surprises, using a slightly different lens than that which we typically employ. In the past, our interests focused primarily on the woods as a context that challenged and promoted children's physical strength, coordination, stamina, and shared play scripts. Possibly due to the age of these children, the frequent, repeated, and extended visits to the woods; our adherence to documenting each experience; and the collaborative sharing of data, we were led here to the more serious consideration of the children's social-emotional life in the natural world.

Summer in the Woods as a Place of Emotion

At the end of the summer in the woods, Emily, Spencer, Dee, and Jeanne reviewed the images and videos we had collected. Although we began by considering the children's patterns of activity in particular areas of the woods, we noted that our discussions kept returning to the social and emotional quality of the children's interactions with peers and with the living objects they encountered. This chapter offers us the opportunity to reflect on this aspect of not only the children's, but also their parents' and teachers' experiences. The editors' invitation to consider emotion as a contextualized response intrigued us, given our view of the woods as a particular place where one experiences unpredictable, multiple, and complex sensations; risks and challenges; and the need to accommodate to the ever-transforming natural environment. Such a physically and intellectually engaging context surely must elicit a wide and diverse range of emotions.

The experiences we are sharing in this chapter took place in Centennial Woods, a sprawling and densely forested woodland, located one-half mile from our doorstep. Emily and Spencer wanted the children to experience the woods together and in the process, develop a network of interdependent peer relationships. Of course, they also had many questions: How would "living in the woods" unfold with such a young group of children? Were they taking on more than was practically manageable? How would the families react?

What follows is a discussion of this experience as a very particular and rich context, a place of risk, challenge, and transformation. How did children approach and negotiate the emotional complexity of living a school day in the woods? How did the families respond emotionally to the "idea" of their very young children inhabiting such an environment for full days? And how did teachers experience this ambitious enterprise emotionally?

Children's Voices

> "House, house, new house!" Elle calls as Dee approaches the campsite after the children and teachers have settled in. Her wide eyes and high-pitched voice betray her excitement as she motions for Dee to come quickly. Dee responds, "You have a new house?" Elle answers loudly, "Yeah . . . sleeping!" Dee is led to the new tent where Elle eagerly shows her how to work the large zippers that close the flaps. Elle smiles as she explains that this is where they will be napping.

Elle's greeting is a harbinger of the emotional quality of the experience the children will share over the course of the summer. Her excitement is palpable as she shows Dee what will be their base camp, a place where they will gather to begin their day with classroom rituals, eat their lunch, and take their naps. Dee, too, is delighted, as much by Elle's excitement as by the scene before her. We take note of Elle's affect and confidence as she leads Dee to the camp and demonstrates the workings of the tent zipper. In retrospect, Elle's excited invitation introduces the woods as a place where giggles and laughter will be heard throughout the summer as the children encounter and explore the natural world. Hidden from the first moments, however, was the intensity of experiences that would both challenge and delight the children, producing a tension of emotions, a desire to help, and a heightened awareness and connection to their surroundings. We would come to see the woods as a socio-emotional context where children support each other as they relate to the diverse life-forms of the natural world.

A Place of Discovery

The natural world presents endless opportunities for full-bodied exploration and new discoveries that often involve noise and disorder. The following observation shows how the children responded to a familiar path that had been transformed by several days of rain:

> The children walk along a path in the woods and although some areas have dried out, many areas are thick with mud. Deep in the woods Daniel and Conner find a low area that has the appearance of a giant mud pond. They begin to slide their feet on the surface, and laughter mixes with squeals of delight and occasional raised eyebrows as their feet glide out too far from underneath them. They stomp their feet and watch the mud splash around their boots, legs, and each other as they intermittently work to stay upright!

This unexpected discovery in the woods leads the children to investigate the different ways of interacting with the muddy surface. Their shouts and laughter suggest the joy of their antics while playing with the elements of the transformed surface that produce both resistance and slipperiness. When suddenly their feet slip too far and their balance is threatened, their expressions suggest a rush of surprise and anxiety as they work to stay vertical and move at the same time! We also wonder if their reactions may reflect a bit of toddler humor as they splash each other, defying what might normally be unacceptable behavior.

FIGURE 7.1

A Place of Challenge

Self-selected challenges also show us how persistent children can be, even when facing risks. The following observations detail how two children respond to mastering challenges that they set for themselves:

> The children stop in the depths of the woods where they revisit a large fallen tree whose trunk meets the ground at a steep incline. The top of the incline where the tree has uprooted on a small hillside is particularly bumpy and slippery. Emily stations herself near the roots while Spencer stands to the side of the trunk. Spencer speaks to Sarina as she scales the trunk of the tree. "Remember it was very slippery the last time we climbed this tree and some friends tumbled off the side." Sarina is undeterred and continues climbing, even as her rubber boots occasionally slip backwards. As she climbs, Sarina stops to brush away some bush branches that hinder her path. When Sarina reaches the top, she is greeted by Emily who exclaims in a loud voice, "You did it!" Sarina jumps down onto the ground, tumbling as she lands. She rolls over and smiles broadly as she looks up at Emily, who exclaims, "Ta-da!"

In this vignette, Sarina sets out to reach the top of the fallen tree trunk. She appears confident, despite losing her footing on the trunk's slick surface and needing to push away branches that block her path. She reaches the top, jumps to the ground, and reacts with an expression of accomplishment:

> Elle also decides to climb the fallen log. As her feet slide backwards on the log, she says, "Muddy." Elle hesitates as she gets closer to the top, looking straight ahead. Emily intervenes: "What's your plan, Elle? Tyler's right behind you." Elle begins to climb and continues to slip. She furrows her brow and starts to cry. Elle lays flat on her stomach, and Emily crouches close by and offers a hand . . . Elle reaches for Emily's hand, but it isn't quite close enough. When she places her hand on the side of the log, loose dirt begins to peel away, but she continues toward her goal. Her eyes are focused on the top and her facial features appear frozen. She moves her knees forward even as they continue to slip. Elle slowly inches her body along until she reaches Emily and then reaches to use her as a support. Emily says, "I'm going to move my body back 'cause I want you to keep going." For a brief moment after Elle arrives at the top, she reaches out and uses Emily's body to turn herself around. Emily now is encouraging others. "Help me get down," says Elle. Emily points and tells Elle that Sarina went this way. There is a moment where Emily helps to steady Elle and then Elle walks down the small hill created by the roots until she reaches firmer ground.

Elle seems unsure of her ability to accomplish her goal. At any time, she could have decided to get off the tree trunk with Emily or Spencer's support, but instead she continued. Her cry suggests she is afraid, perhaps of losing her balance or of falling. She persists, however, and in the end, she overcomes the physical and psychological challenges, reaching the top of the tree trunk and ultimately stable ground.

These observations and others like them have contributed to our sense of the woods as a place where the children sought out experiences that challenged their skills and sense of effectance. Whereas Sarina seemed confident as she scaled the tree, Elle appeared less sure of herself. Sarina's smile signaled accomplishment, whereas we considered Elle's cries an expression of uncertainty or fear. Nevertheless, with verbal encouragement, she persists until she reaches the top. The children's emotional responses and social interactions varied widely as they tested their skills and experienced the physical and psychological challenges of the woods. In addition, each situation required the children to gather their personal resources, to consider their options, and to act. In our little school, as hard as we might try, our classrooms rarely offer children such an authentic context where children experience the emotional tension that accompanies the challenge of testing their boundaries of will, persistence, and competence.

A Place to Lend a Hand

The children often looked to their peers for help. Even more significantly, from a socio-emotional standpoint, the children volunteered to help when they perceived someone else in need of support. As we try to understand the meaning of children's responses to their peers' efforts and at times distress, we recall one of the first experiences these children had in the woods when, as 1-year-olds, they were attempting to cross a bridge:

> Elle scoots across the bridge while Mason crawls. The oldest child, Sarina, is walking, and one of the youngest, Sophie, is standing at the beginning of the bridge. She falls down on her bottom several times, getting back up after each fall. Sophie cries momentarily with each fall. Sarina is cheering on Elle as she scoots, when Emily says, "Sarina, maybe we could cheer for Sophie, too." Sarina immediately changes her chant. "Go, go Sophie, go, go." Emily says to Sophie, "Did you hear Sarina? She's cheering for you!" Sarina continues to softly cheer as she pumps her arms up and down. She walks back to stand behind Sophie. Sophie gives a little cry after Sarina passes her and raises her hand momentarily toward Emily. Very quietly, Sarina says, "Watch, Sophie." Emily says, "Sophie, Sarina wants you to watch her. She's trying to show you how to walk across the bridge."

In this vignette, Emily supports Sarina's and Sophie's interaction as she narrates and gives meaning to their behavior. She doesn't directly help Sophie, but rather scaffolds Sarina to support her.

We believe that the teachers' efforts to deliberately verbalize a child's distress and relinquish their own "helping power" contributed to the increasing frequency of the children's efforts to come to each other's aid. Rosenthal and Gatt (2013) discuss the need for teachers to go beyond responding sensitively to children as individuals to supporting children's socio-emotional development. They refer to moments of effective socio-emotional learning in a group setting as being times of heightened emotionality. Teachers can assume the role of "stage manager" at this time, effectively scaffolding children's behavior. It seems probable that this strategy is one way teachers can indirectly promote a group culture in which children act to support each other's well-being. The natural setting can play a significant role as it presents and promotes such opportunities by virtue of the challenges it presents to children of varying skills and experience. The following observation takes place in the same location when most of the children have left the area to begin the trip back to school:

> The children take their last turns climbing the fallen tree trunk and begin to head up the trail. They walk approximately 150 feet when Spencer and Daniel hear a child yell, "Help!" Daniel stops and looks at Spencer, "Sarina?" he asks. Spencer replies, "Yeah, it sounds like Sarina. Maybe she fell off the tree trunk." Immediately Daniel turns and dashes toward the fallen tree.

In this brief exchange, Daniel first alerts Spencer to the possibility that Sarina is either hurt or in trouble. When Spencer confirms Daniel's concern, Daniel doesn't wait for Spencer to act. He dashes off to see why Sarina has called for help and (we conjecture) to help her.

The notion of the woods as a rich and diverse place that challenges young children physically, intellectually, and emotionally may explain in part the children's efforts to help each other. The very fact that the children were constantly encountering obstacles to overcome put them in the position to need help or encouragement. We see the adults as playing an equally significant role in the children's responses to their peers' struggles. Emily and Spencer were very explicit in their responses to children, almost always redirecting the children to each other for potential strategies and/or for words of encouragement. We believe that together, these two factors contributed to the children's awareness of each other's efforts and willingness to lend a metaphorical or literal hand when they perceived that someone needed help.

In another vignette, Mika takes it upon herself to warn others of a bridge that is in a state of disrepair:

> Dee steps up onto the bridge. Mika is ahead of Dee and she turns, putting up a hand in a "stop" motion. She addresses Dee in a stern voice, "Careful, big hole!"

In this instance, Mika seems to be assuming responsibility for assisting Dee. Is she reenacting what she has seen her teachers do in similar situations, or is she acting on a desire to keep Dee safe? Or both? Although we acknowledge the subjectivity of any interpretation, we can say that every day we were in the woods we recorded instances when children needed help and/or comfort, and children helped or comforted with actions or words.

We continue to question the meaning of the children's responses to others. Are the children imitating behaviors they have seen, or are they identifying with and responding to the feelings the other child is expressing? Traditional literature argues that the children in this group are far too young to be credited with empathic responses (Sroufe & Cooper, 1988; Lewis, 1992). In contrast, more recent literature (e.g., Henderson, Gerson, & Woodward, 2008; Henderson, Wang, Matz & Woodward, 2012) suggests that by 18 months of age or younger, children can infer the intent of others and understand that some ways of acting are shared among groups of people. Although not mentioning empathy per se, Trevarthen (2011) argues that by 15 months of age, toddlers can organize themselves into a working team without adult help. Surely this constitutes being able to conceptualize and act on various roles. Research by Thompson (2008, 2012), Jaffe (2007), and de Waal (2005) all document that the capacity to experience empathy or respond empathically begins earlier in development than was previously thought. In other words, these more recent studies suggest that children are becoming social experts by the time they are 2 years of age. Clearly, multiple factors contribute to the development of empathy. Could the social opportunities experienced in nature pose rich provocations for such developmental and interactional advances? The experiences we observed and documented over the summer lend support to this view.

A Place to Connect

> E. O. Wilson (1984) argues that humans have an "innate affinity for the natural world".
>
> (p. 157)

This concept, called *biophilia,* intrigues us and seems related to the children's strong curiosity about, interest in, and displays of affection toward the flora and fauna of the woods. Toads, crayfish, spiders, worms, and fish: All were approached and handled gently as Spencer helped the children learn to handle found creatures with care. Small insects were some of the most treasured objects in the woods. The children spent time finding, observing, and carefully handling them. Inchworms, caterpillars, spiders, and slugs were gently cradled in hands or observed as they crawled over a child's arm. The children often tried to find a critter's home. If that didn't prove fruitful, they would attempt to make it a home by digging a hole in the ground with sticks. Spencer was especially skillful at finding and catching crayfish by hand. The crustaceans' claws fascinated the children. One day, Spencer put leaves in the pincers so the children could touch the body of the crayfish. Offering his expertise to the toddlers, Spencer asked, "Who would like to hold this crayfish? You? Or you?" There seemed to be apprehension among the children, as several declined the offer. Finally, Elle volunteered to carry the crayfish back to the water with Spencer. At the water's edge, she carefully eased it into the stream. On that same day in an open wooded area, we taped the following episode:

> Sarina cups her hands, pretending to hold a crayfish. She calls the children over and asks, "Who would like to hold this crayfish? You? Or you?" Elle steps forward and with great care the girls transfer the imagined crayfish from one hand to the other, making sure to position their fingers so that they will not get pinched.

We interpret this observation as a moment when Sarina and Elle enact an exchange that highlights their regard for each other's well-being and that of the imagined crayfish. Their actions are precise and delicate—actions that we interpret as reflecting a sense of connectivity not only to each other, but also to the natural world. Vygotsky (1967) states that "there are rules stemming from an imaginary situation" (p.10). The rules here involve care and well-being. It seems fair to us to conclude that Elle is empathizing here on some level.

The following observation captures what seems to us to be a similar moment in which the children's efforts may reflect a concern for the well-being of birds that live in the woods:

> The children gather around a small bush, eagerly picking its colorful berries. Their small fingers grasp the fruit and gather it in their hands. Sophie scatters the berries on the ground, calling, "Here, birdie!" Elle scatters the berries saying, "These are for birds. Right? Here go, birdie." Conner picks berries one by one and squishes them against the nearby tree bark. "Juice. For birdies," he declares.

Early during the children's experience in the woods, the teachers taught them that only a few of the berries they found were for people to eat, whereas most were edible for the animals that inhabited the woods. Spencer and Emily told the children that these honeysuckle berries were only for the birds, and hence the children called them "birdie berries." They routinely picked the berries and then threw them on the ground for the birds.

In the previous observation, we see the children acting on their knowledge about the berries. They don't put the berries in their mouths, but rather scatter them on the ground. It's possible that they experience satisfaction in the fine motor act of plucking the berries and, because they've been told that they are not to be eaten, take the opportunity to throw them on the forest floor. These gestures, however, also may signify the children's understanding that birds, like themselves, need food to live. Perhaps they are trying to help the birds by removing and dispersing the difficult-to-reach berries from the bush. And although it's possible that Conner's juice is an example of what Golomb (1974) refers to as an early representational act of "reading off" the squashed berries, it is also conceivable that Conner prepares juice for the birds as an act of intersubjectivity as he considers the possibility that, because he likes juice, perhaps birds do as well. The answers to these questions are debatable, in the best sense of the word, and as such, offer us the opportunity to reflect on the meaning of the children's seemingly simple acts of plucking, scattering, and crushing the honeysuckle "birdie berries."

Taken together, we believe our observations of the children in the woods offer a clear window into the emotional and relational life of toddlers. In her article, *The Wonders of Nature: Honoring Children's Ways of Knowing,* Wilson (1997) argues that children's ways of knowing in the natural world are linked to a sense of wonder. She believes that if fostered at an early age, a sense of connection to the natural world can serve as a lifelong source of joy and learning. Our documentation of the experiences of these very young children, who spent long uninterrupted hours in the woods, suggests it was a time of wonder, joy, and learning; if not for life, then certainly in the moment-to-moment encounters that characterized their present experiences.

Research from Scandinavia (Rosenthal & Gatt, 2013) describes the teacher's role in helping young children learn socio-emotional competence, whereas Moser & Martinsen (2010) cast the outdoor environment as a pedagogical space that promotes relationships among the children. Hyun (2005) reports that young children's perceptions of nature seem fundamentally different from those of adults, in that children experience the natural world directly through their senses and pretend play in a more direct and descriptive manner. These studies resonate with our experience and inform our point of view that the woods is a context where children discover not only the wonders of the natural world, but also related responsibilities and associated feelings that accompany *living in it.* We observed that the act of responding to a perceived need, whether the need is that of a friend, teacher, critter, tree, or bird, was always enacted with a high level of emotional engagement and regard. These expressions of affection and affiliation suggest the unique role the natural world may play in even very young children's developing sense of self in relationship to others—as defined in the broadest, most inclusive sense of the word.

Families' Voices

Emily and Spencer understood that this experience would be as unique for the parents as it was for the children. Well before the first day in the woods, they met with the parents to explain their plans. They also spent one Saturday morning in the woods with the families and children to introduce them firsthand to the environment. In the fall following the summer in the woods, Emily e-mailed the families, asking them to share their perspective on this experience. She asked them to discuss their initial thoughts about their children spending all day in Centennial Woods. She also invited them to share any hesitations they had about the children's experiences.

Six of the seven families responded, with the seventh responding to a second e-mail. Many expressed their initial reactions to Emily and Spencer's proposal with a combination of anxiety and excitement. One parent describes her feelings here, clearly worried about the risks inherent in this undertaking:

> We were nervous, probably more nervous than our e-mails convey, and we had lots of questions. There are so many dangers in the woods (in my mind), and it seemed like Mason would be farther away and harder to reach than I liked if something ever happened. On the other hand, we were excited for him to have this opportunity and to increase his knowledge of the natural world.

Another parent articulates a similar mix of emotions:

> I was impressed and excited for Sarina. However, I could not get my head around the logistics of daily activity, like eating, napping, potty, etc. Also worried about ticks and mosquitoes.

The following was written by a parent who initially kept her child home on "woods days," but over time changed her mind:

> I kept her out of school that summer 1 or 2 days a week not because of the woods but because I wanted to keep her home but also keep her connected to the school. At first, I scheduled them on the woods day, but toward the end of the summer, I realized that she was really missing something, and when I did drop her at the woods, she practically ran down the path. She had such confidence and clearly loved the physical challenges in the woods . . .

On the other hand, this parent's enthusiasm is immediate and unconstrained:

> We were excited and impressed that the school was providing this experience, as it is so in line with our lifestyle and values. I've bragged about it to all my friends and family—that Daniel can navigate and walk/crawl on inclines, around logs, tree roots, rocks, bridges and splash in creeks, pee in the woods, sleep and eat in the woods, learn about water creature, fungi, insects and plants like poison ivy at such a young age. Most childcare centers do not stray far from designed "nature" surrounded playgrounds, but Centennial Woods is wild, unplanned, REAL, and an evolving natural setting. It was important for us as parents and biologists to instill a love and respect of nature in our children and were thrilled to hear that the school would take a lead in our parenting goals . . . We were also a bit relieved because as working parents, our only time remaining to immerse our child would be busy weekends, and we never make it out in nature as often as we

would like due to errands and other planned activities. So, so happy about the option.

In general, most parents responded with emotion-laden descriptions that reflected a mix of excitement and concerns about safety. It is interesting to note that the parent just quoted identified these expeditions as in line with their "lifestyle and values." The extent of other parents' experience in and valuing of the natural world may well have played a role in the degree to which they experienced their children's outings as a source of anxiety. Although Emily's questions did not probe these variables, we know that many of the parents who reported concerns about the risks of the natural world do not spend their leisure time hiking or camping, suggesting the possibility that at least for some, their emotional discomfort came from a fear of the unknown and/or a lack of knowledge about the outdoors.

Many parents, even those who expressed mild or no concern, indicated that they felt some hesitation about their children spending full days in the woods, particularly in regard to risks associated with getting bitten by mosquitoes and ticks or tripping or falling. One parent separates her excitement about the "idea" of spending full days in the woods from the real risks it presents:

> We had no hesitations in supporting the idea overall. We were somewhat concerned about poison ivy and ticks, but that didn't stop us in the slightest.

FIGURE 7.2

One parent responds:

> No hesitations necessarily, as I trusted her teachers, just a little nervousness because it was such an unknown space . . .

This parent's response captures what appears to us to be the vital role that trust played in the parents' willingness to support this initiative despite their emotional anxiety and fear of the unknown. Another parent summed up the role that trust played in his reaction when he wrote:

> Not hesitations but questions—at that time they were all potty training—how would that work? How would naps work? We had faith in you [Emily] and Spencer and the really great students you had at the time to figure it out, but I really wondered how you'd deal with those challenges.

A parent expands on the role that trust played to include the children when she wrote: "She [her daughter] and her peers had a lot of trust in each other and in their teachers!" Another parent implies a similar bond of trust among the children when she remarks on the extent to which the children supported each other:

> I liked the social development the kids developed in the woods. It was so interesting to see how they helped each other and/or coached each other. The physical challenges were so different, it seemed they all just took on a different level of responsibility. The social structure seemed very different to me compared to the classroom or play yard.

Parents also commented on how ambitious this undertaking was ("I think my initial thought was wow, how are they going to do that?"). They wrote about how impressed they were by Emily's and Spencer's decision to offer this opportunity to the children (. . . and [we] thought that you guys were very brave for taking this on . . .")

As a sort of embedded epilogue to the "Children's Voices" section, we close this discussion with a parent's description of pick-up at the end of a day in the woods. It brings to mind our observations of the quality of the children's emotional expressions, ones that we, too, had we thought of it first, would have chosen to describe as "sparkling":

> As we would walk him back along the path to the parking lot, he'd be non-stop talking about the hiking, playing in the stream, the animals that were spotted in the woods that day, or the frogs that were caught. He always was sparkling and smiling when he relived the day.

Teachers' Voices

During the summer in the woods, we focused on the children's interactions with each other and the natural world. Although the teachers "appeared" in our observations, our intent was to record the children's experience and, as a result, our documentation of Emily and Spencer's experience is limited. Consequently, we asked them to respond to several questions regarding the quality of their experience in writing by recalling and reflecting on their feelings and how they changed over the course of the summer. We probed for particular situations that elicited emotional responses and asked them to reflect on the woods as a context in which emotions are experienced and expressed.

"Freedom, wonder, excitement, and joy." These are the words Spencer uses to describe his experience of the summer in the woods. He shares childhood memories in which he and his brother spent entire days in the woods behind his house, days that "established in my consciousness that the woods are a space of freedom, where the structure and limits of the adult/built environment fall away." The idea of freedom recurs in Spencer's reflections when he writes, "The sense of unfettered freedom acts as a catalyst for wonder and exploration." Spencer also remarks on the significance of both time and adult comfort level as elements that contributed to the quality of their shared experience:

> Spending full days in the woods was the only means to allow for the temporal space necessary to provide the children with authentic woods experience. Also, our sense of comfort in the woods allowed us to provide children with much greater spatial freedom than the built environment.

Emily, too, describes a sense of excitement as she and Spencer planned this initiative and the role that time plays in her vision of what the children would do. She writes:

> I was excited to be able to spend the whole day in the woods with Spencer and this group of children and not have to rush anywhere.

She elaborates by explaining her vision that children would have time to master physical challenges, explore new paths, and have control over the experience. And, like the parents, Emily acknowledges some concerns:

> I remember also feeling hesitant about the unknown. Did we remember to bring everything that we needed? What happened if the bugs became a big issue? What would happen if kids weren't able to/didn't want to nap? These things were enough to make me a little worried in the beginning, but after the first few times, all those worries went away.

Once Emily's concerns are laid to rest, she describes her experiences in the woods as different from those in the classroom:

> Walking down to our campsite in the morning, it was as if a sense of calmness would come over me. I was able to think about the day and was excited for what was to come. It didn't ever feel stressful, as it can many times in the classroom. Even the day that we got "lost" as we hiked on a new path—if we still would have had to walk back to school, that would have set us up for a stressful/long walk back. Being that we only had to find our way back to our campsite, it was a fun adventure that we were able to laugh about once we returned.

Emily brings a new perspective to our thinking about the experience of spending full days in the woods when she shares her reflections on how it affected the relationships among the teachers:

> I think excitement came out in the playfulness of teachers. Teachers got to spend a lot more time together, and that was different [from] being at school. We all ate meals together (children and teachers) and got to share in conversation about what the day would bring. Our sense of community became even stronger. Children and teachers were able to share in experiences together, working through challenging experiences and celebrating accomplishments.

And so Emily captures our thoughts about this ambitious and complex undertaking. Perhaps its real power rests in the fact that all the protagonists—parents, children, and teachers—were taking risks, supporting each other, sharing their excitement and uncertainties, and ultimately celebrating their accomplishments as a genuine community.

Final Thoughts

Documenting the children's experiences led us to an appreciation of the woods as a context that provokes a range of emotional expressions. Although there were moments when the children cried in response to what appeared to be frustration and even exhaustion when confronted by the woods' physical challenges, their interactions with each other were predominately characterized by exchanges of laughter, smiles, and gestures of support. Whereas the adults in their lives were concerned with the risks that the woods presented, the children's connectivity with others (including the "other" of the natural world) predominated. Perhaps the "psychological benefits" (Wilson, 1984) of the natural world rest in their ability to create a sense of unity. This is a place where we experience ourselves in communion with others, whether the other is our peer, our teacher, a tree where we lean to catch our breath, or a fungus that draws us in with its sensory-rich display of color, smell, and texture. The challenges, beauty, and diversity of the natural world make us leap, pause, ponder, relish; laugh, cry, frown, smile. We can hardly imagine a more profound, provocative, and emotionally evocative environment than that which we inhabited during the toddlers' summer in the woods.

References

Clay, R. A. (2001). *Green Is Good for You*. Retrieved from www.apa.org/monitor/apr01/greengood.aspx

Crain, W. (2001). How nature helps children develop. *Montessori Life, 13*(3): 22–24.

de Waal, F. (2005). The evolution of empathy. *Greater Good*. Retrieved from http://greatergood.berkeley.edu/article/item/the_evolution_of_empathy

Goldhaber, J. (2010). Valuing children as citizens of their community and stewards of the natural world. *Innovations, 17*(2): 13–21.

Goldhaber, J., & Smith, D. (2008, June). *Observing Children in the Natural World: What Can We Learn?* Presentation at The South Dakota Infant/Toddler Project, South Dakota State University, Brookings, SD.

Golomb, C. (1974) *Young children's sculpture and drawing*. Boston, MA: Harvard University Press.

Hart, R. (1979). *Children's experience of place*. New York, NY: Irvington Publishers.

Henderson, A. M. E., Gerson, S., & Woodward, A. L. (2008). The birth of social intelligence. *Zero to Three, 28*(5): 13–21.

Henderson, A. M. E., Wang, Y., Matz, L. E., & Woodward, A. L. (2012). Active experience shapes 10-month-old infants' understanding of collaborative goals. *Infancy, 18*(1): 10–39.

Hyun, E. (2005). How is young children's intellectual culture of understanding nature different from adults? *Environment Education Research, 11*(2): 199–214.

Jaffe, E. (2007). Mirror neurons: How we reflect on behavior. *APS Observer*. Retrieved from www.psychologicalscience.org/index.php/publications/observer/2007/may-07/mirror-neurons-how-we-reflect-on-behavior.html

Kaplan, R., Kaplan, S., & Ryan, R. L. (1998). *With people in mind: Design and management for everyday nature*. Washington, D.C.: Island Press.

Kellert, S. R. (1997). *Kinship to mastery: Biophilia in human evolution and development*. Washington, D.C.: Island Press.

Kellert, S. R., & Wilson, E. O. (Eds.). (1993). *The biophilia hypothesis*. Washington, D.C.: Island Press.

Lewis, M. (1992). *Shame*. New York, NY: The Free Press.

Little, H., Wyver, S., & Gibson, F. (2011). The influence of play context and adult attitudes on young children's physical risk-taking during outdoor play. *European Early Childhood Education Research Journal, 19*(1): 113–131.

Melhuus, C. (2012). Outdoor day-care centres—a culturalization of nature: How do children relate to nature as educational practice? *European Early Childhood Education Research Journal, 20*(3): 455–467.

Moser, T., & Martinsen, M. T. (2010). The outdoor environment in Norwegian kindergartens as pedagogical space for toddlers' play, learning, and development. *European Early Childhood Education Research Journal, 18*(4): 457–471.

Norris, J., Smith, D., & Gandini, L. (2009, November). *Responsive Materials for Supporting the Infants' and Toddlers' Curriculum: Nature's Atelier*. PowerPoint presented at National Association for the Education of Young Children Conference, Washington, D.C.

Olds, A. (1985). Nature as healer. *Children's Environments Quarterly, 6*(1): 27–32.

Rosenthal, M. K., & Gatt, L. (2013). Learning to live together: Training early childhood educators to promote socio-emotional competence of toddlers and preschool children. *European Early Childhood Education Research Journal, 18*(3): 373–390.

Sebba, R. (1991). The landscapes of childhood: The reflection of childhood's environment in adult memories and children's attitudes. *Environment and Behavior, 23*(4): 395–422.

Sroufe, L. A., & Cooper, R. G. (1988). *Child development: Its nature and course.* New York, NY: Alfred A. Knopf.

Taylor, A. F., Kuo, F. E., & Sullivan, W. C. (2001). Coping with ADD: The surprising connection to green play settings. *Environment and Behavior, 33*(1): 54–77.

Taylor, A. F., Kuo, F. E., & Sullivan, W. C. (2001). Views of nature and self-discipline: Evidence from inner-city children. *Journal of Environmental Psychology* Retrieved from http://faculty.une.edu/cas/szeeman/GK-12/articles/ViewsofNature.pdf

Thompson, R. (2008). The psychologist in the baby. *Zero to Three Journal, 28*(5): 5–12.

Thompson, R. (2012). How emotional development unfolds starting at birth. *Zero to Three Journal, 32*(3): 6–11.

Trevarthen, C. (2011). What young children give to their learning: Making education work to sustain a community and its culture. *European Early Childhood Education Research Journal, 19*(2): 173–193.

Vygotsky, L. S. (1967). Play and its role in the mental development of the child. *Soviet Psychology, 5*(3): 6–18.

Wilson. E. O. (1984). *Biophilia.* Cambridge, MA: Harvard University Press.

Wilson, R. (1997). The wonders of nature: Honoring children's ways of knowing. *Early Childhood News.* Retrieved from www.earlychildhoodnews.com/earlychildhood/article view.aspx?ArticleID=70

COMMENTARY

John Nimmo

UNIVERSITY OF NEW HAMPSHIRE

The stories of toddlers negotiating slippery mud, rocks, and gravity in Smith and Goldhaber's chapter left me with an impression of emotional intensity and authenticity. Along with the toddlers' joy of accomplishment and tenderness in helping a friend, I also felt their cries of frustration and apprehension in not knowing how to navigate the terrain. Something about the woods evoked these emotions.

Where the Wild Things Are

The natural world is unpredictable and untidy in its complexity. It is an authentic, rather than prepared and regulated environment. Children witness and respond emotionally to the unfolding rhythms of nature with its changing colors, textures, and sounds. Smith and Goldhaber use the term "wild" to distinguish the setting for the toddlers' adventures from other spaces like gardens and natural playgrounds (p. 113). It is an important distinction. In the book *Wild Law* Cullinan (2011) writes: "'Wild' . . . is synonymous with unkempt, barbarous, unrefined, uncivilized, unrestrained, wayward, disorderly, irregular, out of control, unconventional, undisciplined, passionate, violent, uncultivated, and riotous" (pp. 29–30). He argues that we need to discard the false dichotomy between civilization (regulation) and nature (wild) and embrace the need for both dimensions in human experience.

The authors' observations of children in the wild draw our attention to the significance of risk. Risk leads to a range of emotions, including surprise, fear, excitement, and anticipation. At a Norwegian forest school I visited, a teacher introduced herself as the risk assessor. Her role was to look at how children could best experience the challenges of a woods environment—very different from a safety inspector. Likewise, the teachers in the chapter accepted the inherent risks of the wild as an opportunity for greater freedom of movement, space, and time.

Connection to Place

The stories of toddlers and teachers in this chapter conjure up images of journeying to special places. Smith and Goldhaber talk about the sense of unity the toddlers experienced as they encountered shared obstacles and discoveries, which became opportunities to show empathy and provide help and encouragement. I also see this unity as linked to a shared sense of place. Together, they mapped the lay of the land, the places to be careful, and the creatures they might encounter. For the toddlers, this experience was soaked with what they heard, felt, touched, smelled, and tasted; they shared a connection to that place.

Jinan Kodapully offers his insights from more than a decade of observing village children in India. These children know the sounds of birds and the smell of the berries to eat; the natural world is a part of their daily lives. He reflects: "The way [these children] explore the world of senses is by interaction with nature, and the world of nature through senses. Senses are a two-way tool—to know the outside *and* the inside" (Kodapully, 2014, p. 3). Likewise, Andy Goldsworthy (1990), known for his dynamic sculptures inspired by and made from materials in nature, conveys the sensorial connection with place that he needs for inspiration:

> Movement, change, light, growth, and decay are the lifeblood of nature, the energies I try to tap through my work. I need the shock of touch, the resistance of place, materials, and weather; the earth is my source. I want to get under the surface. When I work with a leaf, rock, stick, it is not just the material in itself, it is an opening into the processes of life within and around it.
>
> *(p. 1)*

For the children and the artist, the complexity and authenticity of natural spaces arouse a range and depth of emotions.

I wonder about our (adult) separation from the natural world. This leaves us as the observer who enters natural spaces rather than being part of that world. As the authors note, toddlers display a comfortable affinity with the wild; they are part of nature, not separate.

As adults, how do we rebuild our sense of place? Berg (1995) talks about the importance of developing an awareness of one's bioregion, the geographical zone of where you live that includes distinct and interdependent natural features—a watershed, plants, animals, climate, and so on. He says, "The concept of a bioregion is uniquely useful for putting ourselves back into nature instead of on top of it" (p. 5). A sense of place is important to our identity as individuals and as members of a community. In part, this connection requires confronting the fears we have as adults about wild places.

Fear and Trust

Parents are understandably anxious about the uncertainties of their toddlers spending a day in the wild woods. Given the many negative images of "wild" in industrialized societies and the cultural disconnection from nature, it is no surprise that parents felt apprehension as well as excitement. The trepidation of some parents in this chapter reflects differences in their experience, knowledge, and cultural values. Smith and Goldhaber's observations affirm that trust can ease these fears. The parents placed trust in teachers, whom they believed cared for and knew their children. Based on their prior relationships, they trusted in the teachers' skills, knowledge, and passion for nature. The authors' observations point out the importance of considering the range of emotionality for parents and teachers, not to deny these feelings, but to think about how they can be a healthy presence in home–school relationships.

Teachers also grow through opportunities to stretch their comfort level. As professionals, they are more explicitly aware than parents are of the ways that discomfort and challenge can lead to their growth as educators. The teachers in the chapter felt at home in the woods and saw it as an environment with much potential for children's exploration. They modeled a relatedness and comfort with being in nature. Torquati and Ernst (2013) found that pre-service early childhood students reported only moderate levels of connection to and comfort with nature and a clear preference for taking children into natural spaces maintained by humans. We need to encourage teachers to develop their relatedness to nature and to take the emotional risks involved in engaging children in natural and wild spaces.

Parting Thought: Finding Wild Places

I worry about the tightening social range and spatial mobility of children (from home base and into the neighborhood) in industrialized societies, particularly in urban areas (O'Brien, Jones, & Sloan, 2000). Increasingly, we keep children within the walls of childcare programs or home. How can children find wild and natural spaces where they can roam, play, imagine, take risks, and feel connected? We need to stretch our understanding of how unregulated and unprepared (wild) spaces evoke emotionality for both children and adults. Although the image of children frolicking through pastures of flowers is an attractive one, the reality is likely to be, and should be, more complex, more challenging, and more fully human.

References

Berg, P. (1995). *Discovering your life-place: A first bioregional workbook.* San Francisco, CA: Planet Drum Foundation.

Cullinan, C. (2011). *Wild law: A manifesto for earth justice* (2nd ed.). White River Junction, VT: Chelsea Green Publishing.

Goldsworthy, A. (1990). *A collaboration with nature.* New York, NY: Harry N. Abrams, Inc.

Kodapully, J. (2014). *Traditional Knowledge or Nature's Knowledge?* Retrieved from https://indepdendent.academia.edu/JinanKodapully

O'Brien, M., Jones, D., & Sloan, D. (2000). Children's independent spatial mobility in the urban realm. *Childhood, 7*(3): 255–277.

Torquati, J., & Ernst, J. A. (2013). Beyond the walls: Conceptualizing natural environments as "third educators." *Journal of Early Childhood Teacher Education, 34*(2): 191–208.

PART III

Understanding Emotion within Roles and Relationships

8

CRITICAL FRIENDS WORK THROUGH THE EMOTIONS OF BEGINNING TEACHING TOGETHER

David E. Fernie[1]

WHEELOCK COLLEGE

> "Right now. I'm focusing on everything. I've got a new book full of . . . every time I had an idea I write the idea down. . . . And it's huge and I can't keep track of it all . . ."
>
> —*Dustin*

> "Two days after I was offered the job I had this nightmare that I was doing a lesson and the principal and somebody else was watching and they told me that 'you're not allowed, leave here, we don't think you're ready for this. . . . So we're going to find someone else."
>
> —*Ashley*

For Dustin and Ashley, two new early childhood teachers in the first weeks of their first professional teaching jobs, teaching clearly is not solely or even primarily a cognitive act. Both from the very beginning and over time, the quality of teachers' emotional experience matters: Teacher and administrator "burnout" and the high attrition rate for new teachers (up to 50% in the first 5 years in urban settings) have been linked to the emotional dimensions of teachers' experiences and to accountability pressures intensified in the era of the federal No Child Left Behind Act (Henke, Chen, & Geis, 2000; National Commission on Teaching and America's Future, 2003). This alarming attrition rate alone dictates that we must better understand teachers' emotional experience. More hopefully, research also suggests that teachers' emotional engagement and satisfaction with their role is a primary factor in their job satisfaction and retention. Hargreaves (1998) expresses the essential and critical nature of teachers' emotional experience well: "Teaching cannot be reduced to technical competence or clinical standards. It involves significant emotional understanding and emotional labor as well. It is an emotional practice" (p. 850).

As the quotes from Dustin and Ashley demonstrate, the transition from completing a teacher preparation program to teaching as a novice professional is clearly a challenging one. Program completion means (hopefully!) a new job and career; typically, this will mean that a new teacher then enters an unfamiliar school as a stranger—with new colleagues to work with, administrators to work for, and children to teach. Especially in our urban schools, they often encounter the challenges of heightened accountability, resource retrenchment, and children and families who struggle with intractable poverty conditions and related impacts. It is a transition that might be characterized as a huge "leap of faith."

It follows, then, that the first year of teaching is when teachers' emotions and stressors run highest and when they need the most support to make a strong start. The first year is not a warm-up year: It sets the tone and structure for teachers' role and their experiencing of classroom life, and it is the time when their professional identity and "learning to feel as a professional" develop in an interwoven fashion (Madrid & Dunn-Kenney, 2010; Madrid, Baldwin, & Frye, 2013). It is also when teachers will either hold on to innovative ideas from educator preparation programs or give them up and adopt more traditional ideas. And research suggests that teachers who make a strong start are those most likely to remain effective educators (The New Teacher Project, 2013).

Recently, induction-year programs are trying to support new teachers, but many focus on skill development and downplay or even ignore the emotional experience of new teachers. There is also a growing recent interest in creating innovative online and face-to-face venues for dialogue during the induction year, such as "Professional Learning Communities" and the TLINC concept advanced by the National Commission on Teaching and America's Future (http://nctaf. org/tlinc/). Despite these promising new efforts and developments, we still know too little about the emotional lives of new early childhood teachers during this transition period and about how to best support them through it.

As I describe in this chapter, a promising opportunity to document new teachers' voices and garner support for them arose when my college was awarded a federally funded project grant intended to increase the diversity of the early childhood teacher workforce. A competitive application process yielded diverse cohorts of mature career changers and community-based early childhood professionals committed to social justice work and urban schools, who then engaged in an intensive 2-year program, which included a yearlong internship in an urban elementary school. The program's (and participants') goals were to achieve a state licensure credential to teach ages 3 through grade 2 in public schools, a master's degree in early childhood education, and teaching jobs in urban school districts.

Close to the end of their program, I had the pleasure of getting to know members of the project's first cohort by teaching a course on action research for them. After the summer semester completion of their master's, these new graduates were to take additional evening coursework that fall semester, leading to an additional state credential; consequently, these new graduates/new teachers would be back on campus taking coursework with familiar peers just as they began their first professional teaching jobs.

I saw this as a unique opportunity to explore the emotional side of what could be addressed in induction/first-year support. For novice teachers, graduation typically means cutting ties with, or at least greatly reducing interactions with, trusted student peers and higher education professors from their pre-service programs; further, graduation implies the optimistic and questionable notion they are now ready to go forth and be effective in their new classroom settings. Here was an opportunity to create support and continuity for our program participants in the transition from teacher preparation program to first professional job.

Given my research interest in the emotional lives of teachers and my desire to continue to support members of this cohort, I invited five new teachers (Dustin, Paula, Andre, Lina, and Ashley) to join with me as "Critical Friends" (Dunne, Nave, & Lewis, 2000; Bambino, 2002) in 1-hour-long group conversations each week throughout the semester, just prior to their evening class. Although there is research literature documenting the value of mentoring by more experienced teachers and new colleagues in the job setting (Whitebrook, Bellm, & Schaack, 2013; Kochan & Trimble, 2000), there is little research on this venue for support, that is, having new teachers engage in continuing dialogue with a familiar college professor and trusted program peers experiencing this same life transition.

The format of these conversations was informal, and the purposefully "open" goal was for us to engage in dialogue about this transition and whatever issues were arising for them during it. The conversations were videotaped and transcribed.

From participating in the group and reviewing videotapes, it became apparent to me that the first 8 weeks constituted a cohesive whole, a first and most intense phase in their emotional lives as new teachers. Conversations during the second half of the semester differed in both tone (lighter and with more humor) and topic (more focus on pedagogical strategies and classroom management). Interested in what was going on in their emotional lives in this critical very first phase, I then reviewed the videotapes and transcripts from the first 8 weeks multiple times to develop a coding system for salient themes and to identify exemplars throughout the data.

In the following sections, four common tensions or themes that challenged these five new teachers are presented, with an attempt to capture both common emotions they felt as they traveled this new, uncertain terrain, as well as differences due to personality and situation. In a final section, I focus on how the "Friends" learned to feel differently as they experienced and weathered this transition together.

Nascent Professionalism Meets the School Culture

When hired into their teaching roles, the "Friends" collectively felt the satisfaction, joy, and relief of achieving their professional goal. This no doubt felt validating of the hard work and the personal (and often familial) sacrifices that enabled them either to advance their early childhood career or to change careers into this field.

Simultaneous with these positive emotions, the Friends' first weeks posed various versions of the following significant challenge and tension: to integrate their personal ideals and the strategies endorsed in their graduate preparation with the established practices and structures in their settings. This tension and the anxiety it provoked were perhaps most challenging for the four Friends hired into pre-kindergarten or primary-grade classrooms in urban public elementary schools, as described next.

Paula, a Haitian American woman and a leader in the early childhood community, was hired into a full-time K–1 (4-year-olds) classroom in a school that, due to low performance on district-wide standardized test scores, had been designated a "turnaround school." What that designation brings with it is a limited time frame to improve scores, along with more intensified oversight procedures and professional development initiatives. Describing her situation under this "watch" status, Paula explained at our first Friends group conversation, "I'm in a turnaround school which . . . means . . . whenever they're under pressure, which then means that I'm under pressure, which then means the children are under pressure." For a new teacher, this contextual pressure adds a new and intimidating dimension to the transition process.

Andre, a Latino male and also an experienced teacher of young children who was hired into a K–1 classroom in an urban school (one not under watch), came quickly to question whether a formalized curriculum approach developed for older children could be extended in a developmentally appropriate way to his 4-year-olds, as he was charged to do:

> Andre: The school that we're in, we're trying to do, like, our workshop model for K–1.[Laugh] . . . so I'm not sure how that . . . one, I'm not sure if it's developmentally appropriate [laugh], but two, like, it's definitely not "NAEYC appropriate". . . . but yeah, so I'm kind of like struggling with that myself.

The other two Friends hired into public schools, Lina and Ashley, were hired into long-term substitute roles, a common hiring circumstance that created different challenges and emotions in the attenuated transitions to their "own" classrooms. Lina, an experienced early childhood practitioner and leader in the wider non-public school community, was hired into a substitute role in the same school where she had her internship. Already known and well liked within this school, the plan was for her to serve initially as a substitute wherever needed, along with spending time in the classroom she was to take over in November during the regular teacher's maternity leave. An upbeat person by nature, Lina was very happy to be hired in a familiar school, and saw this initial "itinerant" role as an opportunity to establish a wide presence in the building and to hone a range of skills as she encountered various classroom situations. Subbing in the first 2 months in both primary and upper-grade classrooms, and even in educational settings outside of her licensure specialty or expertise, such as a special education classroom, the library, and a bilingual Vietnamese classroom, Lina generally reported feeling both challenged and successful in these diverse venues.

Yet hearing her peers talk in our group conversations about their "own" classrooms created conflicting feelings too:

LINA: I started reminiscing about everybody talking about their classrooms and setting up and I was trying to appreciate all the different classrooms that I'm seeing and all the different ways teachers are setting up and then I got overwhelmed by that. . . . You know, I grew a little envious. Like, gosh, I do kind of wish I had my own classroom. I'd be settled. I'd be struggling with whatever and figuring it out . . . But it would be just one classroom. . . .

Yet when Lina proactively volunteered in August to help her pregnant colleague set up the classroom Lina would later take over, her colleague's mention of what "place" in the curriculum Lina would probably start with in November provoked an unanticipated emotional reaction.

LINA: As soon as she said, "Okay, so you'll probably be at Unit 3 for math" and she gave me the pace and guide for the year [laugh], I started to get butterflies. That I said . . . was, like, Oh, I'm a teacher [laugh]. I'm going to be responsible for making sure students . . . learn these . . . meet these milestones and get . . . learn these different things and I . . . I got a little hot. We opened the window. I was like, wow! . . . I didn't expect that feeling, but it happened.

For Lina, as was often the case for other Friends, the emotions that arose during this time were mixed and changeable, as both the enormity and attraction of "being in charge" and even the anticipation of it provoked feelings of being anxious yet eager, overwhelmed yet stimulated.

Ashley, a white female new to early education, was hired directly into a long-term substitute role in a Spanish bilingual classroom shortly after the school year began, so she joined the Friends group a couple of weeks after her peers. The path to hire had already been especially anxiety provoking for her because she had interviewed widely without success and then had to work through a frustrating and slow bureaucratic paperwork process. By the time the approved offer to hire finally came, Ashley, a career changer from graphic design, confided that she was seriously contemplating a job offer in her former field.

Her first weeks were spent "shadowing" and supporting the assigned classroom teacher, who would return the following fall. Ashley's status as "teacher-in-waiting" during these weeks created subconscious worries of inadequacy, as in the nightmare she describes at the opening of the chapter. Ashley, like Lina, experiences conflicting sentiments in her substitute role, aware of the value of "shadowing to see how things are done," yet also feeling less the professional and more the apprentice because it is not yet her classroom.

ASHLEY: I'm like freaking myself out and then . . . and I also feel like I'm right back in student teaching because, basically, I am . . . the teacher's there. . . .

Sharing the classroom, Ashley feels unsure of how to make the right moves in her teaching and unable to make her own mark as a competent professional in the classroom. Although the teacher never explicitly tells Ashley not to do things her own way, Ashley feels the hierarchy and "hears" implicit messages to conform to current school practice, conflicting with her desire to create a classroom culture consistent with her beliefs and the tenets of her graduate program:

ASHLEY: And it's almost like the unlearning of everything we've learned here at Wheelock when you're kind of going by what you've learned and someone is saying "No."

As described earlier, each of the Friends hired into public schools were confronted during the first 8 weeks with the daunting task of managing both the tensions between their idealized advanced conceptions of teaching and the realities they encountered in their settings and the strong and mixed emotions provoked in this enormous transition. The task was essentially to create continuity between two cultures in conflict—the institutional culture of their early childhood higher education preparation, with an emphasis on developmentally appropriate practice (Copple & Bredekamp, 2009) and constructivist curriculum, and that of a large urban school district, with formal curriculum packages and the current intensification of accountability pressures.

But even for Dustin, the one Friend hired as a lead teacher in a private preschool in another East Coast city (and who joined us each week by Skype), there was considerable practical and psychological distance to travel in these first weeks from the demands of his student/intern role to the responsibilities of his lead teacher role:

DUSTIN: I'm not doing well . . . because I don't have the goals that I want, and I don't have the structure that I might . . . it's a lot of things I want to achieve all over the place, and so I almost don't know how to measure . . . whether I'm being successful or not. And that . . . creates a lot of anxiety in me. Also it makes me think constantly about work . . . I almost never think about anything else.

Struggling to Make Time and Still Have a Life

As Hargreaves (1997) reminds us, "Time is a chronic problem in almost all kinds of teaching. It comes with the territory" (p. 97). But the problem of time is perhaps never more apparent than in teachers' first months on the job. Pressing tasks include setting up their classrooms, procuring materials and resources within and outside of the school system, making curriculum plans, establishing new relationships with children and adults, setting up assessment systems for accountability, etc. For the new teacher, as Dustin laments earlier, the list seems endless and all of these tasks may feel (and may in fact be) critical to accomplish. And without effective mentoring and supervision, there is no one to tell you what to do and when and how to do it.

Dustin, comments by Skype in our first session, "My wife . . . I'm explaining to her what's going on . . . been going on. She has an analogy of I'm building the plane while flying it and that's how I feel, I guess." There is so much to do and so much to figure out. And, as Paula (somewhat) humorously remarks in one of our first Critical Friends sessions, "It will be a long year if I don't figure things out" [laugh]. The conundrum for new teachers, however, is that figuring it out requires more time than they have available.

The result of trying to create the essentials of high-quality classroom life in scarce available time, while simultaneously doing classroom life each day, is that the Friends often felt disorganized, rushed, and anxious during these first weeks:

DUSTIN: Well, I haven't gotten a chance to think about what the issues are. Like, I'm still kind of confused about exactly what the problems are and I want to make sure I have this big plan and I've got goals.

Echoing the cultures-in-conflict tension, several Friends expressed frustration that elements of early childhood philosophy and practice that they personally valued or that were stressed throughout their graduate program couldn't be fitted within the limited "face time" and preparation time that a 24-hour day and a 7-day week offer:

DUSTIN: I trust myself to make good plans and to improve myself if I have time and I . . . I think one thing that's getting to me is that I don't feel like I have the time to make those plans.

For Andre, a self-described "people person," what is missing is the time to build close relationships with families, like the ones he had built in previous teaching roles in childcare:

ANDRE: If I'm working late and going to school and have staff meetings late and then I . . . I need some time to plan in between . . . like, when am I going to meet families?

Regardless of whatever critical elements they were trying unsuccessfully to force-fit into available time, the result for the Friends was exhausting days of teaching followed by nights of planning, mandatory meetings, and/or professional development sessions, with the latter two more prevalent in schools under formalized pressures to improve, such as Paula's. As a result, the Friends often shared the lament that their combined work–personal life agenda is too full and too imbalanced in the direction of work:

PAULA: And I . . . you know, my own personal life, sort of balancing that. I've taken so much advantage of my partner and I gave him a surprise last night because I felt really bad. And he won't complain. . . . And I tell him you might not talk to me but the eyes do . . . And so I tried to make a gesture to show him that I know that my life has sort of become a burden on everybody (pause). . . . See, now I am going to get emotional (pause). . . . Anyway . . . I am trying to find a way so that he can have his breathing time and my life doesn't sort of take over. . . . It's wearing me out, all in a nutshell.

In another particularly poignant moment, she laments the temporal (and hopefully temporary) estrangement she feels from her youngest child, a toddler:

PAULA: I saw him last night and felt, like, oh my God, he looks like the strangest baby . . . that I don't know this boy.

I call this emotion, connected to scarcity of time, *relational guilt*. Similar to what Alan Davies (1989) calls *depressive guilt* and Madrid and Dunn-Kenney (2010) call *persecutory guilt,* this is the feeling that they are burdening or not meeting the needs of the people they love and are responsible for. One form of this phenomenon, evident earlier, might be called *family relational guilt,* emanating from the perceived impact of this transition on family members, spouses/partners, and their own children. A second form might be called *student relational guilt*—the feeling that they are letting down the young children under their care because they are struggling to get control of their professional and personal lives. And as new teachers performing a complex role, they feel, perhaps rightly and even inevitably, that they are doing a less-than-perfect job in helping children to learn and benefit from early education.

For these new teachers, time is a thief. It robs them of attending to their lives outside the classroom. It robs them of the opportunity to create an orderly transition to teaching through which they might feel some sense of control. And it robs them of merited feelings of satisfaction with the tremendous efforts, accommodations, and accomplishments they are making in these first 8 weeks.

Children as a Source of Positive and Negative Emotions

For these new teachers, the classroom has become the center of their lives, and at the center of the classroom life are teachers' new relationships with children and their families. In these very first weeks, the emotional satisfactions of teaching young children can be a joy, a compensation for the struggle, and a necessary reminder to keep the "eye on the prize" of supporting young children. Dustin, teaching more advantaged children in an urban preschool, comments:

> It just seems a little bit difficult to start but at the same time I'm really excited about the children. It's not exactly the population that I had hoped for but, that said, it's very, you know . . . the kids are great and it's in many ways, easy . . .

After a day of substituting as the librarian, Lina "glows" in talking about one child's response to her:

LINA: She wrote me a note at the end and she said "Dear Ms. Thomas: I love you as a substitute and a library teacher. I love you as a daughter to me (sic)." It was the, I swear, it was the best way to end my day. I . . . I really just felt so . . . and she's in third grade, too, but she gave me the biggest hug and, you know, just *that* was confirming, like . . . I still meet their needs even though I feel like maybe I didn't do it as well as I could of if I was a librarian [laugh] . . .

The satisfaction of watching and helping children learn also surfaces in the Friends' conversations. Seeing qualities in a student that remind her of her son, Paula offers the following empathic and self-questioning reflection:

PAULA: He wants to answer every question, very bright kid but he has a real hard time, too, regulating his want to participate, his need for attention and so I have to get kind of creative and . . . I was sort of asking myself in the moment, did I handle this . . . I made a decision and then my mind says "Was this right? Was this the right tone of voice? Is this the way that you should have treated this person?"

The desire to treat children well, often accompanied by student relational guilt and self-doubt, motivates the Friends to strive to make the right teaching moves, to demand the best from themselves, and to self-monitor teaching decisions to those ends on behalf of their young charges. As Paula points out, "This is the only K–1 (4-year-olds) classroom they will have."

In addition to these positive emotions, teaching children in these settings poses challenges and concerns as new teachers work simultaneously to meet the needs of the whole class and of individual children or a small group of children who, due to the impact of poverty or difficult family circumstances, may need additional support or social experience to participate and benefit more fully:

ANDRE: You know, we're in *a low-income area* but the population of children that we work with, I think, are really high-need and there's certain

children in my classroom that I think need like, you know, play therapy,
like small group . . . social-emotional skill-building type activities.
And I can do that, but I can't do that and manage the classroom at
the same time. So it's really . . . that's something that I'm trying to
figure out . . . how to get them, the children, the help that they
need, the support that they need, like, calm them down and give
them strategy . . . you know . . . ways for them to like . . . just, just
help them cope with the day and help them kind of, like, regulate
themselves.

Andre's concerns underscore the fact that many urban and underfunded
schools lack the needed resources of counselors and mental health professionals
and are not oriented to supporting the social and emotional development and
needs of children. And he personally feels stuck between the rock and the hard
place of addressing some children's more evident social and emotional needs while
managing the whole class.

In addition, there is the difficult situation of individual children who are troubled or troubling, whose problems are complex and deeper than their school
behavior, with socioeconomic, familial, or psychological dimensions to them. (See
Danforth & Smith, 2005, for the fuller analysis of their situation, which is beyond
the scope of this discussion.) In any event, both new and experienced teachers often encounter children who variously are disruptive to the orderly flow of
classroom life, seek much attention, seem disengaged from school activities, or are
resistant or unresponsive to the typical rewards and punishments intended to shape
"good" behavior.

I call these children *focal children* due to the sustained, focused attention they
demand and elicit from teachers. When a teacher is drawn to spending inordi-
nate time dealing with a child who disrupts group times, or runs away from the
playground, or hurts other children, the whole ecology of the teaching–learning
situation changes and suffers. And it is not unusual to have more than one such
child in a classroom.

Especially for new teachers, these children can evoke a feeling of helplessness,
an inability to help them and to limit their impact on others and the learning
environment. Several of the Friends spoke of such situations and what it evoked
in them. In one session, Ashley described chasing after a child who ran away from
the playground, her embarrassment while running by parents congregated on the
street, and her relief when he heads for the front door to the building:

ASHLEY: He luckily runs to the front door and rings the bell to get in. So he
went in, I followed him in, and when we walked in, he yelled at me "I
hate you. I want you to die. I hope you get shot" and [laugh] and then
he said, "I hope you go to heaven" [laugh]—which, I think he meant,
I hope you're in heaven and not here.

During these first weeks, children were a source of a wide range of positive and negative emotions for the Friends. In early childhood and elementary teaching, teachers' commitment to an ethic of care and to loving children are strong values underlying practice and teachers' decisions to enter the early education field (Goldstein, 1997). When positive emotions are expressed and reciprocated between children and new teachers, the satisfaction is profound and sustaining. But when these emotions are negative and one's politicized intention to improve the lives of children and families feels unrealized, teachers can feel sad and even disheartened. According to Hargreaves (1994), "The more important that care is to a teacher, the more emotionally devastating is the experience of failing to provide it" (p. 145).

Surveillance and Pressure versus Support and Supervision

New teachers' work, of course, brings them into interaction with a range of adults as well as children. The quality of these diverse interactions, the power relations embedded within them, and the quality of attention paid to these novice teachers engendered a range of positive and negative emotions among the Friends.

The inevitability of being watched or noticed as a new teacher translated for some Friends into feelings of being under surveillance (Madrid & Dunn-Kenney, 2010). Surveillance is defined as "monitoring" or "watching over" a person or a group of people (p. 392). For teachers, feeling watched over (and subsequently internalizing that feeling) can flow from any number of sources within the ecology of the school setting—other teachers, parents, principals, or other supervisory personnel.

As previously described, Ashley's time as "teacher- in-waiting" fueled these feelings with respect to her colleague (despite Ashley's positive regard for her) and contributed to making Ashley feel constrained, tentative, and reticent to do things her own way.

In schools under heavy accountability pressures, and especially in schools under formal surveillance procedures, the feeling of being watched may be inescapable and intense for new teachers. In her "turnaround school," Paula speaks of getting her work done so that she is happy with it, but also "so that people around me, who are all looking, all seeing, all listening, and all talking aren't necessarily reporting negative things about me, and I'm also trying to work towards ignoring what other people might be saying because, if I'm thinking about that all the time, then that's going to add additional stress."

In this statement, Paula struggles with this feeling of surveillance—getting her work done in part to diminish this dynamic and related fears and minimizing the stress of what might be said about her by ignoring what others might be saying. A thoughtful and somewhat private person, Paula takes a stance toward the feelings engendered by surveillance: "I am going to guard myself, protect my emotions." But as a consequence, this protective stance, even when justified, also may limit access to adult sources of potential support in the school environment.

Although colleagues and parents may contribute to the feeling of surveillance, the ethic and pressure often flow from the top. Casual comments and even the absence of positive feedback from administrators and supervisors can fuel a new teacher's internalized fears of surveillance, as Paula's recounting of an anecdote reveals:

PAULA: One of the children had gotten up to use the bathroom and he was really taking a while to go back to his mat and (her paraprofessional classroom aide) said "go sit, sit." But she kept saying the word "sit, go sit." And the principal walked by and said "Is there a dog in there?" or "Is there a dog around here?" or something like that. And so, what I got from that was, if that is her response and the way that she's analyzing and articulating her opinions of this one statement that the "para" made to the child, you know, how are other things being perceived and analyzed? And so I felt like the pressure went up even higher . . .

What a person in power says, even in an offhanded way, can make a difference, positive or negative, to a new teacher. In contrast to Paula's situation, Lina recounts a casual encounter when the principal was surprised to see Lina subbing in a particular classroom:

LINA: The principal was looking for the (regularly assigned) teacher and she came in and she said, "Gosh, you're everywhere" [laugh]. It's like "Yeah, I'm pretty pliable" [laugh] . . . But she was, like, "That's really good, thanks" and she walked out.

Lina often spoke positively of the support she felt from adults in her school, which complemented the previously noted compliments of children. Regardless of the source, the support of some other adult or adults in the school seemed to make a difference in how the Friends felt in their setting. In counterpoint to the "sit, go sit," Paula describes her relationship with her paraprofessional in the same Critical Friends session:

PAULA: Umm . . . I'm glad I have the para that I have in terms of personality . . . she comes in, whatever needs to be done, whether I . . . so I might not even see it, she sees it and she gets it done.

Supportive feedback, too, took different preferred forms for different Friends. For some, constructive criticism from supervisors or assigned mentors would have to be balanced in its tone between supportive remarks and suggestions. For others, direct comments and pointed suggestions were preferred. For Dustin, the latter delivery style would be especially helpful in calming feelings of uncertainty and anxiety during these beginning months, when things felt overwhelming and when measuring and feeling the progress or success he aspires to felt especially elusive:

DUSTIN: Like basically, any time I think about school . . . but especially before I am, I'm going to go. . . . Am I doing the things I need to do today to be prepared to be good and then to improve? I don't really know for sure and that scares me, and that I might be getting bad habits and just not doing what I set out to do, you know. . . . Anything I do I want to be great at, just like all of you. . . . I would prefer to be in a situation where somebody said "here's what you need to do" and I'll do those things.

One final and important source of support felt by the Friends concerns the interactions within the Critical Friends group, which will be elaborated next in describing how the Friends gradually came to feel differently in these first 8 weeks.

Learning to Feel Differently through Reappraisal

As mentioned earlier in this chapter, the conversations among the Friends shifted in content and tone over the 8 weeks presented in this analysis. Over this period, the group's focus shifted increasingly toward classroom issues—to pedagogy, to focal children, and to problem-solving the practical problems shared by the group. At the same time, analysis of these hour-long conversations revealed that the Friends were gradually learning to feel differently in their professional roles—less overwhelmed, less anxious, more settled, and more effective. In this section, the focus is on interpreting how they learned to feel differently—on the internal, external, and social "work" accomplished by individuals and the group through the interwoven processes of reappraisal, recognition, and reconciliation.

Sutton (2007), reviewing work from a social-psychological perspective on the common emotions of anger and frustration experienced by teachers, describes a process of *reappraisal* over time in which additional information allows teachers to feel differently about their anger and the situations or persons that provoked it. Throughout this volume, we take the view that emotions are more than internal states; they are fluid, dynamic, and negotiated constructs that are performed, produced, and reproduced in ongoing social interactions. Taking this wider view, I attempt to demonstrate next the different aspects of the nexus of thought, action, and social interactions that led to reappraisal of some difficult emotions for the Friends.

First, a caveat is in order. In the previous sections, positive as well as negative emotions were evident among the Friends. But positive emotions, such as feeling joy and satisfaction in caring for children or appreciation of colleagues' support, do not require reappraisal. Rather simply put, the way to feel better as a new teacher is to feel more positive emotions and less negative emotions, though the latter may, of course, be very instructive. For this reason, the work described in this section concerns how the Friends learned to feel differently as they diminished their negative feelings of inadequacy, uncertainty, and generally feeling overwhelmed during this phase of their transition.

The process of reappraisal involves two related but somewhat distinct components, in my view. Reappraisal often begins (and ends in some instances) with *recognition or recognizing*. Here, I refer to the internal, more cognitive process of noticing anew, gaining new personal insight, or incorporating the alternative or balancing perspective of others. It is "re-cognizing" the feeling. For example, Andre, focusing on the relationship between curriculum planning and what then actually transpires in classroom daily life, shares with the group a sports-related metaphor of effective, responsive teaching that occurred to him as an "aha moment" one day:

ANDRE: You have this plan in mind of like, okay, we're going to run to the right side. What I'm telling you is the reflective piece is really important because you could be planning to go to the right side but the reality is that you don't know how the defense is going to react. You don't know what's going to happen on the ground and the reflective piece is what's really important. So . . . you might have these ideas in your head and you might have that anxiety in your head but the fact that you're, like in reality, you're sitting there, going, you know, this isn't right. Let me try to do *this*. Let me change *that*. Let me tweak *this*. *That's* what's really important because what's happening on the ground will end up, like, *that's* what's going to make it effective (emphases added).

Andre describes how this metaphor led him from anxiety to a vision of effectiveness. Interestingly, Andre's insight sounds much like Schön's (1983) observation that effective teachers are not just reflective, but are able to reflect quickly and naturally in the moment as they work with children—to learn the strategy of "reflection in action."

Recognition also came in the form of self-awareness of one's emotional tendencies, a critical step toward self-monitoring and modifying how one feels:

DUSTIN: One thing I wish about myself and that I've really been working hard on, but have not made a lot of progress in, is divorcing the reflectiveness and desire to improve from the feeling of anxiety. I wish I could have the one without the other . . . and that seems really hard for me.

Recognition also comes socially, when the value or legitimacy of Friends' comments or perspectives is recognized, a phenomenon that is widely evident in these conversations. Challenged by the prospect of subbing in an unknown array of classrooms, Lina "hears" Paula's balancing observation of the value of this situation, which elicits the group's (and then Lina's) agreement:

PAULA: I think you're definitely going to get a good practice of your bag of tricks.

LINA: [Laugh] Uh huh.

PAULA: You know, what works for you; how you respond on the spot to kids you don't know.

LINA: Yeah.

ANDRE: Right.

PAULA: And so, imagine when you get to know them better . . .

ANDRE: Yeah, that's true.

PAULA: How easier things will be interacting with them . . . like that. So . . .

LINA: That's definitely a positive way to look at it . . . great perspective!

Friends frequently offered insights from their particular experience in these weeks that comforted their peers and helped them to put things into a wider (and calmer) perspective.

Over these 8 weeks, the pervasive feeling of being overwhelmed diminished as the group came to embrace an ethic of manageable progress—change and improvement taken one step and one day at a time. And just the articulation of this insight seemed to be comforting to the group:

PAULA: So, I'm in the process of trying to meet the expectations that are there and be realistic about what I can do at the moment and working towards making improvements in the process. I can't change everything in one day.

A second form of reappraisal leading to more positive feelings came when members moved beyond recognition to *reconciliation*—to actions and strategies that made them feel better or more effective in their setting. Dustin describes a practical strategy to reconcile the gradual ethic of progress with his pressing desire to improve and to meet high personal standards:

DUSTIN: You know . . . Paula, what you're saying reminded me of . . . an idea that had come when I was talking to somebody else about this . . . Say, for example, I want to do a really great . . . I learned how to do really great read-alouds and I don't feel like I'm getting time, like I think I mentioned on my blogs, to even like select good books . . .

LINA: Um . . .

DUSTIN: Or let alone think about each book and think, what will kids be able to understand from this? How do I get them to the deepest understanding of it? And that's frustrating. But then I thought, okay, well, if I can't do it for everything at least I want to practice the good habit once a week. So I'm going to . . .

LINA: Yes, yeah.

DUSTIN: Be okay with doing crappy read-alouds most of the week [laugh]. But at least that one . . .

DAVID: Oh wow, you're really going to nail that one!

LINA: Yeah [laugh].

DUSTIN: And I'm really going to read a good book, reading carefully, thinking of questions, putting them on sticky notes. Put them on that book and then, like, I'll start to build good patterns slowly, albeit not as fast as I want.

DAVID: Hmm.

LINA: Yeah.

DUSTIN: And that, I think, might be a good strategy for me.

LINA: [Clapping]

DAVE: Yeah!

PAULA: Uh huh.

Next, Paula reconciles the desire to meet expectations of the school culture while improving in ways that feel true to her values and professionalism. This begins with recognition (and acceptance) of the situated meaning of lesson plans in her turnaround school, but then leads to reconciliation through her actions:

PAULA: But I don't think there's enough time for me to process learning the curriculum . . . because our goal is to work as quickly as possible to get it, the lesson plans, done by the Wednesday before the following week, so we can send it to our principal—and so that's the goal. The goal isn't really for me to process information and learn it.

Yet, knowing that planning in her experience and graduate preparation is deemed critical to intentional teaching, Paula reconciles this difference by adapting a two-part planning process:

PAULA: So this weekend was the first weekend where I really tried to sit and process from the plan that we sent to our principal and I realized, [laugh] you know, I need my own script. I need to go from this sort of summary of things to do my own way, you know, how am I going to approach my kids when I do this?

In her adaptive planning process, Paula accepts the reality that lesson planning serves the school's accountability and oversight procedures while maintaining planning as a bedrock strategy consistent with her professional ideals. This reconciliation is a "both-and" action that meets the school's expectations without defaulting to a diminished idealism.

During these first 8 weeks of professional teaching, the Critical Friends group was a place for social support, dialogue, friendship, and comfort; a place to "dump" fears and express anxiety and, in the process, to enhance feelings of collegiality and shared experience. Reappraisal within the Critical Friends group involved a collective noticing, listening, thinking, acting, and feeling in ways that brought the reality of their teaching situation and the ideals they desired to achieve as professionals into better congruence. Through reappraisal and its twin processes of recognition and reconciliation, these new teachers earned small victories and moved toward resultant feelings of control and ownership over what initially felt overwhelming to them in their first 8 weeks.

Summary and Conclusion

Given that all of teaching is "an emotional practice" (Hargreaves, 1998, p. 850), it almost goes without saying that the first weeks of professional teaching will be especially daunting and especially emotional. Today's public and legislative atmosphere of heightened accountability adds another layer of pressure, especially for teachers in urban and underfunded and/or underperforming districts—the very districts in which new graduates (generally), and our most socially committed new teachers in particular, will find their jobs.

In this chapter, the common conditions, issues, and tensions of this transition and the emotions yoked to them were described for five new early childhood teachers. Although their situations and personalities varied, all were challenged to live their professional ideals, to find enough time for work and home, to notice the joy and cope with the heartbreak of young children's situations, words, and actions, and seek and find support in their settings. All this, they brought and shared in the Critical Friends group of trusted peers and a supportive professor.

As these teachers move forward and gain experience, some conditions and emotions no doubt will endure. For example, time will always be an issue because there is always more for a teacher to work on and to do. And as Hargreaves (1997) notes:

> Teaching is a caring profession. In an endless job, this means that teachers can never quite care enough. Teachers are therefore always haunted by feelings of guilt and inadequacy. At its best, the guilt comes from endless aspiration [that] is a spur to dedicated professionalism. At its worst, it can turn altruistic enthusiasts into self-denying martyrs and cheerless workaholics.
>
> *(p. 79)*

In contrast to the extremes of this best-to-worst continuum, the present analysis suggests that when new teachers' efforts are supported by the dialogue, exchange, and support of a Critical Friends group, they can learn to feel differently and better through reappraisal and can gain a modicum of emotional control over the tumultuous and anxiety-provoking beginnings of professional teaching in urban schools. In this considerable accomplishment, perhaps they have navigated in the direction of a path that will lead them to successful future teaching and a long-term professional career as an early childhood educator.

Note

1. The author thanks the members of the Critical Friends group for their courage to teach and participation in this project. The author gratefully acknowledges the support of Wheelock College and, in particular, the support of the Gordon L. Marshall Fellows Program that made this project possible.

References

Bambino, D. (2002). Critical friends. *Educational Leadership, 59*(6): 25–27.

Copple, C., & Bredekamp, S. (2009). *Developmentally appropriate practice in early childhood programs.* Washington, D.C.: National Association for the Education of Young Children.

Danforth, S., & Smith, T. (2005). *Engaging troubling students: A constructivist approach.* Thousand Oaks, CA: Corwin Press.

Davies, A. (1989). *The human element: Three essays in political psychology.* Harmondsworth, England: Penguin.

Dunne, F., Nave, W., & Lewis, A. (2000). Critical friends groups: Teachers helping teachers to improve student learning. *Phi Delta Kappa Center for Evaluation, Development, and Research Bulletin, 28*: 1–9.

Goldstein, L. (1997). *Teaching with love: A feminist approach to early childhood education.* New York: Peter Lang.

Hargreaves, A. (1997). In conclusion: New ways to think about teachers and time. In Adelman, N., Walking Eagle, K., & Hargreaves, A. (Eds.), *Racing with the clock.* New York: Teachers College Press.

Hargreaves, A. (1998). The emotional practice of teaching. *Teaching and Teacher Education, 14*(8): 835–854.

Henke, R., Chen, X., & Geis, S. (2000). *Progress through the teacher pipeline: 1992–93 college graduate and elementary/secondary school teaching as of 1997* (Statistical Analysis Report). Washington, D.C.: National Center for Education Statistics.

Kochan, F., & Trimble, S. (2000). From mentoring to co-mentoring: Establishing collaborative relationships. *Theory into Practice, 39*(1): 20–28.

Madrid, S., & Dunn-Kenney, M. (2010). Persecutory guilt, surveillance and resistance: The emotional themes of early childhood educators. *Contemporary Issues in Early Childhood, 11*(4): 392–401.

Madrid, S., Baldwin, N., & Frye, E. (2013). "Professional feeling": One early childhood educator's emotional discomfort as a teacher and learner. *Journal of Early Childhood Research, 11*(3): 274–291.

National Commission on Teaching and America's Future. (2003). *No dream denied: A pledge to America's Children.* Washington, D.C.

The New Teacher Project (2013). *LEAP year: Assessing and supporting effective first year teachers.* NY: The New Teacher Project.

Schön, D. (1983). *The reflective practitioner: How professionals think in action.* NY: Basic Books.

Sutton, R. (2007). Teachers' anger, frustration, and self-regulation. In P. Schutz (Ed.), *Emotion in education* (pp. 259–284), Burlington, MA: Academic Press.

Whitebrook, M., Bellm, D., & Schaack, D. (2013). *Supporting teachers as learners: A guide for mentors and coaches in early care and education.* Washington, D.C.: American Federation of Teachers Education Foundation.

COMMENTARY

Barbara Seidl

UNIVERSITY OF COLORADO, DENVER

David Fernie's study examining new teachers' emotional lives during their first months on the job highlights the importance of providing support for new teachers as they enter what is often a highly anticipated, but extremely pressurized and stressful position. As a teacher educator whose work has been concerned with the preparation of teachers for over 20 years, I have often marveled at the degree to which people are willing to ignore the relational and emotional quality of teaching. Think about or remember (if you've ever been a teacher) or imagine (if you have not) being in an intimate relationship with 20 or 30 children, sharing their ups and downs, their very different hopes and dreams, strengths and needs, likes and dislikes while simultaneously trying to get them all moving in the same direction toward mandated learning outcomes. Add to that beautiful mix substantial and increasing pressure to produce higher test scores and blame and public humiliation when this does not happen. Few other professions exist within such an emotionally charged domain.

It should be obvious that a new teacher's emotional responses to the pressures, demands, and joys of their work are worth attention, yet this is often not the case. As Fernie points out, an absence of concern and support for how new teachers are processing the emotions they experience during this time leaves many vulnerable to less-than-positive shifts—from reverting back to transmission models of curriculum to blaming children and families for the angst, frustration, and lack of effectiveness that they feel, which is a normal and common experience during this time.

My response to Fernie's chapter is situated within my own commitment to building upon the positive emotions of care and love that drive many people into teaching (Bullough Jr. & Young, 2002) and that I see as strengths, as well as my ongoing desire to create caring environments that support the continued growth and well-being of teachers. Toward these ends, I take up two points in relationship to Fernie's work. I first discuss the recent return of the language of emotions in the larger social and scientific research communities and the impact of emotion and emotional intelligence on a teacher's health, well-being, tenacity, and effectiveness. I then briefly identify the manner in which the Critical Friends space that Fernie created supported these teachers' emotional intelligence in ways that can ultimately lead to greater pedagogical effectiveness and longevity.

A recent emphasis on the role of emotions in the health of the body and mind in areas such as neuroscience and psychology (Fredrickson, 2013, Fredrickson, Cohn, Coffey, Pek, & Finkel, 2008; Heaphy & Dutton, 2008; Kok, Coffey, Cohn, Catalino, Vacharkulksemusuk, Algoe, & Fredrickson, 2013) has brought renewed legitimacy to the language of emotions in the conversation around education, teaching, and learning. It is now well understood that positive emotions such as joy and love, especially love, have extensive physical and psychological benefits (Fredrickson, 2013) and, conversely, negative emotions and the accompanying stress are toxic to the mind and body. In fact, "although it is known that long-term or chronic stress can affect the brain's learning and memory region, a new finding discovers short-term stress, lasting as little as a few hours, can also impair brain-cell communication in these critical areas" (Chen, Dubé, Rice, & Baram, 2008). The fact that the brain's emotional and executive areas are interconnected (Goleman, 2008) means that when teachers are under stress, even for short periods, their ability to make decisions, plan, and organize their work is compromised. The teachers in Fernie's study communicated this relationship between negative emotions, stress, and feeling overwhelmed. In their experiences of surveillance in turnaround schools and as they wrestled with inappropriate curricular mandates, diverse relational demands, and too little time, they experienced exhaustion and an inability, as one participant put it, to establish the structures and goals that they knew were important.

At the same time that the language of emotions has made its way into mainstream and scholarly conversations, the idea of emotional intelligence (EI) has also become popular as a framework to explain positive outcomes in connection to the abilities to recognize, process, regulate, and leverage emotional information in order to promote emotional and intellectual growth (Mayer, Roberts, & Barsade, 2008). Although there are numerous models, EI in general is characterized by self-awareness, self-management, social awareness, relationship skills, and decision making associated with the well-being of self and others (Goleman, 2005). The more capable a person is of understanding, expressing, and regulating their emotions, the more likely they are to be healthy and productive, experience positive relationships (Ciarrochi, Chan, & Bajgar, 2001), and avoid burnout in high-stress environments (Görgens-Ekermans & Brand, 2012). Perhaps most importantly, individuals with high EI have a level of self-awareness that allows them to interrupt and challenge negative thoughts that lead to negative emotions in order to reassign productive meaning to emotional experience (Feldman & Mulle, 2007).

Teachers like those in Fernie's study often have well-developed emotional intelligence in the contexts in which they are familiar and have experience. However, as we see with this group, the predictable negative emotions, such as guilt for not living up to their ideal, sadness over circumstances their children face, anger at the system, or fear of failure, create a context for stress that begins to challenge their psychological and emotional well-being. Short-term and chronic negative emotions can begin to generate a recurring cycle of negative thoughts and emotions: As Lantieri (2009) puts it, "Distress kills learning, creating a downward spiral of one stress reaction after another" (p. 12). Left unchecked, these stressful emotions can begin to overwhelm EI (Gohm, Corser, & Dalsky, 2005), interfere with their ability to learn, and become the reason that many new teachers leave the field in the first years of their careers.

How do we support teachers' EI as they encounter these predictable challenging experiences and emotions? How do we help them manage and reduce the stress that threatens their ability to grow as teachers? All too often, new teachers are required to go through this turbulent time alone when research demonstrates that the opposite is needed. Environments found to be linked to stress reduction and increased EI are characterized by support and trust and are those in which positive emotions and positive social connections are leveraged (Kok, et. al. 2013; Lantieri & Nambiar, 2012). In addition, given that feelings or emotions follow beliefs and perceptions, such environments provide support for assessing and/or reassessing interpretations of experience and emotion and reassigning meanings that lead to a greater sense of agency and efficacy (Feldman & Mulle, 2007). In short, positive connections that "broaden and build" psychological and emotional health (Fredrickson, 2013) and support for interrupting and reframing the negative thought–emotion cycle are important for shoring up EI under stressful circumstances.

The Critical Friends group that Fernie established with these new teachers provided a space that supported the conditions described earlier. Within the group, participants with a shared, positive experience co-created a space of trust and mutual support as they worked together to frame and reframe their emotions and challenges, or as Fernie maintains, reappraise and learn to feel differently about what they were experiencing. Evidence that Fernie provides in his analysis indicates that, over time, they drew upon their emotional intelligence to self-assess, identify and regulate their emotions, read the social context of their work place, and reframe their challenges to gain control over their emotions and their work.

In conclusion, in an era in which the teaching profession "greens" with the increased retirement of veterans (Ingersoll, 2012) and as we move to stem the loss of new teachers, it is important for the field to understand that the need for emotional support is perhaps as critical as the need for pedagogical support. Fernie's findings demonstrate a straightforward and highly achievable approach to this critical need in the extension of an already established, trusting, and positive community of support and begs the question of the degree and nature of partnership between university and district during the first years of teaching.

References

Bullough, R. Jr., & Young, J. (2002). Learning to teach as an intern: The emotions and the self. *Teacher Development, 6*(3): 417–431.

Chen, Y., Dubé, C. M., Rice, C., & Baram, T. (2008). Rapid loss of dendritic spines after stress involves derangement of spine dynamics by corticotropin-releasing hormone. *The Journal of Neuroscience, 28*(11): 2903–2911.

Ciarrochi, J., Chan, A., & Bajgar, J. (2001). Measuring emotional intelligence in adolescents. *Personality and Individual Differences, 31*(7): 1105–1119.

Feldman, J., & Mulle, K. (2007). *Putting emotional intelligence to work.* Danvers, MA: American Society for Training and Development Press.

Fredrickson, B. L. (2013). *Love 2.0: How our supreme emotion affects everything we feel, think, do, and become.* NY: Hudson Press.

Fredrickson, B. L., Cohn, M. A., Coffey, K. A., Pek, J., & Finkel, S. (2008). Open hearts build lives: Positive emotions, induced through loving-kindness meditation, build consequential personal resources. *Journal of Personality and Social Psychology, 95*(5): 1045–1062.

Gohm, C. L., Corser, G. C., & Dalsky, D. J. (2005). Emotional intelligence under stress: Useful, unnecessary, or irrelevant? *Personality and Individual Differences, 39*(6): 1017–1028.

Goleman, D. (2005). *Emotional intelligence: Why it can matter more than IQ.* NY: Bantam Books.

Goleman, D. (2008). Introduction. In L. Lantieri (Ed.), *Building emotional intelligence. Techniques for cultivating inner strength in children* (pp. 1–4). Boulder, CO: Sounds True.

Görgens-Ekermans, G., & Brand, T. (2012). Emotional intelligence as a moderator in the stress-burnout relationship: A questionnaire study on nurses. *Journal of Clinical Nursing, 21*(15–16): 2275–2285.

Heaphy, E. D., & Dutton, J. E. (2008). Positive social interactions and the human body at work: Linking organizations and physiology. *Academy of Management Review, 33*(12): 137–162.

Ingersoll, R. M. (2012). Beginning teacher induction: What the data tells us. *Kappan, 93*(8): 47–51.

Kok, B. E., Coffey, K. A., Cohn, M. A., Catalino, L. I., Vacharkulksemusuk, T., Algoe, S., & Fredrickson, B. L. (2013). How positive emotions build physical health: Perceived positive social connections account for upward spiral between positive emotions and vagal tone. *Psychological Science, 24*(7): 1123–1132.

Lantieri, L. (2009, Spring). Social emotional intelligence: Cultivating children's hearts and spirits. *Lilipoh, 14*: 11–15.

Lantieri, L., & Nambiar, M. (2012). Cultivating the social, emotional, and inner lives of children and teachers. *Reclaiming Children and Youth, 21*(2): 27–33.

Mayer, J. D., Roberts, R. D., & Barsade, S. G. (2008). Human abilities: Emotional intelligence. *Annual Review of Psychology, 59*: 507–536.

9

EMOTIONAL INTERSECTIONS IN EARLY CHILDHOOD LEADERSHIP

Nikki Baldwin

UNIVERSITY OF WYOMING EARLY CARE AND EDUCATION CENTER

> "I don't have the luxury of losing it. I have to be the one who keeps it together."
> —*Emma, childcare center director*

What does this quote reveal about an educational leader's understanding of the role of emotion in her work? Is the expression of emotion a "luxury" that directors must not indulge in? If this is the case, how has it come to be so? Recently, Jill, another female director of an early childhood program, echoed Emma's feelings:

> It's so much worse if *we* unravel . . . It seems like a teacher is allowed to have a moment, allowed to come in here and raise their voice and cry and just be all frustrated. But we have to recognize our power. It's really almost like we're not allowed to. When you're in a position of power, you can't really do that.

Jill's reference to the expression of emotion as "unraveling"—something that directors aren't "allowed" to do because of their position of power—echoes Emma's understanding of the expression of emotion as a demonstration of a director's loss of control, or "losing it," and as something that must be regulated by those in leadership positions. This chapter seeks to understand more about how this plays out in the lives of three early childhood administrators.

The view of emotion as something that must be controlled if you are in a position of power is a consistent theme in early childhood administrators' understanding of the role of emotion in their work. As an early childhood administrator, having directed programs for the last 15 years, I navigate this debate on emotion every day; in many instances, I have found myself arriving at the same conclusion as both Emma and Jill about the place of emotion in my own work. Yet, I have been troubled by what has felt like a double standard for my behavior. I focus on supporting teachers in their work in a very emotion-laden profession, yet I don't allow myself to "lose it" or "unravel."

On one particularly stressful day recently in my center, I chose not to restrain my emotion in an interaction with a teacher. What followed was initially a cathartic experience for me: Letting go and expressing emotions I had been feeling for months provided an incredible sense of freedom and release. However, the resulting care and effort it took to attempt to repair the relationship with this teacher due to my lack of restraint made it clear to me, once again, that the tension between the expression of emotion and the need to control emotion in leadership is very real and extremely complex.

The work of Erving Goffman (1959) and Arlie Hochschild (1975) has offered me insight into the pressure I feel to control my emotion at work in order to maintain a certain sense of order and harmony. Goffman offered a theory of people as social actors who perform in front of others in order to present an idealized version of themselves, particularly in the workplace. In doing so, he argued, we conceal certain things about ourselves that do not fit with this ideal. Goffman also noted a similar pattern in group or team performance in which people play particular parts in order to maintain a desirable impression of the team. In my performance as director, I am expected to behave and express emotions in particular ways. I am also responsible for directing the performance of my staff in order to make a positive impression on others.

Arlie Hochschild (1975) extended the notion of social performance to include emotion, arguing that people are not only motivated to *act* in certain ways to maintain a particular impression, but they also try to *feel* certain things they are expected to feel. This "emotional labor" is something that researchers have studied in teachers who are often expected to have "maternal emotions" such as gentleness, love, and care for the children in their classrooms (Colley, 2006; Goldstein, 1997; Madrid, Baldwin, & Frye, 2013; Noddings, 1984; Shields, 2002).

As a result of my exploration of Goffman and Hochschild, I have come to recognize the tension I sometimes feel about my expression of emotion at work and my own attempts, sometimes successful, sometimes not, at performing emotional labor in order to act the part of the good educational leader. I can identify moments in which I act in ways I am expected to act, regardless of how I am feeling. I also can identify moments in which I find myself working to *feel* the things a "good leader" should feel.

My insight about the emotional labor I perform, however, only addresses one aspect of the way emotion affects my work. In my personal reflections, it also has become clear that it is not possible to "remove" emotion from my work. Rather, emotion permeates everything I do. I also believe that my emotion is more than simply acting, or trying to feel in certain ways. How I feel at work, and what I do in response, is much more complex. In my efforts to better understand what it means to be a good leader and to recognize the part my emotion plays in my work,

I have had many conversations with fellow administrators over the last 5 years. Most recently, my interest in emotion and leadership has also led me as a doctoral student at the University of Wyoming to complete my own research on the topic.

As I have sought to better understand research on emotion and educational leadership, I have found two revealing trends in the literature. The first trend relates to social research, which studies emotion as a social construction played out in public as individuals interact, influence, and are influenced by one another and by the cultural context in which they reside (Beatty, 2000; Hargreaves, 2000, 2001; Hochschild, 1983; Jaggar, 1989). I have found that the ways *teachers* socially construct emotion in schools is receiving significant attention in the literature (Colley, 2006; Goldstein, 1997; Hargreaves, 2000, 2001; Madrid, Baldwin, & Frye, 2013; Madrid & Dunn-Kenney, 2010; Meyer, 2009; Nias, 1996; Shields, 2002; Tsang, 2011; Tucker, 2010; Zembylas, 2003a, 2003b, 2004, 2005a, 2005b). The construction of emotion for *educational leaders,* however, has received notably less attention (Beatty, 2000, 2001; Beatty & Brew, 2004, 2011; Crawford, 2009, 2011; Hargreaves, 2004; Johnson III, Aiken, & Steggerda, 2005; Stamopoulos, 2012). Although few studies have focused on the emotional experience of K–12 school leaders (Beatty, 2000; Blackmore 1989; Grogan & Shakeshaft 2011; Zorn & Boler, 2007), even fewer have focused on leaders in early childhood. The result has been that "research on early childhood leadership remains sparse and inadequately theorized, while the voice of the early childhood profession remains marginalized" (Stamopoulos, 2012, p. 1).

A second trend in the literature is that the absence of research on the social construction of emotion for education leaders appears to exist because most research on emotion and educational leadership focuses instead on the use of emotion as a management tool or a leadership competency. There is no shortage of literature on ways that educational leaders can use teacher emotion as a tool to increase job satisfaction and morale; decrease teacher stress, anxiety, and burnout; increase teachers' feelings of self-efficacy, commitment, and engagement; and motivate teachers to improve their practice (Foster & St. Hilaire, 2004; Hargreaves, 2004; Leithwood & Beatty, 2008; Moore, 2009).

In addition, research has focused on educational leaders' attainment of *emotional competency,* which is viewed as an essential skill that all successful leaders possess. The rise of the theory of "emotional intelligence" (Goleman, 1995) has led to identifying the ability to manage emotion as a "leadership attribute" (Beatty & Brew, 2004; Johnson III, Aiken, & Steggerda, 2005; Moore, 2009). Researchers have identified competency domains (Johnson III, Aiken, & Steggerda, 2005) related to a leader's emotional "constellation of understandings, skills, and strategies" (Bocchino, 1999, p. 11). Emotion, through this research lens, is something that skillful leaders are able to manage and control as they work with teachers in schools.

What is clearly missing in the literature is a coherent theory of how emotion constructs and is constructed by the daily experiences of early childhood leaders. The field of early childhood offers great potential for the study of emotion in education because of its unique position as an outsider in the U.S. education system. Early childhood education is different from K–12 education in that it has received inconsistent attention from policy makers historically in both funding and regulation (Clark, 2010; Elkind, 1987, 2009; Kamerman, 2007; Kanter, 2013; Lascarides & Hinitz, 2000; Mitchell, 2009; Swadener, 1995). It also emerged from a very different theoretical and pedagogical foundation than the K–12 public school system (Bredekamp, 1987; Koedel & Techapaisarnjaroenkit, 2012; Elkind, 1987, 2009; Lazerson, 1972; Zigler & Styfco, 2004, 2010). This history of difference has resulted in the creation of a wide variety of early childhood programs serving distinctly different purposes, funded with very little uniformity across the country. Although attention to early childhood education has increased in recent years, there has been little consistency in the application of resources among states, counties, and cities (Early Childhood Data Collaborative, 2013). Because early childhood education programs vary so widely depending on location, early childhood leaders' experiences within programs also differ. This provides a rich opportunity for research on the construction of emotion.

My goal as a researcher was to study the construction of emotion for three directors from diverse early childhood programs in my area, the Rocky Mountain region of the United States. I selected participants leading very different programs with unique organizational structures, funding mechanisms, and goals. They also had differing levels of experience and had taken distinctly different professional journeys that led to their current administrative positions. The uniqueness of each leader's story provides an excellent opportunity to study the ways different contexts and different experiences interact to construct emotion. A brief introduction to the three participants in my study follows.

Carolyn

Carolyn is a female executive director of an agency that covers two rural counties in the mountain West, with the purpose of serving children with disabilities and children in Head Start in free-inclusive, part-day preschool classrooms. In addition, the agency provides special education and related services to infants and toddlers in their home environments. This agency covers communities within a roughly 300-mile radius, employs 95 staff in six centers, serves 468 children ages 3–5, and 63 children birth–3. This nonprofit agency is accredited by the National Association for the Education of Young Children (NAEYC) and is responsible to a board of directors and a policy council with representatives from each of the six communities it serves. It also uses a "braided funding" system that blends funding from the Department of Health, Head Start, the State Department of Education, Medicaid, the local United Way, and the two counties it serves. Carolyn has worked for this particular agency since 1989, and has been the executive director for the last 10 years.

Jill

Jill is a female co-director of a high-profile, private, for-profit early childhood program that has received national and international attention for its pedagogy and progressive teaching practices. It is licensed by the state, but has intentionally chosen not to seek NAEYC accreditation, instead aligning itself with other programs that are challenging traditional approaches to teaching young children. Jill is not only co-director of the program responsible for mentoring teachers, but also is a sought-after presenter and consultant who travels frequently in that capacity. Her program is housed in a single building, serves 200 children birth–5 years, and employs 50 staff. Jill has been an employee of the program since 1993 and has been in program administration for most of that time.

Emma

Emma is a female director of a nonprofit, campus-based early childhood program that is part of a statewide community college system. This program serves children of faculty, staff, and students associated with the community college and children of military families from the area. It is housed on campus and is a practicum location for college students taking courses in early childhood education. The program employs 43 staff, serves 90 children, and is accredited by NAEYC. It is funded through parent tuition, a national campus program's grant, special funding for military families, and some additional private donations. Emma had been program director for 1 year at the beginning of the study. She had previously worked in the program for 9 years, and had spent 5 months as assistant director before her promotion to director.

Findings

Although my encounters with social constructionist theories of emotion, influenced by Goffman and Hochschild, led to my initial interest in this study, my findings after months of work with each participant led to a search for other interpretive answers and new ways to represent the complexity of the construction of emotion I was witnessing in the lives of Carolyn, Jill, and Emma.

Conflicting Professional Identity

One finding, for instance, with all three participants was that their professional identities, or the ways they understood themselves as leaders, strongly influenced their construction of emotion. In fact, for Carolyn, Jill, and Emma, tension between what they considered important parts of their identity resulted in emotional responses during the study. The experience of Carolyn, the director of a large disabilities and Head Start program covering two counties, offers an excellent demonstration of this tension at work.

Carolyn believed that an important part of her role as director was maintenance of program funding and accreditation—what she referred to as her "bureaucrat" identity. She also believed strongly that the best way to lead was to be a good listener and put the needs of her staff first—what she referred to as her desire to be an "approachable boss." These two pieces of her identity, the "bureaucrat" and the "approachable boss," collided at one point during the study as she had a deadline to meet during a time when her staff was in need of a great deal of support. She described the conflict:

> All of our grants are due in March and April so this is the time of year that I need to be task-specific and yet I end up working at night and on weekends almost every single night and weekend because the staff is needier.

The "neediness" of the staff was impacting the work Carolyn was able to accomplish during the workday, resulting in an emotional response. Carolyn's choice of her identity as an "approachable boss" over her identity as a "bureaucrat," and the resulting stress on her personal life, was a consistent thread during the study. On one occasion, Carolyn expressed feelings of anger and resentment following a weekend when she was unable to spend the time she wanted with her college-age daughter who was home for a visit. She stated:

> The Head Start grant is due and my daughter was home and I was really angry at the thought of having to work when she was home . . . I still didn't get everything done that I needed to get done, so [I'm] kind of resentful actually.

Although the choice to be the "approachable boss" took an emotional and physical toll, Carolyn continued to choose this part of her identity. At the end of one particularly long week, she concluded:

> I was worn out at the end of the week, but when you look at my time sheet and I've put in twelve and a half hours on Tuesday and Wednesday because I didn't get anything done that I wanted to get done at work. I mean that's why I get worn out.

Carolyn's feelings of anger, resentment, and even exhaustion during the study were more than simply her reaction to a needy staff and paperwork deadlines. They offered a lens with which to examine her identity in conflict. Two important pieces of her identity were made clearer through Carolyn's emotion, the "bureaucrat" and "approachable boss." This finding is in concert with the work of Michalinos Zembylas (2003b), who argues that as emotion is enacted both privately and publicly, this interaction is the location of identity development. Zembylas also deconstructs the notion of identity as not simply an individual's objective interpretation of his or her experiences that develops into a static and finished conception of the self. Rather subjectively, through the practice of emotion, both publicly and privately, the self is "continuously reconstituted" (p. 114). In other words, our identities are constantly changing. Importantly, Zembylas also argues that identity "is fractured, multiple, contradictory, contextual, and regulated by social norms" (p. 113). The tensions within Carolyn's identity, and the choices she made to resolve it, fit well within this description.

Context as a Constructing Force

Another finding in the study was that historical discourses that created each program's unique identity, or the local micro-context, greatly influenced participants' construction of emotion. Jill, for instance, spent much of her time during the study reflecting on the effectiveness of her leadership approach in a school that openly resists traditional trends in early childhood. The school's intentional construction of itself as different from traditional early childhood programs is an important part of its history. The process of change it underwent, from traditional approaches to a more progressive philosophy, is a story often told to visitors in order to demonstrate the program's unique identity.

One feature of Jill's school that influenced her emotion during the study was the creation of a climate of critique and competition as a tool to promote individual teacher and program growth. The most significant representation of this approach is found in the school's yearly hiring process. Traditional methods of hiring allow teachers to rely on a continued contract as long as they have met expectations and passed reviews. Jill's school challenged this approach and created a system in which all teachers participate in a competitive reapplication process each spring. Because of the high-profile status of the program, there is great interest in obtaining teaching positions, resulting in more applicants than openings every year. Jill described how the process impacts some teachers:

> I think it's a good thing, but it's maybe a little bit more unusual that we have far more qualified teachers who want positions than we have positions for. And so, you know, that's unsettling for people because they're worried that at some point they may not have a job. And part of the problem is, sometimes people that aren't offered jobs, it's not that they did anything wrong. You know like somebody that is not offered a job they'll say to their colleagues "My review was great," and I'm like, "Well they did a really good job, but it's in comparison to everybody else."

On several occasions, Jill shared her struggle to decide how to best support teacher growth within this competitive climate. When describing a teacher who had performed well but did not receive a contract, Jill expressed feelings of uncertainty as she reflected on how honest she should or should not have been in her feedback as she mentored this teacher:

> We just had a teacher who we didn't hire. She was at the top of the list of the people who didn't get jobs for the fall and she probably would have made the cut except for that she has a shyer personality. But so we try to, we found ways to tell her, but the more we really struggle is like, I never said like, "you're probably not going to get a position because you're too quiet or you're not dressing professionally enough." Sometimes just, I have such a hard time with that. I don't know if it will be too hard for her to hear those words or if it would have helped her to be sort of more blunt.

Jill's questions about how to best mentor teachers while also preparing them for the hiring process were a consistent thread throughout the study. On another occasion, she commented:

> This is something that is an ongoing struggle for me because a large portion of my role is to support the teachers and I do understand that not everyone's in the same place at the same time and so I need to meet them where they are. But then also I'm responsible for ensuring quality experiences for all the children that go to our school and so then at what point do I say it doesn't matter that you are on this journey, it's still not quality enough for the children. They're sort of . . . they're opposing things.

Jill made choices throughout the study in response to this tension between her mentoring style and her program's unique identity. One tool she used to navigate this emotional intersection was her reliance on her belief in her program's high standards. She said:

> This is kind of a hard thing for us because I think in our field we are always focusing on support. But then I do think that at a certain point we don't have a problem saying somebody's not smart enough to be a doctor. Can we say somebody's not smart enough to be a teacher?

As Jill continued to question the effectiveness of her mentoring approach, she frequently mentioned her school's success as a way to measure her success as a leader. On one occasion, she reflected, "The fact is that every year we still have more qualified people that want to work here than we have jobs. Can't that be also a way to rate what we're creating in the school? That's unheard of for preschool, you know?"

Jill's emotion throughout the study, particularly as she reflected on her work with teachers, was greatly influenced by her school's competitive hiring process, which was both created and embedded within the school's unique history and culture. Although Jill wholeheartedly believed in it, she spent much of her time questioning how to successfully do her job within this structure. In the end, she made choices to use her school's visibility and renown as the ultimate tool in evaluating her success. In this scenario, Jill's emotion provided a lens with which to examine her program's history and culture. The school's choice to resist traditional approaches in both teaching and leadership also provides an opportunity to examine the larger context of early childhood education in the United States. Jill's emotion was powerfully constructed by context—the micro-context of her own program, and the macro-context of early childhood education in the United States.

These findings support the work of Megan Boler (1999) who called for "foregrounding" historically constructed relations of power, values, and ideologies in research on emotion. Boler saw these historical discourses as powerful influences on our construction of emotion, forces that are rarely attended to in research on the topic. The micro- and macro-contexts that influenced Jill's emotion during the study have been historically constructed within relations of power and resistance. The identity of her school, in fact, represents conscious resistance to powerful discourses of early childhood education embodied in the creation and dominance of NAEYC. In this study, historical relations of power and resistance were forces that acted to construct emotion for Jill, Carolyn, and Emma as they acted within this social, cultural, and historical context on both the local, or micro-level, and the societal, or macro-level.

Emotion as a Tool for Reflection and Change

A third finding in the study was that as Carolyn, Jill, and Emma reflected on their emotion during interviews, they began to think critically about what their emotions were teaching them about themselves and their work. This act of critical reflection often resulted in change, most noticeably in Emma, a new director searching to define herself as a leader. At the beginning of the study, Emma described what she saw as her responsibility as a new director working to make changes in her program:

> For a very long time we had a very poor reputation on campus of having difficult teachers and having a negative atmosphere. So you know not only am I trying to support teachers, I'm trying to support a change in culture and our building that is emotionally okay for everyone.

Emma's use of the word "support" is significant, because it demonstrates how she approached enacting this change in culture. In her view, her job as a leader was to "support" teachers and "support" change, all while making sure her decisions were "emotionally okay for everyone."

Later in the study, a situation in which Emma had to discipline a teacher due to inadequate supervision of children resulted in feelings of frustration. As she reflected on her feelings, Emma began asking questions. She shared her initial response:

> I mean this week I think I had a lot of uncertainty about, "Wow, am I really cut out for this job?" Not because I don't think I can do it, but because it's that question of, "Do I want to do this? Is this what I want my life's work to be?" I don't know.

Emma used her emotional response to the discipline situation to question her work, her motives, and the direction she wanted to take in her career. She did not doubt her ability to do the job, but was uncertain about whether being a director was something she really wanted to do. She had achieved a professional milestone with her promotion, but after having spent a year dealing with situations like the supervision incident, she was asking herself, "Do I want to do this?" Later, she shared her response to her feelings of uncertainty. She took action in several ways:

> After my rough week I've done lots of thinking and reading and trying to find some resources, and have been really . . . I think as far as emotions go, really trying to figure out what do I want to do "big picture," and where am I going? And then how do I bring everybody with me? So I think that's been a little emotionally exhausting lately.

In response to her emotion, Emma looked for answers in literature on leadership and critically reflected on her struggles and her decisions and how they impacted her teachers and her center. She reflected on her identity as a leader, seeking to find her direction—"Where am I going?"—and then defined how she intended to approach leading others—"How do I bring everybody with me?"

As a result of her study and reflection, Emma's understanding of her identity as a leader began to shift. She evaluated what her emotional responses to situations revealed about her and her work, and then actively challenged her thinking, looking for new ways to respond. She stated:

> I realized [that] I have this, almost being motivated by fear sometimes. That my decision making is motivated by fear, and that is the worst place to be operating from. Fear of repercussions, fear of people being unhappy and leaving our program, fear of being the bad guy, fear of making a mistake, or you know, fear of not knowing everything.

In Emma's perspective, making decisions motivated by fear was "the worst place to be operating from," so she consciously chose to reframe her emotions. Emma described her new approach:

> I feel like I have made a move from being scared to do the right thing to feeling more confident in my ability to make decisions. This has been so

refreshing because I no longer have to contemplate everything. I have been addressing issues head-on as soon as they happen and I have realized that it is so much better to be in the thick of the problem, actively dealing with it rather than imagining all the possibilities of how I could handle it and how everyone may react . . . definitely a change that has been so beneficial for me.

Emma equated her fear with inaction. She no longer wanted to spend her time "contemplat[ing] everything" and "imagining all the possibilities." Instead, she chose to approach challenges such as the supervision incident in a new way. She used two phrases that demonstrate her newfound intent to take action: First, that she was now "addressing issues head on"; and second, that she wanted to "be in the thick of the problem, actively dealing with it." This "head-on," "thick of the problem" approach was, in her mind, the opposite of her previous fear-induced response of "imagining all the possibilities of how I could handle it and how everyone may react."

On one occasion, Emma used another interesting phrase to describe the way she felt in her previous experiences when struggling with frustration and fear. She described feeling "bogged down." She explained:

> Some of the stuff that I get bogged down in decision making is the emo-tion of it. And I imagine, you know, why is this happening? Or how could I really help them? And it turns into this . . . that I'm really trying to please everyone and I'm trying to make sure that everybody's okay and find all of these win-win solutions for everyone. And I think in recognizing that there are always going to be challenges . . . that when there are challenges it's not a representation of our program necessarily, or how I'm doing as a leader. That sometimes decisions just have to be made.

This quote reflects a distinct change in Emma's approach to leadership from her comments at the beginning of the study. She initially talked about her need to "support" her program and "make sure everybody's okay." Now she argued that she no longer felt the need to "please everyone," and she argued "when there are challenges it's not a representation of our program necessarily, or how I'm doing as a leader." Emma demonstrated a new acceptance that challenges are to be expected rather than feared and a new confidence that "sometimes decisions just have to be made." Emma's conscious choice to change her thinking and feelings about her work as a result of her reflections on her emotion reveals how powerfully emotion can inform a director's work and impact not only her sense of identity, but also her program and the teachers she works with. This conception of emotion as a tool to access individual agency, or our ability to make choices, is supported by Zembylas (2003b), who argued that agency is present in how we choose to understand our emotions, in the ways our understanding is expressed, and in the choices we make in response.

Emotional Intersections

As the three key findings in this study suggest, emotion is extremely complex and constructed by a number of factors that all intersect in sometimes unpredictable ways. Our identity or continually changing understanding of ourselves is a force clearly present in the construction of emotion. It is also a force, as demonstrated in this study, changed by emotion and our response to it. Historically constructed discourses of power and resistance, embedded in our local context and our society, also act as forces that construct emotion. Other people, with whom we interact every day, with their own changing, contradictory, and multifaceted identities, undoubtedly also act as a force in the construction of emotion. I have come to understand emotion as the result of the intersection of each of these forces. The image of an intersection allows for the messiness that is clearly present as these forces exert different levels of influence in any given moment to construct emotion.

As early childhood leaders go about our daily work, we construct emotion as a result of all that we encounter and the choices we make in response. This influences how we understand ourselves as leaders, which, in turn, impacts how future encounters and emotions are enacted. This continual cycle of construction, enactment, and reconstruction of emotion is as much a real and tangible part of my experience as any of the responsibilities in my official job description. Yet, this process often goes unnoticed as I move from task to task during a busy workweek. Although many early childhood leaders encourage the practice of critical reflection in their teachers (Madrid, Baldwin, & Frye 2013), our own emotion is something that we may feel we don't have time to reflect on (at best), or is something that we believe we must repress (at worst).

The emotional labor early childhood leaders must perform in order to keep emotion underground results in stress and high instances of burnout, and undoubtedly makes us less effective leaders. However, a different alternative in response to our emotion has yet to be offered. New research supports the need for early childhood teachers to have opportunities to reflect on their emotional experiences (Beatty, 2000; Boler, 1997; Fernie, this volume; Krum and Geddes, 2000; Madrid, Baldwin, & Fry, 2013; Tsang, 2011; Winograd, 2003; Zembylas, 2005a, 2005b), yet their leaders are not being afforded the same opportunity. One result of this double standard is that leaders are emotionally marginalized, constructed as emotional outsiders within our own programs. If this is the case, then we are experiencing marginalization not only institutionally, by working in a field with outsider status, but also as individuals leading others within this field.

The most powerful finding in this study is the potential for me and other early childhood leaders to use emotional intersections to inform our work every day. Each story demonstrates what can be understood when an effort is made to examine how our emotion is constructed. If we take time to reflect on our emotion, looking for potential insight into historical discourses in society and our programs and our identity as well as the identity of others, it has the potential to powerfully enhance our understanding of each force. Identifying and examining emotional intersections also allow us to turn the critical lens on ourselves by revealing the choices we are already making and the potential to make different choices for our good, the good of our teachers, and the programs we lead.

References

Beatty, B. R. (2000). The emotions of educational leadership: Breaking the silence. *International Journal of Leadership in Education, 3*(4): 331–357.

Beatty, B. R. (2011). Leadership and teacher emotion. In C. Day & J. C.-K. Lee (Eds.), *New understandings of teacher's work: Emotions and educational change* (pp. 217–242). New York: Springer.

Beatty, B. R., & Brew, C. R. (2004). Trusting relationships and emotional epistemologies: A foundational leadership issue. *School Leadership & Management, 24*(3): 329–356.

Blackmore, J. (1989). Educational leadership: A feminist critique and reconstruction. In J. Smyth (Ed.), *Critical perspectives on educational leadership* (pp. 63–87). New York: RoutledgeFalmer.

Bocchino, R. (1999). *Emotional literacy: To be a different kind of smart.* Thousand Oaks, CA: Corwin Press.

Boler, M. (1997). Disciplined emotions: Philosophies of educated feelings. *Educational Theory, 47*(2): 203–227.

Boler, M. (1999). *Feeling power: Emotions and education.* New York: Routledge.

Bredekamp, S. (1987). *Developmentally appropriate practice in early childhood programs serving children from birth through age 8, expanded edition.* Washington, D.C.: NAEYC.

Clark, J. (2010). The origins of childhood. In D. Kassem, L. Murphy, & E. Taylor (Eds.), *Key issues in childhood and youth studies* (pp. 3–13). New York: Routledge.

Colley, H. (2006). Learning to labour with feeling: Class, gender, and emotion in childcare education and training. *Contemporary Issues in Early Childhood, 7*(1): 15–29.

Crawford, M. (2009). Getting to the heart of leadership: Emotion and educational leadership. London: Sage.

Crawford, M. (2011). Rationality and emotion in education leadership—enhancing our understanding. In C. Day & J. C.-K. Lee (Eds.), *New understandings of teacher's work: Emotions and educational change* (pp. 217–242). New York: Springer.

Early Childhood Data Collaborative. (2013). Retrieved from www.ecedata.org/

Elkind, D. (1987). *Miseducation: Preschoolers at risk.* New York: Alfred A. Knopf.

Elkind, D. (2009). History. In *The wisdom of play: How children learn to make sense of the world.* New York: Community Products.

Foster, R., & St. Hilaire, B. (2004). The who, how, why, and what of leadership in secondary school improvement: Lessons learned in England. *Alberta Journal of Educational Research, 50*(4): 354–369.

Goffman, I. (1959). *The presentation of self in everyday life.* New York: Anchor.

Goldstein, L. S. (1997). *Teaching with love: A feminist approach to early childhood education.* New York: Perer Lang Pub.

Goleman, D. (1995). *Emotional intelligence.* New York: Bantam.

Grogan, M., & Shakeshaft, C. (2011). *Women and educational leadership.* San Francisco: Jossey-Bass.

Hargreaves, A. (2000). Mixed emotions: Teachers' perceptions of their interactions with students. *Teaching and Teacher Education, 16*: 811–826.

Hargreaves, A. (2001). Emotional geographies of teaching. *Teachers College Record, 103*(6): 1056–1080.

Hargreaves, A. (2004). Inclusive and exclusive educational change: Emotional responses of teachers and implications for leadership. *School Leadership & Management, 24*(2): 287–309.

Hochschild, A. R. (1983). *The managed heart: Commercialization of human feeling.* Berkeley, CA: University of California Press.

Hochschild, A. R. (1975). The sociology of feeling and emotion: Selected possibilities. *Sociological Inquiry, 45*(2–3): 280–307.

Jaggar, A. (1989). *Gender/body/knowledge: Feminist reconstructions of being and knowing.* New Jersey: Rutgers University Press.

Johnson III, R., Aiken, J., & Steggerda, R. (2005). Emotions and educational leadership: Narratives from the inside. *Planning and Changing, 36*(3&4): 235–252.

Kamerman, S. B. (2007). *A global history of early childhood education and care.* Education for All Global Monitoring Report 2007. Strong Foundations: Early care and education. United Nations.

Kanter, B. (2013). *Why Preschool Matters.* Retrieved from www.parents.com/toddlers-preschoolers/starting-preschool/curriculum/why-preschool-matters/

Koedel, C., & Techapaisarnjaroenkit, T. (2012). The relative performance of Head Start. *Eastern Economic Journal, 38*(2): 251–275.

Krum, S. M., & Geddes, D. (2000). Catching fire without burning out: Is there an ideal way to perform emotional labor. In N. M. Ashkanasy, C. E. J. Hartel, & W. J. Zerbe (Eds.), *Emotions in the workplace: Research, theory, and practice* (pp.177–188). Westport, CT: Quorum Book.

Lascarides, V. C., & Hinitz, B. F. (2000). *History of early childhood education.* New York: Routledge.

Lazerson, M. (1972). Early childhood education: The historical antecedents of early childhood education. *Yearbook of the National Society for the Study of Education, 71*(2): 33–53.

Leithwood, K., & Beatty, B. (2008). *Leading with teacher emotions in mind.* Thousand Oaks, CA: Corwin.

Madrid, S., & Dunn-Kenney, M. (2010). Persecutory guilt, surveillance and resistance: The emotional themes of early childhood educators. *Contemporary Issues in Early Childhood, 11*(4): 388–401.

Madrid, S., Baldwin, N., & Frye, E. (2013). Professional feelings: One early childhood educator's discomfort as a teacher and learner. *Journal of Early Childhood Research, 11*(3): 274–292.

Meyer, D. (2009). Entering the emotional practices of teaching. In P. Schultz & M. Zembylas (Eds.), *Advances in teacher emotion research* (pp. 73–91). New York: Springer.

Mitchell, A. (2009). 4 good reasons why ECE is not just important, but essential. *Exchange, 187*: 8–11.

Moore, B. (2009). Emotional intelligence for school administrators: A priority for school reform? *American Secondary Education, 37*(3): 20–28.

Nias, J. (1996). Thinking about feeling: The emotions in teaching. *Cambridge Journal of Education, 26*(3): 293–310.

Noddings, N. (1984). *Caring: A feminine approach to ethics & moral education.* Berkeley, CA: University of California Press.

Shields, S. (2002). *Speaking from the heart: Gender and the social meaning of emotion.* Cambridge, MA: Cambridge University Press.

Stamopoulos, E. (2012). Reframing early childhood leadership. *Australasian Journal of Early Childhood, 37*(2): 42–50.

Swadener, B. B. (1995). Children and families "at promise": Deconstructing the discourse of risk. In B. B. Swadener & S. Lubeck (Eds.), *Children and families "at promise"* (pp. 17–49). Albany, NY: State University of New York Press.

Tsang, K. K. (2011). Emotional labor of teaching. *Education Research, 2*(8): 1312–1316.

Tucker, S. (2010). An investigation of the stresses, pressures and challenges faced by primary school head teachers in a context of organizational change in schools. *Journal of Social Work Practice, 24*(1): 63–74.

Winograd, K. (2003). The functions of teacher emotions: The good, the bad and the ugly. *Teachers College Record, 105*(9): 1641–1674.

Zembylas, M. (2003a). Caring for teacher emotion: Reflections on teacher self-development. *Studies in Philosophy and Education, 22*: 103–125.

Zembylas, M (2003b). Interrogating "teacher identity": Emotion, resistance, and self-formation. *Educational Theory, 53*(1): 107–127.

Zembylas, M. (2004). Emotion metaphors and emotional labor in science teaching. *Science Education, 88*(3): 301–324.

Zembylas, M. (2005a). Discursive practices, genealogies, and emotional rules: A poststructuralist view on emotion and identity in teaching. *Teaching and Teacher Education, 21*: 935–948.

Zembylas, M. (2005b). *Teaching with emotion: A postmodern enactment.* Charlotte, NC: Information Age Publishing.

Zigler, E., & Styfco, S. J. (Eds.). (2004). *The Head Start debates.* Baltimore, MD: Paul H. Brookes Publishing Co.

Zigler, E., & Styfco, S. J. (2010). *The hidden history of Head Start.* New York: Oxford University Press.

Zorn, D., & Boler, M. (2007). Rethinking emotions and educational leadership. *International Journal of Leadership in Education, 10*(2): 137–151.

COMMENTARY

Holly Elissa Bruno

Emotions, like a breeze off a lake, the impact of a child's smile or her melt-down, continuously pass through, over, and all around us. Emotions, like a breeze, are fluid, dynamic, and can be forceful, fanciful, or both. One thing about emotion is certain: Each emotion provides useful information about where we stand in the moment and the choices we can make as a result.

We dedicate ourselves to helping children grow and mature in all ways, paying special attention to their social and emotional development; however, rarely do we have a curriculum for adult social-emotional development. Perhaps some of us assume that by reaching adulthood, our social and emotional development is complete? If I were to make that assumption, I would be way off the mark! I am 68 and still learning about the world of emotions. Daily, I bump into issues that invite me to learn and grow or to fall back on old, often not so mature ways. For me, developing emotional literacy is a lifelong process that involves paying attention to the world of unspoken, and often unacknowledged, feelings that originate within each of us and between us. If you have ever been given (or given someone) "the look," you know the power of unspoken emotion.

Nikki Baldwin's chapter tells us in a compelling way that by paying attention to our emotional dynamics, we can make informed and life-changing choices. The "emotional intersections" Nikki mentions is a useful way of naming the opportunity that emotional discomfort gives us, including directors Emma, Jill, and Carolyn, to step back, acknowledge, observe, and grow.

Emotions Empower and Inhibit Our Actions

Every early childhood educator I know has a passion to make a difference. Our deeply felt emotions help determine the pathway each of us will take toward helpful change:

- Jill's quest is to lead a unique, stand-out, innovative organization.
- Emma wants dearly to "support" her hard-working teachers.
- Carolyn's desire is to limit her "bureaucratic" role to have time for what she truly loves, mentoring.

Despite their commitment to make a difference, all three professionals are held back by forces that feel, in the moment, impossible to manage. In Emma's world, for example, her gentle, supportive stance inhibits her from directly addressing underlying conflicts. What holds Emma, Jill, Carolyn, me, and perhaps all of us back from fulfilling our quest is often the very same force that eventually frees us to get the job done: Our emotions. Emotions both empower and inhibit our taking action. At these often provocative "emotional intersections," we have the opportunity to make choices that can change the direction of our professional lives.

When Emotions Create Expectations

When we experience and/or hold onto a feeling long enough, that emotion sets like cement into an expectation. Expectations for ourselves help us "keep our eyes on the prize" and to be consistent in our treatment of others. We feel good about ourselves when we honor these familiar and comfortable emotions. For example, Emma expects to be happiest at work when she helps her teachers be the best they can. Carolyn feels good about herself when she limits the time she devotes to bureaucratic tasks so she can give most of her time to mentoring.

Expectations can limit and define the roles we play:

- Emma expects herself to play the "supportive" role; therefore, she cannot "make anyone unhappy."
- Jill believes she has to hire teachers already at a state of excellence, rather than to hire people with potential.
- I expect that, by waiting until my deadline is bearing down on me, I will be energized to complete the task.

When we allow our expectations to set the standard for the decisions we make, our behavior is predictable and aligned with our past desires. That's the good news. Neuroscientist Jeffrey Schwartz (2002) puts this process into scientific terms: "The brain registers sensory information, processes it, connects it with previously stored sensory experience, and generates an output" (p. 367). That "output," our action, predictably aligns with our expectations. Once formed, habits dictate our choices.

When Expectations Restrict Our Creativity

What happens when our quest (of heartfelt desires) changes as we grow more into the complexity of our jobs? The expectation that once helped us make decisions may now become a hindrance to our professional growth, inhibiting us from spontaneously paying attention to our feelings in the moment. This becomes an issue, especially when those feelings contradict the roles we have established for ourselves.

Here's the bad news: An expectation is a resentment waiting to happen:

- If Emma expects herself to be supportive, how can she confront a teacher's long-standing inappropriate behavior, especially if that teacher has the "my way or the highway" attitude?
- If Jill's chosen role requires her to hire only seasoned teachers, how can Jill meet her unstated quest to help promising but less experienced teachers develop?
- If I expect deadlines to run my life, I write my own prescription for burning out.

Expectations control our reactions and rob us of spontaneity. To rephrase an adage: "Holding a resentment is like swallowing poison and waiting for the other person to die."

Our field's commitment to emergent curriculum, the practice of being spontaneous and flexible enough to help each child explore her curiosity in the moment, captures this tension between set expectations and fluidity. A teacher who prefers the structure and predictability of lesson plans may have difficulty "dropping everything" or altering expectations to follow a child's fascination with a fluttering butterfly. We have choices at these emotional intersections. As Nikki Baldwin clearly states, the tension between our past emotions and our present feelings can lead to a professional breakthrough. The question is: Are we open to change? Surprisingly, change is not the problem; our resistance to changing is the issue. Our emotions have the power to both inhibit and inspire our actions.

Help from Neuroscientists

Fortunately for us, technological advances, especially the f MRI (functional magnetic resonance imaging) machine, make it possible for scientists to identify where emotion is born, how it affects our brain, and what power we have to work with, rather than be played by our emotion (Goleman, 2006). What matters here is that we have essentially two neurobiological ways to respond to and foresee threats or challenges in our lives. We can either:

- Respond automatically to the surge of adrenalin and/or cortisol activated by our amygdala gland with a fight-or-flight reaction
- Gain perspective on the threat by taking steps to activate our prefrontal cortex, or the brain's executive function.

According to neuroscientist Louis Cozolino (2006), the more we deal with uncomfortable feelings (another way to describe emotional intersections) by taking a step back to gain perspective, the more adept our brains become at acting wisely rather than rashly in both the moment and the long run. Cozolino advises: "As we mature, our amygdala matures with us. It seems to be much more gentle with us and is less activated by fear and anxiety." (Interview by author with Dr. Cozolino, *Heart to Heart Conversations on Leadership,* BAMradionetwork.com).

By using calming techniques, such as taking a deep breath, counting to ten, or reminding ourselves not to take issues personally, we strengthen our capacity to calm our pounding heart and racing mind. We can switch ourselves over from our autonomic system's unthinking and rapid breathing response, triggered by our amygdala, to our executive function's more measured and soothing approach (Bruno, 2012).

In each moment, especially in stressful moments, we can "take a sounding" by stopping our multitasking ways to pay attention to our feelings. If Carolyn's buttons are being pushed (another way to describe the impact of the amygdala) by the drudgery of paperwork, she can in the moment notice, rather than deny, her anger. Carolyn can ask: "What's going on here? What's causing my anger? What choices do I have?" Carolyn can set a time limit she will spend on paperwork or take breaks from her bureaucratic tasks to interact with her team. How many directors do you know who refresh their spirits by rocking a baby in the infant room or reading to preschoolers?

Acknowledging more quickly and more often the useful data our feelings give us, we can both identify and act upon our emotional intersections more quickly. All three directors got to the point of considerable discomfort before making the decision to change their expectations for themselves. Thanks to these neurobiological principles, we can learn from our emotions in the moment, using them as part of our personal and professional "emergent curriculum." We do not have to wait for grave discomfort to act upon our emotional intersections.

Using All of Your Intelligences

Many adults still define intelligence by our scores on the IQ test. Frankly, the IQ test measures only one aspect of our intelligence: Our ability to be logical. As early childhood professionals, we acknowledge that the development of a child's social and emotional intelligence is every bit as essential as the child's ability to perform on academic tests. IQ, in short, prepares us for academic tests; EQ (emotional quotient) prepares us for the tests of life. Paying attention as adults to the wealth of useful data our emotions signal is to exercise emotional intelligence (Goleman, 2011). EQ is far more than a capacity or a skill. EQ is a way of living that embraces the importance of relationships while acknowledging all the unspoken languages we speak, including neuron to neuron.

When Nikki Baldwin talks about the value of learning from emotional intersections, she is giving us a useful example of how necessary EQ is for educators. Emotions are always present and available to provide us with information; our job is to pay attention to how we feel and learn from our feelings, sooner rather than later. Our social-emotional development is a lifelong process. Robert Frost (1920) reminds us lyrically that we often have to decide between one path and another, even when we cannot predict where either path may lead. At these emotional intersections, we have the opportunity to choose "the path less travelled by" and to discover that path "has made all the difference." The next time you find yourself at an emotional intersection, may you choose a path that uplifts your professional life.

References

Bruno, H. E. (2012). *What you need to lead: Emotional intelligence in practice.* Washington, D.C.: NAEYC.

Cozolino, L. (2006). *The neuroscience of human relationships: Attachment and the developing social brain.* New York: Norton.

EQ-I Emotional Quotient Inventory. Retrieved from www.mhs.com/product.aspx?gr+io&prod-eqi&id=overview

Goleman, D. (2006). *Social intelligence: The new science of human relationships.* New York: Bantam Dell.

Goleman, D. (2011). *Emotional intelligence: Why it matters more than IQ.* New York: Bantam.

Frost, R. (1920). *Mending Wall.* Retrieved from www.internal.org/Robert_Frost/Mending Wall

Schwartz, J. (2002). *The mind and the brain: Neuroplasticity and the power of mental force.* New York: Harper.

Society for Neuroscience. Retrieved from http://apu.sfn.org

10

PROMOTING PEER RELATIONS FOR YOUNG CHILDREN WITH AUTISM SPECTRUM DISORDER

The LEAP Preschool Experience

Phillip S. Strain and Edward H. Bovey

UNIVERSITY OF COLORADO, DENVER

In this chapter, we describe 3 decades of research aimed at improving the social skills and relationships experienced by preschool-age children with autism spectrum disorder (ASD). This research has focused on the utilization of typically developing peers as agents of intervention, culminating in a comprehensive treatment model, the Learning Experiences an Alternative Program for Preschoolers and Parents (LEAP) Preschool, that embodies much of the learning from this line of inquiry. Initially, we will provide a brief portrayal of the social and emotional issues experienced by young children with ASD. Next, we provide the reader with a detailed description of how the LEAP model directly influences the social skills, relations, and emotional development of *all* children in the program. Finally, we provide a brief synopsis of outcomes for children who have participated in LEAP.

Social and Emotional Challenges for Young Children with Autism

Spend just a few minutes in any preschool with typically developing children and you will see children conversing with each other, playing together with toys and materials, smiling, and laughing with the joy of some new discovery with a "best" friend. By contrast, young children affected by ASD are observed to avoid other children and sometimes they scream and cry as others approach them. Sharing a toy and playing a game together are foreign notions. In addition, we know that children affected by ASD have difficulty expressing and understanding emotional displays (e.g., smiling, frowning, laughing, etc.). In fact, delays in the social-emotional domain are one defining diagnostic indicator of ASD.

LEAP Model Development and the Translation of Precedent Research

In order to create a proper context, we begin this section with a general description of the LEAP Preschool Model followed by specific strategies within the model used to build and maintain children's peer relationships.

Program Description

The LEAP model was designed with the purpose of creating a program that would be replicable by public school districts and fiscally sound. Traditionally, LEAP classrooms have included three to four young children with ASD and eight to ten typically developing preschoolers in a split-session (morning and afternoon) class format. Although these numbers do vary across replication sites, to fully benefit from the peer-mediated interventions utilized, a minimum ratio of two typically developing peers for each child with ASD should be maintained. Although various staff configurations can be found across replication sites, we strongly encourage a co-teaching arrangement with an early education teacher and an early childhood special education teacher. No matter the staffing format, at least three adults must be present in LEAP classrooms each day. Speech and language specialists, occupational therapists, and classroom assistants are also typically involved as team members.

Special Features

The LEAP model has a number of unique features. These features include the following:

1. Inclusion begins full-time from day one. Children with ASD are provided with the necessary level of prompting and support to participate in *all* classroom activities.
2. The design of LEAP classrooms begins with establishing a high-quality setting for typically developing children. Sites often use *The Creative Curriculum for Preschool* (Dodge, Colker, & Heroman, 2002) and/or *The Storybook Journey: Pathways to Literacy Through Story and Play* (McCord, 1995) curricula for this purpose. LEAP has also been implemented effectively in classrooms utilizing a variety of other preschool models and curricula, including High Scope and Head Start programs. These sites represent replications in which the "typically developing" children come from backgrounds that put them at risk for developmental problems and in which these children come from ethnic, racial, and language minorities. In the context of this programming, systematic intervention is embedded in typical preschool routines (e.g., circle time, free play/centers, snack, small groups, etc.).

3. Typically developing children play a major intervention role in LEAP. The children are provided with comprehensive training, such that they can facilitate the social and communicative behaviors of peers with ASD.

4. Learning objectives are written in such a fashion that teaching continues until generalized behavior change is achieved. Learning objectives are further described according to relevant prompting hierarchies. Thus, program data are collected on children's behavioral movement toward independent performance, not in terms of percent correct, teaching trials accomplished, or similar indices.

5. Intensity in the LEAP model is not defined by hours per week that individuals are paid to deliver service. We believe that the algorithm defining intensity is complex and includes for each developmental domain of concern the following factors: (1) number of opportunities to respond, (2) the functionality of objectives chosen, (3) the selection of an instructional method that maximizes children's engagement and minimizes errors, (4) the competence of staff to deliver with fidelity the chosen intervention, and (5) the use of data systems and decision-making rules that minimize children's exposure to less-than-optimal interventions.

6. LEAP utilizes a *variety* of science-based intervention approaches, including: (1) peer-mediated interventions, (2) errorless learning, (3) time delay, (4) incidental teaching, (5) pivotal response treatment, (6) picture exchange communication system (PECS) (Frost & Bondy, 1994), and (7) positive behavior support.

7. Because LEAP has always been implemented in concert with public school entities, there are no strict criteria for enrollment. However, research protocols have resulted in a rather complete diagnostic/child assessment process for enrolled children. Children participating in efficacy studies have met diagnostic criteria for "early childhood autism" on the *Diagnostic and Statistical Manual* (APA, 1980, 1987, 2000).

Social Skills Curricula Designed to Impact Peer Relationships

Based upon our prior studies of preschoolers with and without friends, LEAP has focused on a limited but potent set of social skills we directly teach to children in the classroom. The skills include:

1. Getting your friend's attention
2. Sharing—Giving something to a peer
3. Sharing—Asking a peer for something
4. Play organizers
5. Giving compliments

Getting attention from a class peer often occurs in a casual fashion among typically developing children. Sometimes attempts are successful; other times they are not. However, to be successful in getting the attention of peers with ASD and to maximize the effectiveness of social overtures, LEAP teaches a multisensory social initiation that includes three distinct components: (1) looking at the peer, (2) tapping the peer on the shoulder, and (3) saying the child's name.

As indicated earlier, sharing is actually two discrete skills that are taught independently. The first skill that is taught is giving. This skill, as they all are, is initially directed toward the typical peers. The goal is to increase the frequency of peers giving highly desired objects to the targeted children with ASD, thus increasing the social responsiveness of the children with social deficits. Asking a peer for something is then targeted, and the children with ASD are encouraged to use their emerging language/communication skills to request highly preferred objects from their peers.

Among preschoolers, play organizers are usually composed of "Let's" statements, such as, "Let's play trucks" or "Let's play princess, you get the tiaras." Children are taught to initiate play organizers and to respond to others' play organizers as well.

Giving compliments represents a minor diversion from the precedent research that indicated the influence of affectionate behavior on friendships. We elected not to include affection per se, as the only topography of this class of behaviors that related directly to friendships was its occurrence following some injury (physical or emotional) by a child. Although preschoolers are predisposed to complement each other on items of clothing or appearance, in our curriculum, we teach children to compliment actions and accomplishments, such as building a tower or drawing a picture.

One of the fundamental lessons from our precedent research is that children can engage in very high rates of discrete behaviors that impact friendships but *never* have a friend. It is equally essential that children engage in extended encounters involving at least four social turns and that they initiate interactions at least 30% of the time. In LEAP, therefore, intervention continues until children reach these vital patterns of interaction, and objectives are written accordingly.

Teaching Social Skills in the Inclusive Classroom

Now that we have identified the key social skills that lead to the development of friendships and meaningful relationships, we will describe the classroom instructional strategies put in place to support children's acquisition, naturalistic utilization, and generalization of peer-mediated social skills. Instruction is delivered using four distinct components: (1) direct group instruction, (2) creating planned and naturally occurring opportunities for children to practice the skills, (3) adult prompting of children to use the skills in context, and (4) reinforcing children's spontaneous utilization of the targeted skills.

Direct Group Instruction

Direct instruction of the targeted skills occurs during large group (circle) time. Instruction is delivered to all children in the classroom, not just the typically developing peers, using a multistep instructional procedure first outlined in Strain and Kohler (1998) and expanded upon here. In addition to direct instruction from the adults, visual cues (pictures) are used to assist in describing the skills. These pictures can then be used throughout the classroom as visual prompts for children to engage in the targeted skill(s).

Describe the Skill

The first step in delivering the social skills instruction is to provide a brief description of the skill and why it is important. For example, the teacher might say, "Today we are going to talk about *getting your friend's attention*. Sometimes, you want to play with a friend, but they don't know you want to play with them. A great way to start playing with your friend is to get their attention first. To get your friend's attention, we want you to do three things: look at your friend, tap them gently on the shoulder, and say their name."

Demonstrate the Right (Correct) Way with Another Adult

The next step is to demonstrate the skill for the children. When demonstrating, it is important to first do it with another adult so you can eliminate the potential for errors and clearly show the children how to do the skill. Start by inviting a second adult up to the front of the group with you. Instruction then continues by demonstrating how to get a friend's attention using the three skills. It is important to be animated and clearly demonstrate each of the three skills used to get a friend's attention. During instruction, cue the children to provide the key steps in getting attention prior to demonstrating the skill. For example, you could say, "OK, let's pretend I want to get Courtney's attention. What do I need to do to get her attention? I need to (pause, point to your eyes and wait for a child or children to answer)," and then respond, "Right, I need to look at her. Then, I need to (pause, point to your shoulder, and wait for the children to respond)," and then confirm, "Right, tap her on the shoulder. And last, I need to (pause, point to your mouth, wait for the children to respond)," and then confirm, "Right, I need to say her name. OK, let's see if I can do it correctly. You guys tell me if I do it right." The second adult then turns away from the teacher and pretends not to pay attention to her. Props (toys) can be used to demonstrate a child playing. The teacher then clearly demonstrates each component of the skill, and the second adult responds by looking at the teacher. Then ask the children, "Did I do it right?" or "Did it work?" and let the children respond and cheer.

Demonstrate the Wrong Way

After demonstrating the skill the correct way, allow the other teacher to try to use the skill. Prior to this demonstration, you can again review the steps with the children as described earlier. However, when demonstrating the skill, this time, the second adult purposely omits a step or does something blatantly wrong and the teacher will *not* respond. If the children do not notice the omitted step immediately, the adults can cue the children by asking, "Why didn't it work? What did I do wrong?" and then allow the children to correct you. Once the children have provided the missing or incorrect step, demonstrate the skill correctly and then ask the children if it worked. Allow the children to respond and cheer the successful attempt.

Child Demonstrates with an Adult

The next step is to select a typical child and invite them up to the front of the group to demonstrate using the skill with the teacher. Prior to the demonstration, remind the children of the steps. Selecting the "right" child here is important, as you want someone who has a high probability of demonstrating the skill correctly. Once the child demonstrates the skill, the adult responds appropriately and you can again ask the children, "Did she do it right?" and allow the children to cheer for their peer. If the child misses a step, wait and don't respond, as it is likely that another child in the group will remind the child of the missed step. If this does not occur, the second adult can provide additional cueing to the child to perform the skill correctly.

Child Demonstrates with a Peer

The last step in providing the social skills instruction is to invite a target child (child with social/emotional delays) up to the front of the group and to have the typical child practice the social skill with their peer. Teachers should again cue the children to list the steps in getting their friend's attention and then ask the child to try it with their peer. You can position the children so they are facing away from each other and then cue the typical "model" to get their friend's attention. If the child does all the steps and the peer responds by looking, cheer and celebrate. If the child does the skill correctly but the peer does not respond, an adult should prompt the peer to respond to their friend's initiation. If the typical peer forgets a step or does not engage in the targeted skill, the adults should prompt until the skill is performed. Finally, nonresponses by the target child can also provide an opportunity to teach persistence to the child initiating the interaction. Because the target of these social overtures will be a population of children with marked social skills delays, the typical children need to know what to do if they do not get a response on the first initiation.

Creating Practice Opportunities Throughout the Day

Now that we have identified key social behaviors to teach and established a systematic instructional protocol to teach the skills, we need to examine the classroom day to identify both routine, embedded practice opportunities and naturalistic opportunities for children to use the targeted social skills. This two-part approach ensures the help needed to promote children's acquisition and generalization of the targeted skills and encourages utilization across classroom activities and routines.

Embedding Social Skills Opportunities into Classroom Routines

Routines can be defined as "events that are completed on a regular basis" (Ostrosky, Jung, Hemmeter, & Thomas, 2003). To apply this idea to social situations requires that social interactions occur both on a regular basis and in a planned and predictable way. To do this successfully, we look at establishing specific "routines within routines" that create clear expectations, predictability, and consistency around peer-to-peer interactions within activities of the daily classroom schedule (Strain, Bovey, Wilson, & Roybal, 2009). The first step in this process is for the classroom team to sit down together, go through their daily schedule, and ask a basic question, "What do we do for kids every day that they could do themselves?" By asking this question, teams can begin to identify routines within routines that could take on a peer-mediated social component. These routines need to be consistent, in that they happen every day, and predictable, in that they are an established component of how the activity is carried out every time it occurs. In order for these embedded opportunities to reach a meaningful level of intensity, teams should look to embed approximately 100 of these planned, peer-mediated opportunities into a child's program day (Strain & Hoyson, 2000). For example, when children arrive every day, they complete a sign-in activity where they put a photo of themselves on the school picture to indicate they are here in school and they write their name on the sign-in board. This routine, which is often adult mediated (a teacher would invite each child over to complete the activity), can easily be set up as a peer-mediated activity. After the first child signs in, they can look at the student photos and pick one that is not yet on the school picture. The child then takes the photo of that student, finds the child, gets their attention, and gives them their picture while providing the instruction to "go sign in." Doing this, each child will engage in two planned, routine social interactions (except the first and last child, who will only get one peer interaction) every day, and because they are part and parcel of the arrival routine, they are going to happen consistently. Table 10.1 outlines an entire day's sequence in which a preschool team has identified large numbers of embedded social opportunities.

Circle time is another excellent opportunity to embed peer social interactions, as most circle times include songs that have props or materials that go with them. By selecting a child to pass out and/or collect the song props, you can create another 14 peer social interactions (in a class of 15 students).

TABLE 10.1 Embedded Social Opportunities for Ben

Classroom activity	Type of opportunities	Teacher (T)/peer (P) facilitation	Number of opportunities
Arrival	Saying "hello"	T-Verbal prompt P-Reciprocal "hello"	12
Table time	Sharing/requesting art materials	T-Verbal prompt P-Initiate request/ grant request	13
Circle time	Pass objects to peers by name	T-Verbal prompt P-Accept item	24
Centers	Sharing/requesting toys/materials	T-Verbal prompt P-Initiate request/ grant request	17
Snack	Ask for food from peer	T-Verbal prompt P-Grant request	12
Story	Passing story props to peers by name	T-Verbal prompt P-Accept item	12
Dismissal	Saying "goodbye"	T-Verbal prompt P-Reciprocal "goodbye"	12

Supporting Naturally Occurring Peer-Mediated Interventions

During center time, children are given the opportunity to choose their play activities and engage in child-directed, child-choice play in a variety of learning centers. During this time, we utilize peer-mediated strategies, focusing on the specific social skill taught during the large group time. To encourage the use of the targeted social skill, teachers spend additional time setting up centers to facilitate peer-to-peer interactions. One way teachers do this is by limiting the number of centers open in the classroom and limiting the number of children who can play in each center. Limiting the number of students in a center not only ensures that children will be dispersed around the room, it also encourages children to problem-solve and ask for turns. Additional modifications are made within each center to support and promote peer interactions. For example, the sand table can be pulled out from the wall so children can stand across from each other instead of next to each other. This face-to-face orientation encourages and facilitates peer interaction. In addition, the materials in the sand table are limited—one or two shovels and one or two buckets and funnels, instead of having buckets and shovels for each child. Limiting materials in this way supports sharing and turn-taking behaviors and encourages children to interact.

Prompting Children to Use Targeted Social Behaviors

Even after the classroom team has examined their routines to create embedded peer social opportunities and organized center time to facilitate naturalistic peer-mediated opportunities, it is likely that classroom teachers will also need to be highly attentive to children's social interests and, at times, engage in direct prompting of children to engage in the targeted social behaviors. As with all naturalistic teaching strategies, observation of child behaviors and the identification of ideal teachable moments are paramount. Teachers need to be able to identify opportunities of shared interest and joint attention and capitalize on them while being mindful of not interrupting ongoing peer-to-peer interactions. In general, adults should approach prompting of peer interactions using a least-to-most approach, starting with general prompts (e.g., "Remember to play with your friends") and proceeding to more specific prompts (e.g., "Get Ella's attention and give her the marker."). Because this intervention is targeted to children with marked social delays, one important component of prompting children is to remind them to be persistent if their initial social bids are ignored or unsuccessful.

Using Reinforcement to Support Acquisition of Peer Social Behaviors

The final component of teaching peer-mediated social behaviors is the effective use of a variety of reinforcement strategies (Strain, Schwartz, & Bovey, 2008). Reinforcement must be used both to encourage the typical peers to use the targeted skills with the children with ASD and to reinforce the children with ASD for responding appropriately to the social bids of their peers. To achieve these outcomes, we have successfully implemented a token reinforcement system—the Super Star—across classroom populations. The advantage of using a token reinforcement system in this situation is that it allows teachers to reinforce social behaviors immediately with a Super Star as they naturally occur in the classroom and to individualize the reinforcers through the use of a "treasure chest" of selected items at the end of the day.

Time to acquire and use each skill will vary across multiple contexts, and one mistake classroom teams often make in implementing peer-mediated interventions is that they move on from a skill before generalized use is achieved by the majority of the class. For this reason, we recommend that social skills instruction of this kind be dynamic and flexible and not based on providing instruction in each skill for a predetermined number of days. After providing direct group instruction for 2 weeks, we suggest moving to a maintenance phase. During this phase, adults briefly remind children of the targeted skill prior to children going to center time, watch the children for sustained and generalized utilization of the skill, and continue to reinforce the targeted skill with the Super Star system. If children demonstrate frequent use of the targeted skill across a variety of classroom peers and most children are earning a Super Star, then proceeding to the next skill is appropriate. If children's use of the targeted skill decreases in the absence of the direct instruction, then implementing the full instructional protocol for an additional 2 weeks is recommended before assessing children's generalized use again.

Child Outcomes Associated with LEAP Enrollment

The overall research strategy for documenting the efficacy of LEAP has been three-fold. First, we have conducted a longitudinal study of LEAP clients as contrasted with similar children who received an alternative comparison model of early intervention. Summarized results are as follows:

1) Children in LEAP generally show significant reductions in autistic symptoms after 2 years of intervention; comparison children do not (Strain & Cordisco, 1983).

2) Children in LEAP make marked developmental progress on intellectual and language measures; comparison children do not (Strain, Hoyson, & Jamieson, 1985; Strain & Hoyson, 2000).

3) On observational measures taken in school and at home, LEAP children are far more socially engaged and appropriate (Strain, Kohler, & Goldstein, 1996).

4) No negative and some positive (e.g., better social skills, fewer disruptive behaviors) outcomes accrue to typical children in the LEAP model (Strain, 1987).

5) Gains for LEAP children generally maintain following program participation, with 24 of 51 children now enrolled in regular education classes (oldest cohort in college) with no signs of developmental regression (Strain & Hoyson, 2000).

6) Adult family members who participated in LEAP are significantly less likely than comparison families to show signs of significant stress and depression following the early intervention experience (Strain, 1996).

In addition to these enrollment-specific results, we have considered it to be ethically and scientifically necessary to conduct various substudies to demonstrate the efficacy of key model components that represent specific replication training content. These include: (1) teaching typical children to facilitate the social and communicative competence of their class peers with ASD, (2) teaching Individualized Education Program (IEP) objectives within routine class activities, and (3) providing extensive skill training for family members in order to address child behavior issues in home and community settings. The summarized results from these areas of study follow:

1) Typically developing peers as young as 36 months can be taught easily to utilize facilitative social and communicative initiations with their peers with ASD (Goldstein & Wickstrom, 1986; Strain & Danko, 1995).

2) Peers' use of facilitative strategies results in higher rates of communicative interaction for preschoolers with ASD (Goldstein & Wickstrom, 1986; Strain, 1987; Kohler & Strain, 1999).

3) The peer facilitative strategies often produce "day one" effects, suggesting that the delayed social and communicative abilities of many young children

with ASD may be attributable in part to the socially nonresponsive, developmentally segregated settings in which they are most often educated (Strain & Odom, 1986; Kohler & Strain, 1992).

4) For many children who receive the peer-mediated intervention, their eventual level of social participation falls within the typical range for their age-cohorts (Strain, 1987).

5) The potency of the peer-mediated intervention extends across both settings (Strain, 1987; Strain & Hoyson, 2000) and time (Strain, Goldstein, & Kohler, 1996).

6) The naturalistic or incidental teaching used at LEAP to influence cognitive outcomes yields approximately 2 months developmental gain for each month enrolled (Hoyson, Jamieson, & Strain, 1985; Strain & Cordisco, 1983).

7) When compared to one-to-one tutorial instruction, the LEAP incidental teaching model yields more active engagement and more complex developmental skills by children with ASD and their typical peers (Kohler & Strain, 1999).

8) LEAP's parent skill training component produces broad-based and long-lasting effects, including: (a) family use of skills in naturalistic contexts, (b) child behavior improvements in active engagement and challenging behaviors, (c) high levels of family satisfaction with the training program, and (d) decreased levels of stress and depression, especially as families exit the intervention program and move to what they perceive to be less supportive service programs (Strain, 1987; Strain, 1996).

Finally, we have conducted a large randomized, controlled trial (RCT) involving over 250 young children with ASD (Strain & Bovey, 2011). In this study, inclusive preschool classrooms for children with ASD were randomly assigned to receive either LEAP's intervention manuals and training materials or the intervention manuals and 20 days per year of onsite coaching for a 2-year period. Coaching content was driven by the initial and repeated administration of LEAP's intervention fidelity observational scale, the Quality Program Indicators (see Strain & Bovey, 2011). Initial assessments showed that child participants were equivalent at study start on standardized measures of overall developmental functioning, language competence, social competence, problem behaviors, and ASD symptoms. After 2 years, profound differences were noted on all measures in favor of the coaching group. Of particular note, social competence growth by coaching participants exceeded that of comparison children by a 3 to 1 margin.

Presently, the authors are conducting a long-term follow-up on study participants. Preliminary findings strongly indicate that children in the coaching group continue to make excellent progress, with a large fraction now enrolled in regular classes with limited special education support services and with continuing, strong social relations with peers.

Concluding Comments

Although deficits in peer relations are a major defining characteristic of children with ASD, our precedent experimental studies and clinical services in LEAP have shown that this hallmark of ASD need not be a permanent condition. Indeed, the precedent studies have shown that children's level of social participation with peers following our intervention model is identical to that of typically developing children. LEAP outcome studies have shown that these initial results can last up to 6 years post intervention.

It is our contention that these powerful outcomes are achievable only by altering the entire social ecology of children with ASD. This, in fact, is what the peer-mediated intervention accomplishes. Perhaps the best indicator of effect here is not represented by outcomes for children with ASD, but in the attitudes of typical children who have served their preschool peers. As Strain and Hoyson (2000) reported, we have conducted a careful study of outcomes for typical children in LEAP classrooms. When compared to children nominated by teachers as the "social stars" in their developmentally segregated early childhood settings, no differences emerged over a year on measures of overall development and language skills. LEAP's typically developing children come to engage in significantly less challenging behaviors over a 1-year period. However, the most startling differences are in 3-, 4- and 5-year-old children's attitudes toward difference and disability. When the non-LEAP "social stars" see a video of a child putting a puzzle together and the child has been labeled as "not like you," these children attribute the puzzle completion to luck ("bet she can't do it again") or simplicity ("that's a baby puzzle"). By contrast, after 1 year in LEAP, typically developing children respond to this scenario with a simple statement of fact ("she did it"). When the child on the video is unsuccessful, the non-LEAP "social stars" commonly suggest that the child should be punished and that *those* children are no good. On the other hand, LEAP children's most common response is to offer help (e.g., "I could show him how to do it").

These dramatic differences in peer group attitudes reflect two fundamentally different relationship paths. Imagine growing up in an environment where peers see you at less than your best and think you should be punished. Now imagine growing up in an environment where peers "have your back" when you are not at your best. Although we do not deny that children with ASD need to make significant improvements in their social skills to ensure friendships, social-emotional competence is not a solo dance. What potential relationship partners bring to the equation is equally important.

References

American Psychiatric Association (1980). *Diagnostic and statistical manual of mental disorders* (3rd ed.). Washington, D.C.: American Psychiatric Association.

American Psychiatric Association (1987). *Diagnostic and statistical manual of mental disorders* (3rd ed. revised). Washington, D.C.: American Psychiatric Association.

American Psychiatric Association (2000). *Diagnostic and statistical manual of mental disorders* (4th ed.—text revision). Washington, D.C.: American Psychiatric Association.

Dodge, D. T., Colker, L., & Heroman, C. (2002). *The creative curriculum for preschool* (4th ed.). Washington, D.C.: Teaching Strategies, Inc.

Frost, L. A., & Bondy, A. S. (1994). *PECS: The picture exchange communication system.* Cherry Hills, NJ: Pyramid Educational Consultants.

Goldstein, H., & Wickstrom, S. (1986). Peer intervention effects on communicative interaction among handicapped and nonhandicapped preschoolers. *Journal of Applied Behavior Analysis, 19*(2): 209–214.

Hoyson, M., Jamieson, B., & Strain, P. S. (1985). Individualized group instruction of normally developing and autistic-like children: The LEAP curriculum model. *Journal of the Division for Early Childhood, 8*: 157–172.

Kohler, F. W., & Strain, P. S. (1992). Applied behavior analysis and the movement to restructure schools: Compatibilities and opportunities for collaboration. *Journal of Behavioral Education, 2*: 367–390.

Kohler, F. W., & Strain, P. S. (1999). Peer-mediated intervention for young children with autism: A 20-year retrospective. In P. Ghezzi (Ed.), *Seminars in Autism.* Reno: University of Nevada-Reno Press.

McCord, S. (1995). *The storybook journey: Pathways to literacy through story and play.* Englewood Cliffs, NJ: Prentice-Hall, Inc.

Ostrosky, M. M., Jung, E. Y., Hemmeter, M. L., & Thomas, D. (2003). Helping children understand routines and classroom schedules. Center on the Social and Emotional Foundations for Early Learning: What Works Brief.

Strain, P. S. (1987). Comprehensive evaluation of young autistic children. *Topics in Early Childhood Special Education, 7*: 97–110.

Strain, P. S. (1996). *Year 12 report: Peer-mediated treatment of children with autism.* National Institute of Mental Health Grant No. MH37110–11.

Strain, P. S., & Bovey, E. H. (2011). Randomized, controlled trial of the LEAP model of early intervention for young children with autism spectrum disorders. *Topics in Early Childhood Special Education, 31*(3): 133–154.

Strain, P. S., Bovey, E. H., Wilson, K., & Roybal, R. (2009). Leap preschool: Lessons learned of over 28 years of inclusive services for young children with autism. *Young Exceptional Children, Monograph Series #11*, 49–68.

Strain, P. S., & Cordisco, L. K. (1983). Child characteristics and outcomes related to mainstreaming. In J. Anderson & T. Black (Eds.), *Issues in preschool mainstreaming.* Chapel Hill, N.C.: TADS Publications.

Strain, P. S., & Danko, C. D. (1995). Caregivers' encouragement of positive interaction between preschoolers with autism and their siblings. *Journal of Emotional and Behavioral Disorders, 3*: 2–12.

Strain, P. S., Goldstein, H., & Kohler, F. W. (1996). LEAP: Peer-mediated intervention for young children with autism. In E. Hibbs & P. Jensen (Eds.), *Psychosocial treatments for child and adolescent disorders.* Washington, D.C.: APA.

Strain, P. S. & Hoyson, M. (2000). On the need for longitudinal, intensive social skill intervention: LEAP follow-up outcomes for children with autism as a case-in-point. *Topics in Early Childhood Special Education, 20*: 116–122.

Strain, P. S., Hoyson, M., & Jamieson, B. (1985). Class deportment and social outcomes for normally developing and autistic-like children in an integrated preschool. *Journal of the Division for Early Childhood, 10*: 105–115.

Strain, P. S., Kerr, M. M., & Ragland, E. U. (1979). Effects of peer-mediated social initiations and prompting/reinforcement procedures on the social behavior of autistic children. *Journal of Autism and Developmental Disorders, 9*: 41–54.

Strain, P. S., & Kohler, F. W. (1998). Peer-mediated social intervention for young children with autism. *Seminars in Speech and Language, 19*: 391–405.

Strain, P. S., Kohler, F. W., & Goldstein, H. (1996). Peer-mediated interventions for young children with autism. In P. Jensen & T. Hibbs (Eds.), *Psychosocial treatments of child and adolescent disorders.* Bethesda, MD: National Institutes of Health.

Strain, P. S., & Odom, S. L. (1986). Peer social initiations: An effective intervention for social skill deficits of exceptional children. *Exceptional Children, 52*: 543–551.

Strain, P. S., Schwartz, I., & Barton, E. (2012). Providing intervention for young children with autism spectrum disorders: What we still need to accomplish. *Journal of Early Intervention, 33*: 321–332.

Strain, P. S., Schwartz, I., & Bovey E. (2008). Social skills intervention for young children with autism: Programmatic research findings and implementation issues. In S. Odom, S. McConnell, & W. Brown (Eds.), *Social competence of young children: Risk, disability, & intervention* (pp. 253–272). Baltimore, MD: Paul Brookes.

Timm, M. A., Strain, P. S., & Eller, P. H. (1979). Effects of systematic, response-dependent fading and thinning procedures on the maintenance of child-child interaction. *Journal of Applied Behavior Analysis, 12*: 308.

COMMENTARY

Michelle Buchanan

UNIVERSITY OF WYOMING

Over the past 3 decades, Dr. Strain and his colleagues have contributed enormously to our understanding of how to support social competence in young children with autism spectrum disorder through peer-mediated interventions. The Learning Experiences an Alternative Program for Preschoolers and Parents (LEAP) program model presented in this chapter consists of a carefully researched set of intervention strategies that have proven to be effective in increasing and sustaining levels of social participation of children with autism. In 1992, Samuel Odom, Scott McConnell, and Mary McEvoy edited a book entitled *Social Competence of Young Children with Disabilities: Issues and Strategies for Intervention*. This seminal book made the case that peer-related social competence was a critical way for young children to meet social goals, learn from others, develop friendships, and be successful in school and, ultimately, life. The book described a growing body of research demonstrating that early intervention could have a positive impact on children's development of social competence. It was a powerful message, not just because we were learning about successful interventions, but also because providers and consumers of early intervention services were asking questions such as, "What if having a friend is the most important goal on the IEP?" As a field, we were rethinking what we were teaching young children with disabilities and whether our Individualized Education Program (IEP) goals were socially meaningful for children and their families.

Children with autism are often isolated in inclusive early childhood classrooms due to a lack of social interaction with peers. This isolation may be the result of a dynamic set in motion when both children with autism and their peers avoid initiating contact with each other. For children with autism, an accompanying lack of typical play skills and a tendency to send atypical or unclear social messages exacerbates this situation. Behavioral interventions for promoting social participation in the LEAP model include teaching and reinforcing children's social initiations, exchange of objects and verbal compliments, and initiations and responses to invitations to play. Authors report success in seeing an increase in these behaviors, as well as a positive impact on overall development and family satisfaction with the intervention.

Those who work within a behavioral model focus on behavior in their research and avoid cognitive and affective constructs as subjects for study or explanations of behavior. Strain and Bovey do not report whether increases in social participation of children with autism meant that those children experienced a greater desire to interact; seemed eager to share toys, food, or compliments with others; found pleasure in playing with others; and ultimately were able to develop voluntary, reciprocal friendships characterized by positive affect. It is clear that these outcomes are in mind when they put forth the caveat that "children can engage in very high rates of discrete behaviors that impact friendships but *never* have a friend." They address this by assuring that children initiate interactions at least 30% of the time and engage in interactions that include at least four social turns. The assumption inherent in this approach is that the sum and extensive use of social skills taught to young children will result in the development of meaningful relationships, including friendships.

This book examines emotions from the perspective of participants in complex social contexts such as inclusive early childhood education classrooms. Social competence depends on social participation, including sharing thoughts and feelings, having friends, and playing with others. However, sharing, friendship, and social play are more than the sum of their behavioral components. They are emotionally laden, and their authenticity depends on the emotional constructions and experiences of the children. Giving a preferred plaything to a peer simply because you are prompted or reinforced for doing so amounts to giving an object to a peer, not necessarily sharing or showing care for a friend. Children learn to share voluntarily out of care or empathy for a peer who badly wants a toy, or because they experience that sharing can be a pleasurable act for the giver and receiver, or because it leads to interesting play with others.

Likewise, play serves as an important medium for developing relationships in early childhood settings, and social play is a rich emotional experience. Approaches to teaching social play that treat play like scripts or another "task" often fail in the effort to teach spontaneous, creative, cooperative, and pleasurable "playful play" to children with autism (Kasari, Chang, & Patternson, 2013). Friendships are a special form of social relationship characterized by shared positive affect. Buysse, Goldman, West, and Hollingsworth (2008), in a review of research on interventions to promote friendships, suggest that more attention be given to studying what kinds of activities and opportunities foster reciprocal friendships between two children. They recommend setting up cozy spaces for two in the classroom or providing children with multiple sets of toys to encourage shared engagement in play. Recognizing that "having fun together" is an essential function of friendships, they suggest that teachers allow occasional vigorous, silly, noisy, or unorthodox play to support affect in dyadic relationships, especially in the initial development of the friendship. And finally, they propose learning more about what having a friend means for young children, who children choose as their friends and why, and, I suggest, how the emotional experiences and expressions of typical children and children with autism impact the development and negotiation of friendships between them.

In my view, the LEAP intervention model is unique and effective because it sets up a social ecology in an inclusive setting that teaches and actively encourages positive peer relations among all children in the classroom, including those at risk for isolation or rejection because of difference. The message to children is that all are responsible for inclusion. This intervention is about changing social systems, not individuals—not doing things to children with autism, but doing things with them. Children who are socially isolated in classrooms lack *access* to the kinds of reciprocal, pleasurable, caring, empathetic, creative relationships available to typical children. For those children, LEAP interventions open the door to meaningful relationships and relationship-based learning in inclusive settings.

One of the most striking findings from LEAP research is the difference in attitudes between preschool children who are actively encouraged to interact with children with autism throughout the school day and preschool children who are not given that encouragement. Non-LEAP children saw difference as something to devalue or punish, whereas the LEAP children celebrated achievements of their atypical peers and offered help when those peers were struggling. Strain and Bovey conclude by asking the reader to "imagine growing up in an environment where peers see you as less than your best and think you should be punished. Now, imagine growing up in an environment where peers 'have your back' when you are not at your best" (p. 188). Having positive social and emotional experiences in early education settings results in improved quality of life for children in the present; a worthy goal unto itself. However, questions of affect in the classroom are especially important given our evolving understanding from neuroscience that emotion and cognition are subjectively intertwined. We now know that social and emotional experiences children have as members of classroom culture shape cognitive learning (Immordino-Yang, 2011).

This chapter describes a research paradigm and project that demonstrates that carefully planned and intensive classroom interventions can be effective in increasing social participation for children with autism in preschool classrooms, giving all children access to meaningful peer relationships in those classrooms. Other research methods may prove useful in exploring, reconceptualizing, and making visible the emotional underpinnings of social participation and peer relations. How do children construct, experience, express, and manage emotions when they are asked to reach out and interact with atypical and typical peers in their classroom throughout the day? How do children with autism feel about interacting with their peers that they may otherwise avoid? What does friendship look and feel like for typical and atypical preschool children? And how do children develop from performing behaviors adults ask of them to being motivated through empathy, caring, and pleasure of engagement to reach out to peers, typical and atypical, on their own? Qualitative research methods such as case study or ethnography may be especially effective in addressing these kinds of questions.

References

Buysse, V., Goldman, B. D., West, T., & Hollingsworth, H. (2008). Friendships in early childhood: Implications for early education and intervention. In W. H. Brown, S. L. Odom, and S. R. McConnell (Eds.), *Social competence of young children: Risk, disability, & intervention*. Baltimore, MD: Paul H. Brookes Publishing.

Immordino-Yang, M. H. (2011). Implications of affective and social neuroscience for educational theory. *Educational Philosophy and Theory, 43*(1): 98–103.

Kasari, C., Chang, Y-C., & Patternson, S. (2013). Pretending to play or playing to pretend: The case of autism. *American Journal of Play, 6*(1): 124–135. Rochester, NY: The Strong.

CONTRIBUTORS

Nikki Baldwin earned a PhD in curriculum studies from the University of Wyoming in 2013. She has spent the last 15 years in early childhood administration, and continues her work mentoring teachers and undergraduate students as curriculum coordinator at the University of Wyoming Early Care and Education Center.

Steve Bialostok works as an educational and linguistic anthropologist. He is interested in how education has become a kind of governmentality, connecting students' and teachers' subjectivities to the rationality of the market. He examines how everyday language about educational matters becomes inextricably tied to the very tenets of modern capitalism.

Margarita Bianco is an associate professor in the School of Education and Human Development at the University of Colorado, Denver. Professor Bianco teaches undergraduate and graduate courses in special education, educational psychology, and urban community teacher education. Her research primarily focuses on (1) the underrepresentation of students of color in gifted programs, (2) effects of race/ethnicity and disabilities on teachers' perceptions of students' abilities, and (3) teacher pathway programs for high school students of color (see www.Pathway s2Teaching.com).

Edward H. Bovey, MA, is the associate director of the Positive Early Learning Experience Center at the University of Colorado, Denver. He has worked with young children with autism and children with developmental disabilities for 20 years as an inclusive preschool teacher, early interventionist, researcher, trainer, and consultant.

Holly Elissa Bruno, MA, JD, author, attorney, and acclaimed keynote speaker, hosts an online radio program: *Heart to Heart Conversations on Leadership: Your Guide to Making a Difference* on BAMradionetwork.com. Holly Elissa served as assistant attorney general for the state of Maine and assistant dean at the University of Maine School of Law. While working as associate professor and dean of faculty at the University of Maine-Augusta, Holly Elissa was selected "Outstanding Professor." An alumna of Harvard University's Institute for Educational Management, she teaches leadership courses for The McCormick Center for Early Childhood Leadership and Wheelock College.

Michelle Buchanan is a professor of early childhood/early childhood special education at the University of Wyoming. She has more than 30 years of experience in these fields, and her research and teaching interests include the assessment of developmental characteristics of young children, including young exceptional children; children's play and learning; and equity, social justice, and inclusion in early childhood education. Her articles have been published in, among others, *Early Childhood Research to Practice, International Journal of Disability, Development and Education,* and the *American Journal of Play.*

David E. Fernie is an early childhood educator by discipline and has conducted research in several areas: children's understanding of media portrayals, the ethnographic study of teaching and learning in classrooms, and the professional development and technology proficiency of teachers. Much of his research is collaborative in nature. He is co-editor of the Hampton Press volume *Early Childhood Classroom Processes* and the 2011 volume *From Toddlers to Teachers: Learning to See and Understand the School and Peer Cultures of Classrooms.* He joined Wheelock College as dean of education in January 2005 and is currently professor in the Early Childhood Education Department. Previously, he held administrative and faculty positions at Ohio State University and the University of Houston.

Heidi Given is a kindergarten teacher at the Fayerweather Street School. From 1999–2014 she was the mentor kindergarten teacher and research coordinator at the Eliot-Pearson Children's School at Tufts University, and a part-time lecturer in the Department of Child Development. Heidi is an adjunct early childhood education lecturer at Lesley University, as well as a founder and facilitator of the Early Childhood Education Professional Development Consortium—an early childhood–focused professional learning community. Her teaching stance is rooted in inclusive, anti-bias, and culturally responsive practices.

Jeanne Goldhaber is an associate professor in the Early Childhood PreK–3 Program at the University of Vermont. She has worked closely with Dee Smith and the teachers and students at Campus Children's School for many years. Dee and Jeanne are co-authors of *Pinching, Poking and Pretending: Documenting Toddlers'*

Explorations with Clay, as well as of articles and book chapters that reflect their interest in the role that documentation plays in the promotion of reflective practice and collaboration.

Ellen Hall, PhD, is the founder and executive director of Boulder Journey School and director of the Boulder Journey School Teacher Education Program. Ellen travels internationally, sharing the work of Boulder Journey School with educators, policy makers, and child advocates. She serves on a number of boards and advisory committees, including Videatives, Dimensions Educational Research Foundation, World Forum Foundation, and Hawkins Centers of Learning. Her research focuses on children's rights, with an emphasis on children's right to participation.

Tamar Jacobson is chair of the Department of Teacher Education at Rider University and recipient of the 2013 National Association for Early Childhood Teacher Educators (NAECTE) Outstanding Early Childhood Teacher Educator Award. She is author of *Confronting Our Discomfort: Clearing the Way for Anti-Bias* (Heinemann) and *Don't Get So Upset! Help Young Children Manage Their Feelings by Understanding Your Own* (Redleaf Press). More information can be found at www. rider.edu/faculty/tamar-jacobson

Rebecca Kantor, dean of the School of Education and Human Development at the University of Colorado, Denver, brings a robust career as an early childhood teacher, researcher, professor of teacher education, education policy reformer, and public university administrator to her role. Dr. Kantor spent 29 years at The Ohio State University, first as an assistant professor and the director of the lab school and then, over time, in the role of director of the School of Teaching and Learning, along with achieving rank and tenure as a full professor. Her scholarship is focused on the study of classrooms as social contexts for teaching and learning, and reform of the ways we prepare teachers in partnership with schools. Dr. Kantor has published numerous articles, book chapters, and books in her areas of expertise and has been a principal investigator on $17 million of external funding that has supported her research.

Laurie Katz is a professor at The Ohio State University in early childhood education. Her research, teaching, and service have focused on teacher preparation of early childhood educators; inclusion issues; relationships between families, communities, and schools; and narrative styles and structures of young children.

Debbie LeeKeenan was director of the Eliot-Pearson Children's School, the laboratory school for the Department of Child Development at Tufts University from 1996–2013. Past professional experience includes over 40 years of teaching in diverse university, public school, and early childhood settings, as well as consulting on anti-bias education, teacher inquiry and documentation, and inclusive education. She is a published author, and her latest book is *Leading Anti-bias Early Childhood Programs: A Guide for Change,* with Louise Derman-Sparks and John Nimmo. She currently is a visiting professor at Lesley University and an early childhood consultant.

Samara Madrid is an associate professor in the Department of Elementary and Early Childhood Education at the University of Wyoming. Dr. Madrid's research examines the emotional lives of adults and children in early childhood classrooms. She is co-editor of *Educating Toddlers to Teachers: Learning to See and Influence the School and Peer Cultures in Classrooms* and co-author of the Teacher College Press book *On Discourse Analysis in Classrooms: Approaches to Language and Literacy Research.*

Alison Maher, MA, is the education director at Boulder Journey School. Alison coordinates a teacher certification and master's degree program in educational psychology. Over the past 2 decades, she has worked as a presenter and educational consultant in a wide variety of public and private preschool and elementary schools in the United States, Canada, Australia, and Ireland.

Mary Jane Moran is an associate professor in the Department of Child and Family Studies, The University of Tennessee. She teaches courses in contemporary issues in education, early childhood education, and collaborative action research. Her research interests include the education of teachers as classroom researchers, the use of visual literacies as tools for developing critical thinking among teachers, and the design of situated professional programs framed by the creation of communities of practice.

John Nimmo is an early childhood consultant and former executive director of the Child Study and Development Center, and associate professor at the University of New Hampshire from 2003–2013. He is co-author of *Emergent Curriculum* and the recent book *Leading Anti-Bias Early Childhood Programs: A Guide for Change* (Teacher College Press). John's research focuses on children's community participation.

Caryn Park is a lecturer at the University of Washington, Tacoma. After receiving her Ph.D. in education from the University of Washington, she was a postdoctoral fellow and head teacher at the Eliot-Pearson Children's School at Tufts University. She has taught children ages 1.5 to 7 years; mentored undergraduates, graduate students, and beginning teachers; and taught courses on multicultural and early childhood education. Her work on multicultural and anti-bias education for young children appears in publications such as the *American Educational Research Journal* and the *Encyclopedia of Diversity in Education.*

Patricia G. Ramsey is a professor of psychology and education at Mount Holyoke College. She has studied young children's understanding of race and social class and has written several books on multicultural education for young children, including *Teaching and Learning in a Diverse World: Multicultural Education for Young Children*, now in its fourth edition.

Barbara Seidl is an associate dean in the School of Education and Human Development at the University of Colorado, Denver. Her research has focused on community-based teacher education in the preparation of multiculturally competent teachers and the development of pedagogies for critical consciousness.

Dee Smith teaches in the Early Childhood Program at the University of Vermont, and is director of the Infant/Toddler Program at the Campus Children's School. She is actively engaged with Jeanne Goldhaber, Campus Children's School's staff, and students in the study of documentation as a process that promotes inquiry, reflection, and collaboration in their learning community. Dee is interested in how other disciplines inform our understanding of and practice with young children, and how the natural world supports children's development.

Phillip S. Strain is a professor of educational psychology at the University of Colorado, Denver and director of the Positive Early Learning Experiences Center. He has authored over 300 professional papers in the early intervention field, has been the principal investigator of grants totaling over $50 million, and has been recognized with distinguished career awards on three separate occasions.

Melissa Tonachel is a passionate teacher of young children and is committed to the professional development of adults who interact with them. She currently works with the Boston Public Schools Early Childhood Department, collaborating on a project to bring new curricula to life for the youngest citizens in our schools.

Susan Twombly, MS, is the director of the Infant, Toddler Children's Center of Acton, Massachusetts. She has been in the early childhood education field for 40 years, starting out as a Head Start teacher in that program's early years. She was the founding director of the Children's Hospital Child Care Center in Boston prior to coming to the Acton program. Susan has also taught college-level courses and led training workshops on child development, programming for young children, and organizational leadership.

INDEX